THE GREAT WAR AT SEA

J McGuineoW

September, 1976

THE

by A. A. HOEHLING

GREAT WAR AT SEA

A History of Naval Action 1914-18

GALAHAD BOOKS · NEW YORK CITY

Acknowledgment is made to the following publishers for permission to use copyrighted material.

> The Bobbs-Merrill Company, Inc.; from *The Splinter Fleet*, by Ray Milholland, copyright, 1936, by the Bobbs-Merrill Company, Inc., R., 1963, by Sara E. Milholland.
> Hutchinson & Co., Ltd., London; from *With the British Battle Fleet*, by Commodore G. von Schoultz, copyright 1926.

Sources for quotations used in this book are indicated in the bibliography by asterisks.

UNITED STATES NAVY HYMN

Eternal Father! strong to save,
Whose arm hath bound the restless wave,
Who bidd'st the mighty ocean deep
Its own appointed limits keep;
    O, hear us when we cry to Thee
    For those in peril on the sea!

O Christ! Whose voice the waters heard
And hushed their raging at Thy word,
Who walkedst on the foaming deep,
And calm amidst its rage didst sleep;
    O, hear us when we cry to Thee
    For those in peril on the sea!

Most Holy Spirit! Who didst brood
Upon the chaos dark and rude,
And bid its angry tumult cease,
And give, for wild confusion, peace;
    O, hear us when we cry to Thee
    For those in peril on the sea!

O Trinity of love and power,
Our brethren shield in danger's hour;
From rock and tempest, fire and foe,
Protect them wheresoe'er they go;
    Thus evermore shall rise to Thee
    Glad hymns of praise from land and sea.

—William Whiting

Preface

⊕ A person becomes a "survivor at sea" but once in a life-time unless he is quite unlucky. The unusual experience is engraved on memory like none other in the whole mysterious stream of existence.

Generally, the abruptness singles out the event, and imbues it ever afterward with acute shading. The vessel, which a second before was steaming along as normally as could be expected under war conditions, suddenly shudders, alarm bells commence to jangle, whistles blow, people shout and sometimes scream in an undulating, crazy discord. Orders and cries crisscross in a patchwork of sound.

In the case of my own ship, a Liberty, flames fountained skyward into the February night, yellowish red, droning with an insistent, increasing bass. Their tone was one of personal malevolence.

Then, men begin leaping into the sea, willy-nilly, not pausing to consider the temperature. The first over the side will probably be swept beyond hope of saving them. Those who bridle their panic have a better chance. Still others, more terrified yet at the prospect of the cold, dark waters of the North Sea, race aimlessly around the decks or down to their cabins or fo'c'sles.

The waters reach over the decks, sullenly, with surprising quiet and stealth. The ship tilts, hovers on the brink of eternity . . .

In the case of my own Liberty, only two lifeboats were launched through the flaming seas, and no life rafts. One sturdy sailor was picked up by a fisherman far out in the North Sea after dog-paddling for five hours. The Dutch trawler that rescued me landed me in Dover. With my oil-stained khaki shirt and pants and the ludicrously oversized shoes provided by the little vessel's captain, I felt as though I were watching myself in a newsreel—because of the mingled objectivity and unreality of the experience.

In London, the V-1 buzz bombs had lost their sting, but the second "vengeance" weapon, the V-2, was rocketing into the immense city with the regularity of passenger train service and the concussion of the same trains colliding. They echoed like summer thunderstorms which refuse to roll off the horizon and into nothing.

"Sir," a Marine, guarding our navy headquarters on Grosvenor Square, asked, saluting, "aren't you out of uniform?" Quizzically, he eyed the lieutenant's bars hanging from my open collar.

I *was* out of uniform. Some survivors of World War II at sea, however, had struggled ashore even more out of uniform. We were fortunate, even so. Our uniforms could be replaced.

In the accumulating years after Germany had, once again, been pounded into submission, I felt increasingly a serviceman's bond with those cast up, alive, by the seas: in two World Wars. Now, what had been the flickerings out of a history book—the sinking of the *Lusitania*, the battle of Jutland, the loss of the *Hampshire*, the cruise of the *Emden*, familiar names such as von Luckner—assumed a new form and dimension. No longer were the people or their actions impersonal or totally intangible.

What had been a substance of gossamer, out of reach, was now somehow palpable.

Out of this belated understanding and a curiosity to know better my predecessors upon the world's watery battlefields came the seeds which were to grow into this book.

A. A. Hoehling

Contents

Illustrations

THE GREAT WAR AT SEA

Introduction

⊕ The war at sea knew no respite. While land armies along the western front and in other theaters of the Great War paused from exhaustion for periods of rest, the conflict which reddened the seven seas continued until short hours before the armistice was made official. In many ways, the contest on the earth's oceans was more vicious, more merciless, and in the end more decisive than on the battlefields.

More than 3,000 warships—10,000,000 tons of iron and steel—of the principal powers (Great Britain, Germany, the United States, France, Japan, Italy, Russia, and Austria-Hungary) clashed with primitive fury through four flaming years. No armadas in all the world's history ever approximated the size or scope of these mighty fleets. The juggernauts as well as their smaller cousins slugged it out from the steaming tropics to the cold and ice of the Baltic and the gales and blizzards of the inhospitable North Atlantic.

Admiral Alfred Thayer Mahan (the United States naval oracle who died in 1914) had presented a warning and a forecast in his profound book, *The Influence of Sea Power upon History*. He pointed out that both Louis XIV and Napoleon Bonaparte won temporary mastery of the Continent only to lose it because Britain's overwhelming naval strength made her invincible. The American Revolution crackled to its victorious conclusion at Yorktown after England proved unable to maintain control of the waters of the east coast, and the Federal fleet's throttling blockade of the South was probably "the most potent single factor" in the collapse of the Confederacy.

Great Britain believed Mahan. So did the brilliant German admiral Alfred von Tirpitz who from nothing had fashioned the High Seas Fleet in the remarkably short period of two decades. It had not been an easy task in the face of public apathy. France had been roundly beaten in 1871 without the need of a navy.

German infantry, artillery, and cavalry boasted an unbroken record of success with no help from a sea arm.

Kaiser Wilhelm II was empire-minded. He wanted "a place in the sun." As a preliminary to attaining it, he busily set up colonies or cells of "culture" in Asia, in the Pacific, in Africa, and even in South America. When the lid blew off the international kettle in the summer of 1914 he was well on his way to carving out an empire. He had therefore enthusiastically supported the big navy policy of his fiercely bewhiskered senior admiral.

Great Britain went to war with the largest, if not the most modern, navy: 800 fighting ships, grossing 2,713,756 tons, slightly more than twice the naval mass of Germany. The British Admiralty could count 60 battleships or dreadnoughts against 33 operated by her prime adversary.

Without the unremitting labors of Admiral von Tirpitz since slightly before the turn of the century, the odds would have been ridiculously in the British favor. Whitehall, nonetheless, did not make the mistake of underestimating the foe. "Not since the Dutch wars of the seventeenth century," wrote Sir Julian Corbett, the naval historian, "had we had to deal with a first class naval power [beyond the Dover Straits]."

The first effect of hostilities was the disappearance of Germany's vaunted merchant marine from the seas, eloquent enough tribute to Britannia's ruling the waves. Hamburg and Bremen became ghost ports—as empty of passenger or freight vessels as Charleston, Savannah, or Wilmington in the United States Civil War.

Isolated raiders flying the Black Eagle, armed liners as well as cruisers of the imperial fleet, took toll of both Allied and neutral shipping in the early rounds of the conflict. Their success was due, not to their number or to the quality of their armament, but to the skill and daring of their officers and the courage of their highly disciplined crewmen.

Great Britain had early been favored with a stroke of pure luck. Her fleet had been mobilized for annual maneuvers at the time of the assassination of Archduke Francis Ferdinand in Sarajevo. Winston Churchill then followed up chance with calculated judgment. He refused to demobilize the squadrons during the crucial days of July when peace was slipping ever so certainly out of the grasp of Europe.

Thus the Royal Navy was ready overnight to steam to station in the North Sea to bottle up the High Seas Fleet in its great bases: Kiel and Wilhelmshaven. She was able to escort the British Expeditionary Force of 200,000 to France in a few weeks: the "contemptible little British army," as the enemy scoffed.

But Germany did well in the opening months of the war. One U-boat sank three old British cruisers in shooting-gallery succession. The daring act overnight elevated the submarine to a new and formidable standing in the ranks of fighting fleets. One small cruiser, the *Emden* ran amuck in the Indian Ocean, knocking off the truck horses of the sea with casual abandon. The *Kronprinz Wilhelm*, a converted liner, made raiding history by staying at sea continuously in the South Atlantic for approximately half a year before being compelled to seek port for supplies—and internment.

Before 1914 ended, Britain had lost most of a squadron—that of Admiral Cradock—off Coronel, Chile, to the last German squadron still on the prowl, under the command of the gallant if melancholy Admiral von Spee. In lightning turnabout, however, a far more powerful "revenge squadron" was slammed together in England and dispatched at flank speed to the South Atlantic. In a battle off the Falkland Islands in early December, all but one of von Spee's ships were sunk by his implacable adversary, Admiral Sturdee. The German admiral and his two sons went down with them.

So far, the war at sea had been give and take. Britain and France, in a disastrous effort to force the Dardanelles, lost capital ships and transports to submarines, light surface craft, mines, and shore batteries.

Aware that her only hope of victory was by attrition, Germany turned to her underwater fleet. She would sink all merchant ships, Allied and neutral alike, that were bringing supplies to Great Britain. In this, she was almost successful. In April, 1917, German U-boats had sunk nearly a million tons of shipping and had caused the British prime minister to admit, quite candidly, that if losses continued at such a devastating rate

Britain would be forced to ask Germany for a negotiated peace.

Unfortunately for Germany, unrestricted submarine warfare aroused the American public and brought the United States into the war. From that April day when President Wilson asked Congress for declaration of "a state of war," Germany was doomed.

What was a High Seas Fleet tactical victory at Jutland in 1916 could not turn the tide in favor of the kaiser's forces. England lost the greater percentage of ships in that greatest of all sea fights, but she kept her own fleet in existence. When Admiral Reinhard Scheer's mighty vessels limped home, the Royal Navy was still guarding its own isles, the North Sea, and exits into the North Atlantic.

Admiral Sir John Jellicoe, the head of the Grand Fleet, had possibly heeded too strongly Churchill's ominous words: "the only man who could lose the war in an afternoon" was that very commander. In other words, Britain did not dare to gamble with the war at sea or even to hesitate.

While His Majesty's Navy lost a chance virtually to destroy the High Seas Fleet, the latter never again came out in force. And the morale of the German sailors deteriorated through inaction to such an extent that mutiny became an ugly reality in the closing days of the war.

In the last year of fighting, the fresh United States Navy with its new convoy system made certain that the kaiser's Germany, historically dependent on commerce, would be a nation without a navy or merchant marine. Meanwhile, General Pershing, in his crushing Meuse-Argonne campaign, pushed a weary Hun army back toward its homeland.

Out in the cold shifting Atlantic, in the warmer bluer South Atlantic, in the Indian Ocean, on African lakes and deltas, in the Pacific and on lesser bodies of water, including the North Sea and the Red Sea, the High Seas Fleet, her U-boats, anything which once had floated or displayed the Black Eagle, had been shattered and fragmented into oblivion.

The price had been dear, for the victors as well as for the defeated. Of 1,000 warships, grossing a million and a quarter tons, lost in four years of Armageddon, Britain's share was nearly one third. Germany came next, with a toll of 350,000 tons.

The U-boats themselves had suffered in accounting for the greater part of the 7,000,000 tons of merchantmen destroyed. No less than 7,000 officers and men, the finest of Germany's youth, had sailed on the last patrols of 205 submarines. Sacrificed to the war at sea were 34,000 Britons, naval and merchant marine personnel and civilians. The price, indeed, had been dear. But the role of the sea war had been a decisive one.

(1)

The Battling Liners

⊕ "A fateful hour has fallen for Germany," Kaiser Wilhelm told his people on Saturday, August 1, 1914.

In the United States the New York Stock Exchange closed, it was explained, "to avert widespread ruin." The pending America's Cup race between Sir Thomas Lipton's *Shamrock IV* and the defending *Resolute* was canceled.

The complacent mood which had characterized the American reaction to the assassination of Archduke Francis Ferdinand changed. On the preceding day, Friday, experts had been predicting a "localized war" if worse came to worst, and steamship companies had been blandly denying that bookings were being canceled; but on Saturday a notice was slipped into New York newspapers:

All sailings of North German Lloyd steamers between the United States and European ports have been temporarily withdrawn on account of the threatening conditions existing abroad.

Other German lines followed suit. More than 8,000 passages would be refunded, and hotel space in New York was suddenly at a premium as tourists who had expected to journey overseas were stranded. The *Grosser Kurfürst*, which had sailed on Thursday, was ordered back by Telefunken, the German wireless system.

Some of the finest liners to fly the Black Eagle, led by the 49,000-ton *Vaterland*,* were caught at their Hoboken docks. For the moment, they would prudently remain where they were.

*Seized in 1917 by the United States and operated as the *Leviathan*.

It was different with Cunard, White Star, and other British steamship lines. Their operators, for one consideration, felt secure in the knowledge that units of the Royal Navy were already furrowing the seven seas. For another, many of their finest ships were naval auxiliaries. They had to go home and be converted for war, even though this was only Saturday and England was not, thus far, belligerent.

The shaky balance that had been peace was already fragmented beyond repair. On Sunday, the *New York World* reported in eight-column banners:

KAISER MAKES WAR ON CZAR, FRENCH ARMY
ORDERED OUT: ITALY WILL NOT HELP ALLIES
AMERICANS IN PANIC TRY TO QUIT EUROPE

In England an American offered a fellow countryman $1,000 for his third-class passage to New York for himself and his wife. He was turned down. In the Gare du Nord, Paris, tourists rioted in their frenzied efforts to board boat trains for Le Havre, Cherbourg, and Boulogne.

On Monday, August 3, the *New York Herald* proclaimed in bold headlines:

GERMANY'S ARMY INVADES FRANCE:
RUSSIA CROSSES GERMAN BORDER
ENGLAND'S DECISION COMES TODAY

The next day, at exactly 7 P.M., Greenwich mean time, Great Britain entered the war. Having no draft laws, she immediately issued a call for 100,000 recruits between the ages of nineteen and thirty. The Admiralty, upon the momentous declaration, issued its own call and sent out information bulletins. To ships at sea, His Majesty's as well as vessels of the merchant marine, the Whitehall offices transmitted the succinct announcement: "England declares war against Germany."

No further statement was necessary. Masters could tear open sealed orders to learn what to do in an emergency, or in the oldest traditions of the sea, they could rely on their personal judgment. All liners caught in mid-Atlantic blacked out at once.

The procedure was not easy since no portholes had been painted and only makeshift curtains were available.

Most British vessels turned up the steam and raced for home or neutral ports. A few masters improvised zigzag course patterns, without knowing quite what they were doing, why, or just *what* necessarily they were trying to avoid.

The queens, *Mauretania* and *Cedric*, radioed that a German warship was after them, then churned toward Halifax. After hitting speeds in excess of twenty-five knots, the *Lusitania*, sister of the *Mauretania*, both transatlantic record holders, safely raised Ambrose Channel.

Still three days from her destination, Liverpool, when the news crackled over the Marconi, was another famous Cunarder, the 19,524-ton *Carmania*. The ten-year-old liner, of Edwardian grandeur, had sailed from New York in a thunderstorm on July 29 with a passenger list that included at least one German army officer and a cargo of gold. Ports were covered. Oil lamps were lit in passageways suddenly deprived of their electric lights, and candles were placed in the dining rooms and other saloons. Lifeboats were swung out.

As she altered course for Fishguard, on the southwest coast of Wales at the mouth of the Bristol Channel, a second warning was received. It advised James C. Barr, the *Carmania's* sixty-year-old captain, that the enemy cruiser *Karlsruhe* might be lurking at the approaches to the Irish Channel. This would be a rich preserve for intercepting merchantmen steaming in for Liverpool and other Mersey River ports.

The history-making Cunarder was the first big liner to replace piston engines with steam turbines. Three of these unique turbines—working much on a water wheel principle—endowed the *Carmania* with a speed of about eighteen knots, nineteen if pushed.

Barr had developed a real affection for his command, which he often referred to as a "sea-kindly" ship. Famous in his own right, Barr was outspoken as a man and as a skipper. He had served with Cunard almost his entire life. In his early days, while captaining the *Catalonia*, sailing to Boston, he had been questioned sharply by the company's directors as to why he had been a day late on a recent run. This had evoked a lecture by the young captain which had ended with the blunt assertion to his superiors: "That you haven't had an accident at sea has been due not to your good management, but simply to your good fortune! "

Sir Alfred Booth, then Cunard's youngest director, was so impressed that he appointed Barr safety and navigation instructor for the line. While he earned the sobriquet "safe" or "cautious" Barr, he also believed in pinpoint navigation—navigating in a thick fog by the sound of whistling buoys, for example, rather than heaving-to or anchoring. In 1913, Barr made headlines by rescuing passengers in mid-Atlantic from the burning liner *Volturno.*

"The voyage," Captain Barr noted, "has been marked by dominant war talk among the passengers." The voyagers speculated whether "the old boy is after us," thinking no doubt of the "villainous" face, with the waxed whiskers, of Kaiser "Bill."

And so the *Carmania* plowed through the Atlantic. Some passengers remained in a seminumb state of shock, not at all certain they would ever sight land again.

They were not the only Atlantic voyagers with this mortal trepidation. The *Kronprinzessin Cecilie,* also carrying American citizens and gold bullion, turned 180 degrees westward from her course toward Plymouth, England, at the receipt of the news from the powerful Nauen radio. The code that war had been declared was a strangely prophetic choice, Wagnerian in its implications: *"Siegfried Tod!"*

Since the *Kronprinzessin* did not herself wish to be "dead" like poor Siegfried, she streaked back for Bar Harbor, Maine, as fast as she could go. And she arrived there safely.

The *Kronprinzessin* was but one of many units of the kaiser's merchant marine. It was huge, prosperous, and consummately arrogant. The Hamburg-American Line itself counted nearly 500 ships, serving 400 ports to the far corners of the earth, and carried half a million passengers a year. One of the firm's offshoots, the Hamburg-South American Line, was only this year expanding its service, having put into operation a new queen, the 18,710-ton *Cap Trafalgar.* She was 611 feet long (about sixty feet shorter than the *Carmania*) and could drive ahead at nearly twenty-one knots. She was also triple screw, but her main propulsion was conventional—reciprocating engines for two propellers, a low-pressure steam turbine for the third.

Her captain, Hans Langerhansz, a bewhiskered oldster who resembled a benign Tirpitz, had been host to Prince Henry of Prussia on *Cap Trafalgar*'s maiden voyage, in April, to South America. His Highness, a milder-natured brother of Kaiser Wilhelm II, had been on a "goodwill mission."

Her appointments were as heavily in the Charlottenburg Palace decor as those of any vessel which flew the German colors. The many grand saloons, deluxe suites, and a swimming pool, or *Bad*, were capped in Teutonic extravagance by a lofty Winter Garden. Marble pilasters, palms and filigreed tables and chairs gave the ship a ponderous *Gemütlichkeit* second only to the regal prototype itself. The *Cap Trafalgar*, however, was top-heavy, as were the *Carmania* and many passenger liners built shortly after the turn of the century.

One of the war's first casualties, the battleship HMS *Audacious* struck a mine and sank. Here, in a rare action photo, the *Olympic* tries unsuccessfully to tow her to shore. The loss of the *Audacious* was not announced until after the armistice.

As the *Carmania* was caught some 1,000 miles west of Ireland by war's erupting, the *Cap Trafalgar* was off Argentina when the kaiser decided to tussle with his czarist cousin. Assuming that England would soon be in the fray, Captain Langerhansz put in at Buenos Aires, arriving there late at night, August 2. He bid *auf Wiedersehen* to his passengers, ordered cargo off-loaded *"schnell,"* as fast as and maybe faster than possible, irrespective of its destination.

On August 5, *Carmania* was joined by an escort of two cruisers. Her passengers, many of whom had worn their life jackets even to bed, were gaunt-eyed from lack of sleep. Now, with His Majesty's Navy at hand, they relaxed.

The next afternoon, the liner dropped anchor off Fishguard. Her bullion was removed to tenders under heavy Royal Marine guard, along with the German officer passenger. The valuable cargo was packed in small kegs, which reminded the passengers of miniature beer barrels as they were rolled down the gangplanks.

Carmania steamed on up the Irish Sea. She crossed the "Bar"—a sand spit at the mouth of the Mersey River—at flood tide and docked safely at 8 A.M., August 7, to the immense relief of all on board. Six gangways were banged against several decks to hasten baggage off-loading. Sturdier gantries stretched their impressive length sixty feet upward to C (the open promenade) and D (closed) below to remove the first- and second-class travelers.

The ship was at once commandeered by the navy, which catalogued her as an "auxiliary." All first-class passengers were hurried ashore with the exception of one wealthy New York lady who was accompanied by her two children and a German governess. Mrs. Oscar Straus, Jr., would have to stay aboard, along with the third-class passengers, while the governess was cross-examined by ever-suspicious customs and immigration men, augmented now by Scotland Yard and Home Office investigators.

Soon, the distraught lady was weeping and screaming at this unaccustomed treatment. It didn't matter. This was "war, don't you know?" and the German woman along with the hapless voyagers from third-class, or steerage, continued to be scrutinized like so many bacteria under a microscope.

There would be none of the customary activities of turn-around. Laundry carts would not be hovering nearby with literally tons of fresh linen to pamper westbound passengers. The mountains of baggage, the flowers, candy boxes and other bon voyage gifts were not waiting to be trundled aboard.

The Admiralty had other pressing plans for the *Carmania*. At noon, while the third-class passengers were still being subjected to a determined grilling, the big ship was moved from the floating landing stage to her customary Huskinson Dock at Sandon. There an army of workmen impatiently awaited her. In fact, those holding gallon pots of black paint and wide, long-handled brushes went to work even before her lines were secured. Like a circus of monkeys, they swarmed over the ship from twin funnels to Plimsoll mark to smear out her whites and reds and, especially, her shiny brasswork.

The entire smoky Liverpool area became a raucous symphony of noise and rising activity. At Sandon, other greyhounds of the Atlantic already were being converted for war. There was the 45,000-ton *Aquitania*, Britain's largest, which had logged her maiden voyage only in June, flanked by the *Caronia*, occupying *Carmania*'s usual berth. The two—*Caronia* and *Carmania*— were affectionately known in company circles as "the pretty sisters." They had helped to popularize the now accepted transatlantic philosophy of twin vessels, to afford regular, same-class service between England and the United States.

The *Caronia*, however, did not look pretty any more. The painters had completed their blackout, and now cranes were hoisting aboard cannons and range finders, along with miles and miles of heavy hemp rope as shield against shrapnel, small caliber bullets, and spent shells. Peacetime fittings, from chandeliers and first-class saloon bric-a-brac to gymnasium equipment, stuffed chairs, and sofas were hastened ashore in a steady stream —more than 2,000 wagonloads in all.

By mid-afternoon, the *Carmania*'s great bulk had been half splashed over with a pall of black paint. Her furniture, like that of her companion liners, had been snatched from her cabins and public rooms. The veneer had been stripped from the bulkheads, and all drapery and other combustible items had been quickly removed and placed in dockside warehouses. The gymnasium was being readied as a magazine. The nursery, one of the advertised features of the *Carmania* (and also of the *Caronia*) had just been denuded of the eight-foot-long toy boat, the rabbits, dolls, and even the color prints chronicling Aesop's fables on the light blue walls. Tramped under the boots of workmen were the brochures which told of what had once been the youthful heart and soul of this emptied, echoing room:

... if you are a little one you may rock wide-eyed with the fun of it in a sturdy ship of your own, with the name of a very big ship on its bow. When you have tired yourself with that and the other things, the exciting, stimulating things there are to do in the *Carmania* nursery, you have a little nap in one of the twin cribs—or play games sedately at the card tables. . . .

Far from home, in a foreign port where few could speak his language, Captain Langerhansz could not expect the attention being accorded Captain Barr's *Carmania*. The *Cap Trafalgar*, like the Cunarder, however, was also a naval auxiliary with reinforced decks and other appurtenances designed to speed the switch from peace to war. And German merchant-marine masters carried emergency procedure books perhaps even more detailed than those in the comparable safes of British ships. These had been issued during the Agadir crisis between the same two powers in 1911.

The Argentinian authorities, zealous to guard their own neutrality, had searched the large Hamburg-South American liner without finding anything on board that was especially warlike. The officials had been prodded by the British consul in Buenos Aires, who had suggested that the *Cap Trafalgar* held a ballast of 6-inch cannons. This would purportedly be transferred at night to small vessels of the German marine also in Argentine waters.

However, Captain Langerhansz could load up his ship, now empty of passengers and cargo. During the first ten days of August, Langerhansz took aboard 3,500 tons of coal and large balks of timber. Ship's carpenters at once played a staccato symphony with saws and hammers as they shaped the massive wood timbers into shorings for gun positions and certain bulkheads.

Provisions, too, arrived in the cargo nets—in quantities suggesting either a normal sailing with passengers or a long, lonely prowl of the sea-lanes, shunning ports of call. As unostentatiously as possible, painters went to work on the *Cap Trafalgar*'s exterior. Steam fitters commenced loosening the bolts which held one of her three funnels in position. It was a dummy, used only for ventilation.

Habitués of the waterfront could have little doubt that Langerhansz was readying his command for sea. Surely it would be no peacetime cruise. It was rumored, with foundation, that the *Cap Trafalgar* was soon to join up with the *Dresden*, even now crisscrossing the sea-lanes to South America. The twenty-eight-year-old captain of the *Dresden*, Winfried Luedecke, had already intercepted two small British steamers, then with in credible gallantry, released both because he did not possess sufficient accommodations on his cruiser for the passengers, especially the women and children.

And as these activities progressed aboard the *Carmania* and *Cap Trafalgar*, yet another and much smaller ship was herself responding to war orders. Three days ahead of the declaration, the small German gunboat *Eber* cast off from Cape Town and raced toward the protection of her own African colonies.

"I was the second youngest watch officer on board," recalled Lieutenant Otto W. Steffan,* the Telefunken officer. "I really should have remained behind, since I had been in a local hospital with malaria and complications, including blood poisoning. But on this day a shipmate brought orders from the captain to me that we would sail at once because the political situation in Europe had deteriorated so seriously that we must face the possibility of war. They carried me on board!

"It so happened I was the only radio expert. They could *not* leave me behind.

"For three days and two nights our 950-ton vessel thrashed through a howling gale. Our destination was the port of

*Now Admiral Steffan (Ret.) of Litzelstetten, West Germany, he has written his account at the request of the author.

The 11,261-ton International Navigation Company SS *Merion* before and after her transformation in 1914. Unlike other converted liners, however, the *Merion* was a hoax. Renamed the HMS *Tiger*, this "battle cruiser" was more decorative than functional—she carried wooden guns mounted in plywood turrets. She was designed as a decoy to lure German raiders.

Lüderitz in German Southwest Africa. Luckily, on August 1, we arrived there, remaining until the third.

"There we heard of the declaration of war against Russia and France, realizing that we could soon expect to be at war with Great Britain as well. On August 3, we put to sea in the evening. We steered a southwest course, passing not far from a British possession, Gough Island [two thirds of the distance from the Cape of Good Hope to Cape Town] and then steaming for South American waters.

"It was an adventurous journey, for we sailed on without any prospect of finding coal for our bunkers. Without replenishing fuel, we could not reach the South American shores. We were stretching our luck.

"We had encountered only an English four-masted schooner. She was fortunate, since at that time we had no information of Great Britain's entry into the war.

"In the middle of the South Atlantic we met the German collier *Steiermark*. Her captain advised us that England was now our enemy. Thanks to good weather, the *Steiermark* was able to complete the coaling of our bunkers at sea."

The last third-class passengers had picked up their bundles and carpetbags and vanished into the drab port of Liverpool when Captain Noel Grant, of the Royal Navy, came aboard the *Carmania* to take command. A few years younger than the Cunarder's Barr, Grant was a large, corpulent man, a "regular" of no uncertain stamp in His Majesty's Navy.

The naval officer handed the Cunarder's master a typed letter:

Dear Captain Barr:

I have been appointed to command the *Carmania* and am instructed by the Admiralty to invite you to stay on in an advisory capacity. Will you be good enough to let me know?

Barr accepted immediately, volunteering to serve in any position. He was given a temporary commission as commander in the Royal Naval Reserves, and appointed as both navigation and intelligence officer. Grant also wanted "the whole engine-room complement from the chief engineer to the last joiner trimmer." All except one volunteered.

Indeed, her final military complement was reminiscent of her regular transatlantic role. Peter Murchie, the chief officer, would stay, as would the ship's surgeon, the chief steward, the carpenter, blacksmith, plumber, painter, and about fifty ratings, including cooks, waiters, and officers' servants.

Among those called to the colors these heady days of August was William Cowling, thirty years old, of Cornwall. Engaged in the more or less typical duties of a civilian salt, Bill Cowling was quartermaster on a large steam yacht, the *Liberty*.

"We were anchored in Cowes," he recalled, "and on Sunday, August 4, the customs officer came on board and took ten of the crew who were Naval Reserves out of her. We were sent to Portsmouth and all that day and for several days following, hundreds of RNR men were coming into the depots, chiefly fishermen from the north (especially from the Shetland Islands). After some days in the barracks we were sent to Whale Island Gunnery School, off Portsmouth. A good many went to the *Aquitania*. I was drafted to the liner *Carmania* at Liverpool. I had not been waiting long for the van to take our baggage and hammocks to the station when I suddenly saw a chap from my own village, and I said, 'What's on, Tom?,' and he replied, 'I am drafted to the *Carmania*, leaving here for Liverpool.' So I said I was going to her too. You can imagine I was very pleased. When we got to the dock in Liverpool where she was, I was very impressed by her looks, knowing how smart Cunard company ships look. The *Carmania* was painted black even where it looked horrid. There were heaps of fellows working everywhere, about gun fittings and tearing wood out of inside cabins, etc. . . ."

Others of her crew agreed that while the *Carmania* might now be a first-class fighting ship, she was no longer "a pretty sister." She more closely resembled "a floating hearse."

Bulwarks fore and aft on B deck were cut out to allow the guns to train. The *Carmania* would mount 4.7-inch cannons, with a range of 9,300 yards, plus nests of machine guns, largely to repel boarding parties should this unlikely eventuality ever occur.

Armored plates were riveted against her most vulnerable exposures, reinforced here and there with bags of coal and sand. Still not fully satisfied with the stowage capacity of the gymnasium, technicians built platforms into two holds for additional magazine space, together with wide-diameter brass pipes for flooding. Speaking tubes were fitted in the aft steering-gear room, while control telephones were strung to all gun positions and other critical areas of the liner.

A six-foot-long Barr and Stroud range finder was erected on the starboard bridge wing, plus special naval semaphores and searchlights. Eighteen of the Royal Navy's special Maclean collapsible lifeboats were set loosely on the upper decks, intended to float free if the ship went down. It had been hoped to obtain a steam launch, known as a "service cutter," which would have been useful for boarding parties. However, the navy's larger auxiliaries—the *Aquitania*, for example—had already exhausted the stock.

The conversion, accomplished in seven days, represented a "superhuman effort," Captain Grant thought. A "floating hotel of the greatest luxury," Barr seconded, was now "a grim fighting machine, an *interesting* warrior." Her crew numbered 420, including the rather large proportion of 40 officers and 32 petty officers.

On Friday, August 14, the *Carmania* dipped her colors to the house flag atop the Cunard Building as she steamed in sparkling sunshine down the Mersey toward the Irish Sea to "assume patrol in the North Atlantic." In a rollicking mood, her men lined the decks to sing an already popular parody of the German "Wacht am Rhein," which began: "Oh, we'll wind up the watch on the Rhine . . .!"

At almost the same hour which found the *Carmania* pushing seaward, the *Cap Trafalgar* cleared Buenos Aires for Las Palmas in the Canary Islands. Captain Langerhansz, of course, had no intention of making for his declared destination. Since he was in command of a naval auxiliary with no guns, he must rendezvous at sea with one of a number of German navy or merchant ships and arm himself. Already scurrying around in the South Atlantic, playing cat-and-mouse with menacing British forces, were, in addition to the *Dresden*, another cruiser, the *Karlsruhe*, a fast armed liner, the *Kaiser Wilhelm der Grosse* and still another, the 14,000-ton *Kronprinz Wilhelm*.

The *Kronprinz Wilhelm*, commanded by youthful Paul Thierfelder, was closest to the *Cap Trafalgar* as she steamed due eastward in search of a comrade—and weapons. Casting caution aside, Langerhansz wirelessed to all the known ships with which he could possibly rendezvous. From Thierfelder he received an unexpected reply.

It seemed that the *Kronprinz Wilhelm* was infested with rats, taken aboard unwittingly in some recent cargo. Feasting well, they had grown with the speed of amoeba into big, vicious predators. They had killed or chased into the crew's fo'c'sles not only the liner's cats, but several ferrets which Thierfelder had bought in New York. He had left there in haste—and just in time—August 3.

Now, he had clad his fleetest-footed sailors in tennis shoes and double leggings (as bite protection) and sent them into the holds with baseball bats, clubs, and electric torches. The battle continued, the beleaguered master of the *Kronprinz Wilhelm* wirelessed Langerhansz. The arrogant rodents still had the upper hand.

In short, Thierfelder could not spare time from the rat struggle for such distractions as arming another liner. He wished Langerhansz well in his particular quest.

After four days of a fruitless prowl off the Brazilian coast, *Cap Trafalgar* turned south again and steamed back to the mouth of the Plate River, dropping anchor this time off Montevideo, in Uruguayan waters. Langerhansz had finished painting his ship. Otherwise, he was no more ready to assume the role of armed raider than he had been in Buenos Aires.

In the North Atlantic, the *Carmania* had accomplished no more than the *Cap Trafalgar*, other than engaging in gunnery practice, dropping floats for targets. She had stopped two small freighters along the sea-lanes to Europe. They were neutrals, bearing cargo for the United Kingdom.

The medium-sized Cunarder, however, was more fortunate

than her mighty sister, the *Aquitania*, which had been damaged in collision shortly after leaving Liverpool, and forced to return. (She ultimately became a hospital ship.)

After less than a week of gunnery practice, Captain Grant received orders to alter course for Bermuda and join Rear Admiral Sir Christopher Cradock's squadron then forming to search the Venezuelan coast for German merchant raiders and cruisers. These were not only preying on Allied commerce but protecting the kaiser's tenuous lifeline to South America's bauxite, phosphates, and other essential ores and minerals.

Late in the evening of August 22, *Carmania* picked up the dimmed wink of Mt. Hill Light. The broad-beamed Cunarder became the largest vessel to navigate the narrow, shallow North Channel into Bermuda. "After a very exciting series of evolutions," an officer recalled, "she dropped anchor in Shelly harbor."

On August 25, readers of the *London Times* were informed that "the enemy liner *Cap Trafalgar*" had left the Plate August 22 "for an unknown destination . . . it seems probable that she is well equipped to act as a commerce destroyer." The article speculated that she had arrived with "extra guns" stowed below decks.

She was on her way to meet the *Eber*. The Telefunken officer, Steffan, gives this account:

"We steamed northward, reaching, on August 13, lonely, inhospitable Trindade Island, belonging to Brazil,* rearing steeply out of the sea. Here in the following days we rendezvoused with the *Eleonore Woermann* which had been ordered from Douala in the Cameroons to bring us coal and provisions.

"During the night of the 28th of August arrived the *Cap Trafalgar*, the newest liner of the Hamburg-South American Line. We had already heard over the wireless that this ship had

---

*Rocky, mountainous Trindade, 3 miles long, 1½ wide, is situated 1,200 miles below the equator, 500 miles east of Espírito Santo, remote from the usual steamship lanes of 1914. A pirate rendezvous of yesterday, the uninhabited island was dominated by a yellow-gray color. It possessed little vegetation other than dead castor oil plants, remnants of unsuccessful agricultural attempts by both Britons and Brazilians. As unsurpassed sanctuary to twentieth-century raiders, as it once had been to pirates, Trindade Rocks (as some navigators knew the island) had been visited a few days previously by the *Dresden*, coaling in the lee of Nine-Pin Peak.

been converted into a commerce raider, to operate in the South Atlantic. Our *Eber* did not possess the cruising range for such duty, she had never been designed for it. She could make but twelve knots. The *Cap Trafalgar*, on the other hand, grossing 18,000 tons, could steam up to twenty-one knots. She had a disadvantage, however, as we were soon to ascertain: she was an enormous coal-eater!

"With much difficulty and improvisation we transferred both 10.5-cm. [4.1-inch] cannons and the six 3.7-cm. [1.4-inch] machine guns [pom-poms] along with ammunition from the *Eber* to her big sister and finally settled ourselves. We had to get used to the silk sheets and the cabins still smelling of the perfume of the last passengers to leave this luxury liner—memories of peacetime!

"The captain of a United States steamship (the *Berwind*) who offered to provide us with more weapons could appreciate our gratitude, although unfortunately we could not accept. It wasn't the way we did things in the Imperial Navy."

The third funnel was removed completely and the two remaining painted with Union Castle Line colors, black bands on top, red below. The *Cap Trafalgar* now somewhat resembled the *Edinburgh Castle*, though she grossed some 5,000 tons less.

"On September 3," Steffan added, "the new auxiliary cruiser *Cap Trafalgar* put to sea on its first cruise as a privateer. Our stripped-down old gunboat *Eber*, under command of a lieutenant and a few crewmen, was ordered to sail for Bahia and there allow herself to be interned. A demolition device was placed in the engine room, with its detonating key on the bridge—it was to be used if the *Eber* should ever be in danger of capture by the enemy.

"Fortunately, she reached Bahia unchallenged. However, from the moment of her arrival, our enemy must have known of our existence in the South Atlantic.

"We ourselves went cruising along what seemed the normal trade routes. Since we were getting hungry, we hoped, for example, to encounter a French refrigerator ship, carrying meat. We saw nothing.

"A particular frustration was the strength of the enemy's

marine radio. While we listened to the transmission of Royal Navy ships, we still could not take a bearing on them. Fumbling in the dark as we were, it would have been sheer luck to have stumbled onto a prize."

Indeed, Commodore Julius Wirth, small and nervous, the *Cap Trafalgar's* new commanding officer, was prone to frustration: he was impatient with the relative slowness of the liner compared to a real cruiser, and he worried about her towering bulk, which made her an excellent target for the enemy. He was plagued, too, with the suspicion that the *Cap Trafalgar's* masquerade as another ship really wouldn't fool anybody.

Meanwhile, the war at sea accelerated. The British cruiser *Highflyer* caught the 15,000-ton armed liner *Kaiser Wilhelm der Grosse*, once the fastest in the North Atlantic service, in Spanish waters. She sank her in minutes. The cruiser *Königsberg* was playing a cat-and-mouse game off the West African coast with British merchant vessels and warships alike. And 200 miles south of Bermuda, *Karlsruhe* chose to fight another day as she showed her stern to HMS *Suffolk*.

Submarines, on both sides, were scoring their first victories. The Royal Navy's *R-9* sank the light cruiser *Hela* in the North Sea, while a U-boat torpedoed and sent to the bottom of the same body of water the English cruiser *Pathfinder*.

The *Carmania*, like the *Cap Trafalgar*, was herself possessed of a glutton's appetite for coal. By the tedious process of native gangs, like animated human vines, handing up bag after bag of coal, the big Cunarder took aboard 4,000 tons, leaving the entire ship covered with black dust. The new lightweight white tropical clothing which was issued at Bermuda had to be laundered before it could be worn.

On August 29, the *Carmania* sailed to join Admiral Cradock's 5th Cruiser Squadron, then consisting of the *Monmouth*, *Good Hope* and *Glasgow*. A fourth ship, *Cornwall*, had been detached to chase the enemy collier *Patagonia*, which supposedly had just cleared Pernambuco. Captain Grant's orders were to help the *Cornwall* capture the collier, then aid Cradock's major mission of finding the German squadron.

On September 2, the Cunarder passed through the Dragon's Mouths, at the entry to the Gulf of Paria between Venezuela and Trinidad, while the crew marveled at the spectacular mountain scenery. Once more her fast-depleting bunkers were allowed to gorge themselves—at Port of Spain—and she plowed on southward.

Commodore Wirth drove the *Cap Trafalgar* north, east, south, and west off the South American coast for nearly two weeks, crisscrossing the sea-lanes like a lumbering hound which has been sniffing a country field for rabbits. Interception of incessantly heavy radio traffic between British men-of-war gave him great concern. He realized that he did not pack the firepower to shoot it out with an enemy cruiser or even a destroyer.

Finally, he had to coal up once more. He made wireless contact with three colliers, the *Pontos, Eleonore Woermann*, and the American *Berwind*, now under charter. He ordered them to meet the *Cap Trafalgar* Sunday morning, September 13, off Trindade Island.

They rendezvoused on schedule, and started coaling. The crews paused for the night hours, then, Steffan continued:

". . . early on the 14th we were again at our task. The swells were long, and the *Cap Trafalgar*, tugging at her long anchor chain, bobbed up and down. On the port side lay the collier *Pontos*. Coal was spilled from the containers out onto the deck, until we were convinced that the liner was designed to fuel only at a wharf. Coal dust was wafted in the gentle morning breeze down our necks, over most of our bodies.

"The sun rose. Sailors and firemen worked on deck near the guns with sledge hammers and torches to clear all obstructions from the field of fire. There was much swearing on account of the toughness of the metal, and we couldn't help wondering, most earnestly, if we wouldn't have been better off on the *Pontos*, slow as she was, than on the 'show ship' *Cap Trafalgar*.

"At 7 o'clock, the wireless man on watch handed me his headset, and frowned. I listened—and heard strong Marconi signals. I hurried to the bridge and told the captain about it.

"'Neutral or enemy?' he asked. His eyes swept the ship,

which was covered with black coal dust. 'What do you think—run or stand fast?'

" 'Just as fast as we can up anchor and get to sea,' was my answer.

" 'How far away is the fellow?'

" 'Fifty to one hundred miles.'

"Then the captain asked the crow's nest lookout if he could see anything. 'Not yet!' was his answer.

"The loading went on. The light breeze rattled the blocks and tackles and swirled the coal dust about the open hatches. The bunkers were filled, but valuable time had been lost."

About 9:30 A.M., in crystal-like visibility, *Carmania*'s lookouts spotted Trindade to starboard. Captain Grant altered course to south-southwest to bring it dead ahead.

James C. Barr, the *Carmania's* peacetime captain, served on board the ship during the war as navigation and chief intelligence officer.

"Our approach on this bearing," Grant recalled, "was a fortunate accident. The weather was fine and sunny with a moderate breeze from northeast, and a large ship like ours, with a plume of smoke caused by a following wind, might easily be visible thirty miles or more, and this might have given more time to an adversary.

"As our approach was screened by the land from the anchorage, it was not till shortly after 11 A.M. that we, slightly altering course, saw a group of three ships close in to the island and we were apparently seen by them. They were working, for their derricks were topped. But before we had raised their hulls they had separated and were making off in different directions."

The Germans were, indeed, doing just that. Steffan's account of what happened on the *Cap Trafalgar* continued:

"At 11 o'clock, the lookout reported black smoke on the west-northwest horizon. It was time to move. A shrill whistle brought the coaling to a halt! Shovels were thrown aside. Crewmen crawled out of the bunkers, the anchor was hauled in, part way.

"The officers on the bridge studied the newcomer. Was she a merchantman, a warship? As yet, we could not make out her flags.

"Alarms shrilled. 'Buglers sound battle stations!' 'Clear the ship for action!'

"We could soon discern the outline of a gray, large steamship, with two funnels and two masts. The anchor left the sea bottom. The supply ships were ordered away. We turned from the island, hoping to increase the distance from the apparent enemy. While now we could make out his signal halyards, we could not recognize the colors—even so, we were certain we had a fight on our hands.

"When he had closed the distance to five nautical miles, we realized the stranger flew the Union Jack. It was an auxiliary cruiser, even as ourselves."

Orders were crackling the length of the *Carmania*.

"Cooks to the galleys!" It was an old British naval tradition, older conceivably than Nelson's time, that a sailor shouldn't fight on an empty stomach.

"Uniform, dress whites!" Whites were supposed to reduce the infection danger of wounds.

Dr. Harry Clough, the liner's surgeon, was instructed to set up emergency tables and cots in the first-class dining saloon—in case the regular dispensary on lower E deck could not handle possible casualties.

H. W. St. John, senior wireless officer, threw out a continuing series of challenges, both by radio and blinker light. They went unanswered, as the other vessels continued to accelerate. Then, unexpectedly, as Barr was to report:

". . . after running away to the southward for a little while, to clear decks, get up speed, and be sure that we had no supports, he made up his mind to attack, turned boldly to starboard and, steering about northwest, advanced to meet us, both ships going full speed—our speed about sixteen knots. The *Cap Trafalgar* was *certainly* faster.

"Meanwhile, we had sent our crew to dinner, got them back to station again, and were also ready. We had altered course at about 11:50 A.M. to give the island a berth and were steering about southwest.

"It was an ideal summerlike day. The wind being with us made a practical calm and all was very still on board. Captain Grant was calm and alert, spoke little and in very quiet tones.

"I said to him, speaking of our opponent, 'From his confident manner it looks as if he had support behind the land.'

" 'It does,' he replied. 'We shall soon know.' From the control just above us, the officer at the range finder was distinctly audible.

"At about 12:10 the gunnery officer, Lieutenant Lockyer, called, 'In range, sir!' [This was about 8,500 yards.]

"Captain Grant hailed, 'Port No. 1, load blank. Fire across his bow! . . . fire!' "

On the Hamburg-American liner, Steffan noted:

"Events happened rapidly. Next, a bright flash from the ship . . . a geyser of water off our bow. Soon a second shot. We turned now towards our opponent, to come in range.

" 'Hoist flags and pennants!'

". . . and our flags were unfurled at the forepeak in acknowledgment of battle. Deep silence now prevailed throughout the ship, broken only by commands relayed by speaking tube to the gun positions."

The *Cap Trafalgar* replied, in moments "furiously" blazing with all guns that would bear. Smaller caliber, weighing but 28 pounds against the 45-pound projectiles the *Carmania* could hurl, the German shells nonetheless outranged the British by nearly 2,000 yards. They rattled over the Cunarder's masts and rigging.

"Let him have it!" shouted Grant, disregarding the drill book's more formal "Commence!"

"Ready to fight!" replied Lieutenant Peter Murchie, who had been chief officer on the liner.

Stabs of flame and orange flashes* licked angrily from the *Cap Trafalgar*. Her gunners were using a type of shell which did not explode until it had penetrated armor plating. They began to score.

"That first broadside," reported St. John, the wireless chief, Steffan's counterpart, "from the enemy raked the *Carmania* fore and aft in the upper works . . . for most of us it was our first baptism of fire and some indiscriminate ducking took place. I myself remember thinking how horribly mean it was to be so rough.

"The wireless was on the top deck abaft the forward funnel. My assistants, Frank Cook and Rushforth, were on duty but there was no British ship or station within range at the time. Wireless ranges of ships were not more than 100 to 150 miles in daylight.

"I took over the W/T watch and heard the German ship calling for assistance. I knew a little German and loosed off on our transmitter wishing to confuse the enemy operator and any enemy warships listening in.

---

*Both Grant and Barr counted the flashes from the broadsides and concluded that their opponent mounted eight heavy guns rather than two as claimed by Steffan and official German records.

"The *Cap Trafalgar's* operator interrupted his call and sent 'was?' (what?).

"I was a bit rattled at this moment as the W/T cabin was severely shaken by several shell explosions—I replied '*Wie geht's?*' The enemy operator gave this a miss and began calling up his pals again.

"I jammed the communication as hard as I could for a few minutes and then there happened the grandfather of all explosions—the cabin rocked and was filled with smoke and the apparatus ceased to function.

"A couple of 4-inch shells had hit the base of the after funnel and exploded simultaneously, tearing away our aerial connections.

"The three of us went out on deck and tried to clear the aerial leads but could do nothing about it, as the main aerial had been shot away and was a mass of tangled wreckage.

"We had a good view of the conflict just as it was at its hottest. The *Cap Trafalgar* was abeam on our starboard side about 2,000 yards away. She was blazing away at us with her 4-inch guns and pom-poms, shells were screaming overhead, but quite an appreciable number were hitting our upperworks, lifeboats, and funnels.

"One of our starboard guns was hit and the crew knocked out, the gun layer being killed. The gun was quickly remanned and in action again. The two ships were maneuvering around each other at full speed, our captain endeavouring to steer the *Carmania* so that the enemy ship could be ranged on our quarter, thus enabling five of our guns to bear. Our gunners concentrated their aim upon the *Cap Trafalgar's* bow wave and waterline. This eventually had its effect.

"The noise was terrific. In the midst of this inferno the ship's stewards were rendering assistance to the wounded and removing them below. The chief steward calmly distributed lime juice to the perspiring gunners.

"A striking feature of the working of the after guns was the decorative language of the Royal Marine gunners; this could be heard distinctly coming through the intermittent noise of the gunfire; one huge sergeant and a "blue" marine named Dyer, 6 feet, 4 inches, 18 stones, roared out his displeasure in impeccable accents owing to his inability to bring his gun to bear on the target.

"My word, those Royal Marine gunners could swear! It wasn't vulgar. It sounded poetical and inspiring.

"By this time most of the gun crews had stripped to the waist and the scene on deck rather resembled that of Nelson's days: jumpers, tunics, and shirts had been discarded; fire control from the bridge had been destroyed; telephone control to the guns was out of action. Consequently, gunners had to fire independently.

"A shell went through the medical dispensary on the lower deck, shaking up the ship's surgeon, Dr. Clough, and his staff; another swept down a companionway aft and laid out three of the ammunition party; a projectile rebounded from the shield of number one gun and blew the head off a corporal of marines. Then the bridge caught fire and became a mass of flames. The captain and officers in attendance had to retire aft and rig the emergency steering gear and endeavour to control the ship from the stern."

An odd and disturbing circumstance to the damage in the dispensary was the rupturing of an entire store of pillows, sending feathers floating around and around in a vortex which wouldn't readily be subdued. Dr. Clough had been in the midst of a very serious operation: amputation of an arm and leg from a wounded man. He was temporarily blinded by the white storm. In the dining saloon, his assistants were also hard at work, using their emergency facilities.

"All engine room communications were gone," said Barr, "also deck compasses. The rapid spread of the fire called for hurry. Two of the midshipmen saved the standard compass and some of the charts . . . our need was to keep before the wind."

In Captain Noel Grant's cabin, fire, started by a shell which nonetheless had failed to explode, was raging beyond any attempts to subdue it.

On the *Cap Trafalgar* there was mounting destruction. Each salvo from the *Carmania*'s shells had started at least five fires.

"We decided," continued Steffan, "that our fire superiority

was, at best, doubtful. Captain Wirth decided to bring the *Cap Trafalgar* into range of our machine-guns, in order to make all the trouble possible for our enemy.

"I had my combat station aft of our guns. Looking ahead, I could soon see nothing on account of the brown smoke clouds. The first enemy blow had hit the foremast. The shell had then rebounded to the deck and exploded beside the gun and its ready boxes. No man of the gun crew escaped without injury. Assistant Helmsman Schneider became the first of our company to die in the action. His head was blown off.

"Enemy shells and shrapnel tore to bits the flowers in our elegant *Wintergarten*. Marble was torn from the walls. Rubble was heaped on rubble. First Officer Rettberg was injured in the back and thigh by marble splinters.

"Our fire-fighting parties worked bravely to extinguish the many fires about the ship, sustaining casualties as they did so. Their task was made the more difficult because the water and steam lines were all shot with holes.

"Water gushed over the deck, steam billowed up in clouds from the broken pipes. Nevertheless we kept our gun firing effectively until a shot coming in on the starboard made it difficult to aim. Amid fire and heaping rubble, we had to try to clean our gun and get it back into action.

"We were now but 1,800 meters distant from the enemy. We put to good use our machine guns, really intended for limited use in the colonies, until all the ammunition was expended. Soon we were firing with only two cannons, as was the enemy.

"He turned away, burning, leading us to believe we were the victor. However, we kept listing more and more to starboard. A lucky shot, piercing below the waterline, had knocked out a main bulkhead and flooded the engine and boiler rooms so badly that pumps could not control the inrush of water."

Lieutenant Murchie on the *Carmania* decided it was "the bloody fool's undoing" for the *Cap Trafalgar* to keep in machine-gun range, even though this strategy was taking toll of the *Carmania*'s upper structure. Now that it was apparent that the German could outrange him, Grant determined to keep the hot battle raging at even closer quarters.

He executed a pirouette to starboard, bringing other guns to bear and also lessening the effect of the northeast breeze which had been fanning the fires boiling upwards in "purple-glowing clouds."

The enemy passed astern of the *Carmania* at about 2,800 yards. During these moments the cross fire was at its hottest. The two heavyweights were now a little more than a mile apart, steaming parallel—the Britisher at sixteen knots, the German at eighteen—in opposite directions. The *Carmania*, after her graceful circle, was still pounding southward.

On both ships, fire control was directed from the individual guns, telephonic communications having been knocked out. Outside steam lines, too, had been pierced in hundreds of places, their scalding mists hissing in all directions. The water lines had also been ruptured, leaving bucket brigades as the only resource for fire fighting.

The entire *Carmania*, one seaman recalled, "was a medley of destruction." Her decks were knee-deep in expended cartridge cylinders. The port side of her main rigging was shot off and hanging in tatters, the ventilator cowls were ribboned, holes gaped in her superstructure, railings and stanchions were twisted beyond recognition, and fragments of lifeboats, davits—the full and ugly refuse of battle—were everywhere.

On the *Cap Trafalgar* the crew's forward fo'c'sle as well as the entire second-class accommodations were thick with smoke. The palms in the mounting inferno of the *Wintergarten* burned with a yellow flame, sprewing out especially noxious fumes.

A hit in the captain's cabin split the ship's safe open like a burst melon, sending coins clinking in a shower over the deck.

Finally, Lieutenant Steffan received welcome news from Captain Thierfelder on the *Kronprinz Wilhelm*: "Hold out, I am coming . . . ! "

Wounded by shrapnel in the right leg and back, most of his clothes torn off, Commodore Wirth nonetheless continued to "con" his ship, ordering fire directed at the Britisher with those guns which were still in action. The assistant helmsman had been hit in the head, a chief petty officer in the leg, another man in the arm.

34 • The Battling Liners

Although slower in speed and outranged by her opponent's guns, the ex-Cunard liner *Carmania* managed to outmaneuver and sink the German raider *Cap Trafalgar*. This battle took place off the coast of Venezuela and was the war's longest single naval engagement.

One loader threw a last shell into his gun, pressing his elbow against a stomach wound to staunch the pumping of blood. Then he fell dead.

Aboard the *Carmania*, Gunner First Class Richard Edward Pierce, fit and full of fight at forty-two years, refused to be invalided out of the action by an arm wound. He had it dressed, then hurried back to his gun station—to be killed instantly by a direct hit. He left eight children (a ninth, christened Annie Carmania, was born posthumously).

The sailors continued to feed the guns until their hands blistered from the barrels' heat. Around them, flames leaped to mast height. Seemingly insuring the liner's doom, the chemical extinguishers were almost inoperative, "apparently sullied," or defective, according to Barr. However, there remained a few desperate measures still to be employed.

"By blocking all ventilation," he reported, "using water from buckets, baths, and even boat breakers, I was trying to hold the fire, sending frequent messages to the engine room to get the water onto deck service pipes."

Every engineer who could be spared from his principal station below and every officer and man who could leave the guns was pressed into many impromptu fire battalions.

It was now 1 P.M. and the incessant cannonading had been disturbing the quiet of the South Atlantic for nearly an hour. All the seabirds had flapped off from their rocky perches on Trindade. No living creatures, other than the crews of the two ships, witnessed this modern-day encounter of steel leviathans.

"I was still busy with the fire," Barr continued, "when its sudden excess of energy made me look for the causes. I could see that our course had been changed but, being on the port side, could not see the enemy. Firing had ceased and Captain Grant was trying to close. Great sheets of flame from our blazing bridge roared higher than the funnel tops. The fire had attacked the stairway leading below and was spreading.

"I ran aft and, from the boat deck, hailed Captain Grant who was on the after bridge, or wheelhouse, and asked him to keep before the wind if he could, as we were still without water.

"With his extended arm indicating the collier now rapidly closing with the *Cap Trafalgar* which, listing to starboard, had turned sixteen points to port and was stopped, he shouted, 'I want to get that vessel!'

"I replied, 'You will surely lose this one if you don't keep away!'

"When I ran aft the guns were silent, their crews alert and watchful; many of the firemen had ventured on deck and all of those at the after end of the ship could hear the shouted conversation between Captain Grant and myself and see what followed it.

"Reluctantly, Grant gave the order to keep away."

St. John had rigged up "a short-range, emergency antenna." He defied the heat and flames to enter the radio shack and pick up signals from another German vessel "that must have been close at hand."

The *Kronprinz Wilhelm* was indeed near. Thierfelder radioed Wirth that he was no more than ten miles to the southeast; in fact, he could hear the drum-roll of cannonading. In less than half an hour, possibly, he could join forces with the staggering *Cap Trafalgar*. It was, even so, too long.

Not quite three miles to the north of the *Carmania*, the German liner could not wait. She veered to the southeast, indicating that she was attempting to beach. Wirth, almost unconscious from loss of blood, would not strike his colors. However, he ordered two scuttling charges placed in the engine room.

Lifeboats were lowered. Only three made it safely to the water. The great list caused others to be swamped, dumping their occupants into the sea.

"Time," wrote Steffan, "for a final cigarette . . .!

"Then, through the smoke and steam, three cheers for the Kaiser! Hoarsely, we sang the national anthem.

"Two explosions shook the ship. Quickly the order, 'Abandon . . . !' It was all over."

The *Cap Trafalgar*, blazing and spewing like a volcano at the climax of eruption, lay over until her funnels were parallel with the sea. One of her propellers, out of water, continued to windmill. Half of her keel was exposed, like the underbelly of some great dying whale.

Then, unexpectedly, the vessel, boat decks awash, righted herself, the bow dipped under, the stern gradually rose up, up, until it was almost vertical. The scuttling charges exploded. Steffan wrote her obituary:

"*Cap Trafalgar* sank with flags flying. The sea was thick with debris. In such a situation, we couldn't count for sure on our rescue. However, I clung to a plank until the *Eleonore Woer-*

mann, which had not forgotten us, picked me up. During Captain Collmorgen's search he rescued most of the survivors, including wounded."

Nothing now remained except eddies on the disturbed blue sea, wreckage, and the small white dots of lifeboats. *Cap Trafalgar* had, one of the survivors recalled, been "consigned to the stronghold of the sea."

The crew of the *Carmania*, pausing in their efforts to save their own ship and at first awed into silence, now lined the rails to raise a cheer, both for a gallant foe and for the Royal Navy's outstanding victory. An old, slow vessel, outranged by the enemy's guns, had won almost solely because of the superior fighting skill of Captain Grant.

The colliers returned to haul the human flotsam out of the water. Many of the survivors had already been mutilated by the sharks. Even as they worked at rescue, the masts of the *Kronprinz Wilhelm* appeared over the southerly horizon.* It could have been the *Dresden*, Grant and his staff speculated.

Whoever she was, *Carmania* could not fight another battle this day.

As Grant laconically observed, "We were in a very uncomfortable position." In addition to the fires and the widespread destruction, there was a lack of navigational facilities. Steering had to be accomplished from a temporary aft bridge. Charts had all been consumed by the fire.

Ingeniously, Barr rigged the charred remains of a sextant and a compass card on a pillow (for deadening vibration). Through this crude means of direction finding, plus visual observations of the sun and, later, the stars, he steered, "by guess and by God," southward.

The *Kronprinz Wilhelm* did not pursue the Cunarder. She ascertained that the supply ships were picking up the *Cap Trafalgar's* survivors, then returned to the Atlantic sea-lanes. Thierfelder, who in all likelihood had sighted at least the smoke from the burning *Carmania*, never explained why he failed to close in for the kill.

*See Notes and Acknowledgments for this chapter for a postscript on the *Kronprinz*.

The English ship's casualties had been remarkably light: nine killed and twenty-six wounded, four critically. Seventy-nine hits had punched 304 holes in her hull and superstructure. Some projectiles had drilled through three thicknesses of armor plating which had been riveted around the bridge. Her own gunners had banged off 417 rounds.

St. John rigged up a makeshift transmitter and brought the cruiser *Cornwall* belatedly to her aid. He also received congratulations from Sir John Fisher, the first sea lord of the Admiralty: "Well done! You have fought a fine action to a successful finish!"

Later, a naval historian added, "No single ship has been fought to the death in such an historic and Nelsonian fashion." The battle was also to prove the war's longest "single" naval engagement and the only one in which the opponents were very closely matched. And never again would two large luxury liners meet and battle to the death.

St. John himself penned a final amen:

"That evening we had the sad and impressive experience of committing the bodies of our dead comrades to the sea.

"Night had fallen before we had reduced the decks to something like order, and in the starlight we assembled aft while the captain read the funeral service. The bodies slid overboard, quietly accompanied by the sorrowful notes of the 'Last Post.'

"The captain then addressed the ship's company, saying:

" 'Men, you have fought like Englishmen; I am proud of you.' "

The *Carmania* sailed into Pernambuco, where the Brazilians turned their backs while she made extensive repairs. Then she crossed the Atlantic to Gibraltar for further refitting. Captain Barr's "sea-kindly" ship, in her vintage years, had slugged her way to glory. But she wouldn't go back to war until the next spring.

Of the *Cap Trafalgar*'s complement, twenty were dead, including her captain. Most of these, however, had been drowned or killed by sharks. Only a few were lost during the blistering action. The 279 survivors spent more than a week on the *Eleonore Woermann*, steaming this way and that to avoid the thoroughly aroused British Navy. Thanks to good navigation and bad weather, they arrived safely in Buenos Aires. All would spend the remainder of the war interned on Martín García Island.

Meanwhile, Thierfelder, on the *Kronprinz Wilhelm*, had returned to prowling the broad, green lanes of the South Atlantic —and to his crew's unceasing rat hunt. And so the war at sea continued.

Her fight with the *Cap Trafalgar* left the *Carmania* severely damaged, as evidenced by the debris on the bridge. During the battle she suffered 79 hits and 304 holes in her hull and superstructure. Water rushed into the engine rooms causing a list to starboard, and fires blazed on deck.

(2)

Disaster on the Broad Fourteens

⊕ The war was less than two months old when the era of the submarine advanced in one hour from infancy to pugnacious adulthood. On September 22, three hulking British cruisers were swiftly destroyed by a lone U-boat raider in the North Sea. The Great Powers, as well as the lesser ones, including Italy and Japan, took notice and summarily accorded the submarine a respected position in future wars at sea.

The chief agent of the submarine's rise was a daring young U-boat commander named Otto Weddigen. Born in Herford, Saxony, in 1882, he belonged to a family that counted many uniforms in its ancestry and at least one Iron Cross. An uncle had served with distinction in the Franco-Prussian War.

A skilled athlete, Otto compensated for less-than-average height with muscles of iron and very fast reflexes. None could out-distance him in almost any type of race, swimming or track. He was also a wrestler of great strength.

Otto's ancestry, his love of adventure, and his innate qualities of leadership combined to determine his career. He wanted to enter the *Kriegsmarine*, and did.

Avoiding the old-world architecture and atmosphere of the naval academy at Kiel, Otto managed to be commissioned directly into the kaiser's Imperial Navy. His first assignment was to a river gunboat, but he soon switched to submarines. These little "iron coffins" were in their infancy then, but Otto loved them.

He learned their machinery-cluttered mysteries. He staunchly defended this new naval weapon against the barbs of its numerous critics, including the father of the twentieth-century German Navy, the bewhiskered firebrand Admiral Alfred von Tirpitz. "Impractical" and "experimental" were among the least of the criticisms.

At the same time, Otto became somewhat of a legend in his own right. At dusk one evening he leapt into the North Sea to rescue a seaman who had tumbled off the slippery narrow decking of his U-boat. Returning aboard, Weddigen snapped an arm bone.

Two weeks later, the indomitable young lieutenant was, as usual, conducting a gymnastics class for any sailors in Wilhelmshaven who wished to attend. The base commandant, who had been watching the proceedings, finally asked Weddigen if it had not been "difficult."

"Oh, no," Otto Weddigen replied. "I have only *one* broken arm."

By 1914, the now Kapitänleutnant conned his own command, *U-9*, an old-type submarine but, as he liked to describe it, one which had been "built on honor." It exuded much of the beauty of the hand tooling and precision of an antique automobile. He loved his *Unterseeboot*. Besides, it was one of a select as well as unique group. Only twenty-four were commissioned in the entire navy.

Otto also had another love: blonde, slender Irma Prencke of Wilhelmshaven. His courtship was swift during those early months of 1914. It had to be.

"I am forced to draw the sword!" Kaiser Wilhelm had shouted. The response of his subjects was sincere and generally enthusiastic. Repeated in village after village was a solemn and often tearful scene: a son or young father bidding *auf Wiedersehen* to his family at the railway station, going off to join his regiment. Such mass separations hadn't happened since 1870, the last time Germany had fought France.

"Our march to the station was a gripping and uplifting experience," wrote one of them, a Leipzig law student. "Such enthusiasm! The whole battalion with helmets and tunics decked with flowers—handkerchiefs waving untiringly—cheers on every side—and over and over again the ever-fresh and wonderful reassurance from the soldiers. This hour is one such as seldom strikes in the life of a nation, and it is so marvelous and moving as to be in itself sufficient compensation for many sufferings and sacrifices." The author, Walter Limmer, was one of the first to be killed.

Wedding bells sounded from Bavaria to the Baltic, as betrothed hastened their wedding plans. Among them was Kapitänleutnant Weddigen who was married to Irma on August 14 in the military chapel at Wilhelmshaven. There was no time for honeymooning. Instead, Otto readied his little U-boat for "coastal patrol," according to orders.

Across the North Sea, in England as well as in Scotland and Ireland, marriage vows were also being repeated, with an earnestness reminiscent of Boer War days at the turn of the century. The newlyweds hurried out into the streets of empire to be greeted by an exceptionally challenging reminder: posters with the stern, moustached countenance of the earl of Khartoum, Field Marshal Horatio Kitchener, the secretary of state for war, glaring and admonishing, "Your Country Needs *You!*"

Royal Navy Reserves and Fleet Reservists were more numerous than their army counterparts. Recruitment did not pose an immediate problem. Quite the opposite, the Admiralty's only problem was a quantitative one: what to do with those automatically called up by the declaration of war? They ranged from mature officers "on the shelf"—snatched unexpectedly from the humdrum of peacetime middle age—to the youngest rating whose only knowledge of the sea stemmed from occasional drills in some village meeting hall.

An answer seemed to lie in the "ol ' klunkers," semiobsolete warships, which nonetheless floated, mounted guns of heavy caliber, and needed complements disproportionate to their combat potential. Among their number were cruisers belonging to the *Cressy* class, laid down in 1899. Of 12,000 tons each, the four-stackers were 454 feet in overall length, with an ungraceful beam of 69 feet, and a speed—designed at twenty-one knots—which could no longer be resummoned. A 28-foot draft and aging engines combined to slow the cruisers to a little better than half of their intended gait.

However, these reserve "armored" cruisers vaunted a main battery of 9.2-inchers, with punch enough to knock over lesser, newer vessels—and sufficient recoil to soundly jolt their own crews. Their very bulk, it was carelessly reasoned, should deter lesser commands of the enemy, certainly torpedo craft and minelayers, which were to be the particular object of their patrol.

Three of them—the *Cressy* herself, the *Aboukir*, and the *Hogue*—were brought out of the Medway River at the Thames estuary. With the same speed and fervor which had attended the conversion of *Carmania*, the overage ladies of the sea were scrubbed for war.

Barnacles were scraped from their hulls, traces of rust were hidden by dousings of red lead, then the increasingly familiar black-gray war paint was spread on. There was not time even for the customary cacophony of the chipper's hammer. Ammunition and provisions were hoisted aboard; then officers and men filed on—700 per cruiser.

Attached to what was known as the Nore (River) Command of the 7th Cruiser Squadron, the three cruisers were, like so many other ships then in the Royal Navy, local ships. Almost all in their crews lived within walking distance of the Medway. They came from Maidstone and Chatham, from Rochester, Gillingham, and smaller hamlets in the area, whose populace watched with personal pride, and lumpy throats, the outfitting of the *Aboukir*, *Cressy*, and *Hogue*.

This weary but heavyweight segment of the Nore Command had become a family affair.

For the most part, the crews were exceptionally lubberly. However, none of the ships was due ever to steam far out of sight of land, and seasoned regular navy officers at the helms were deemed sufficient to compensate for the inexperience of their commands. They were: Captain John E. Drummond of the *Aboukir*, Captain R. W. Johnson of the *Cressy*, and Captain W. S. Nicholson, of the *Hogue*.

Surprisingly, these cruisers were among the first participants in the war. By September, all three were veterans of the offshore patrol. Their greatest test came when they were allocated to the Southern Force of the squadron to patrol the "Broad Fourteens," the seaman's British term designating an area off the Dutch coast. The entire North Sea was as much a German pond as an English one.

Summer ended abruptly in this uncertain body of water that extends to the Arctic icepack. By late September, whitecaps frothed across the shallow waters, from East Anglia, past the Dogger Bank—an extensive shoal—to Scandinavia and Holland.

This year, an especially severe storm lashed the entire 120-mile stretch of sea from Dover to the Hook of Holland at the approaches to Rotterdam. Its grayish waters became a shifting cauldron of stinging spray and opaque spindrift.

The submarine was used primarily for torpedo attacks on surface ships. But after Germany had demonstrated the U-boat's effectiveness, other countries joined in its construction. Here, in a rare occurrence, the Italian submarine *Medusa* attacks an Austro-Hungarian submarine.

Leipziger Illustrirte Zeitung

On September 19, the Admiralty wirelessed: "The Dogger Bank patrol need not be continued. Weather too bad for destroyers to go to sea. Arrange with cruisers to watch Broad Fourteens."

The next day, off the Maas lightship, Rear Admiral A. H. Christian, commanding the Southern Force of the 7th Cruiser Squadron to which the *Aboukir*, *Cressy*, and *Hogue* were attached, swung westward for Harwich, his flagship badly in need of coal. Captain Drummond, of the *Aboukir*, then became the senior officer of the three remaining vessels, now left without any possibility of protection from a destroyer screen.

The continuing storm augmented a naturally dangerous area, lying between a German minefield to the north and the Dutch coast. There was little room for changes of course. Rear Admiral Christian, however, had already concluded that this defile of seaway, because of its narrowness, was one where the enemy was least likely to prowl. He maintained further that the short sharp wave troughs of shallow waters during storms would preclude submarine operations.

On the twenty-first, however, information was received in London that an enemy force of light cruisers, destroyers, and submarines had been seen from Esbjerg, in the south of Denmark, plowing north. Admiral Sir John Jellicoe, commander in chief of the Grand Fleet, at once organized a northward sweep, up to the Horns Reef. While this operation did not involve the *Aboukir*, *Cressy*, or *Hogue*, it left them isolated.

But early on Tuesday, the twenty-second, the seas fell and all signs pointed to moderating weather. Commodore Reginald Tyrwhitt, aboard the flagship *Lowestoft*, commanding a flotilla of eight destroyers, known as the Harwich Force, put out to patrol with the cruisers and give them protection.

By 6 A.M. the eastern horizon turned from black to a steadily lightening gray. In line, like circus elephants, the *Aboukir*, *Cressy*, and *Hogue* steamed on a northeasterly course, about twenty miles abeam of the Hook of Holland. If continued, the heading would put them aground on the North Holland coast, approximately at Ijmuiden. The present course, however, with a southwest wind and following sea, allowed the big ships to ride easily.

In Berlin, navy chieftains had, with great reluctance, ordered the diminutive U-boats to patrol. The handful which were ready to cast off moorings were distributed between the North Sea, on one side of the Jutland Peninsula, and the Baltic, on the other. To military men, they appeared too fragile, too inconsequential, even for coastal work.

Weddigen's days since the beginning of the war had been spent in familiarizing himself with his own submarine and the charts of his hunting grounds—the area just beyond the low sandy Frisian Islands, the dreamlike Borkum Reefs, and loaflike Helgoland. This barren, rocky plateau reared out of the North Sea like an afterthought in the creation of Europe.

Then, at last, came his first patrol. His *U-9* ground out into the gale-lashed seas on the twentieth. He paused only long enough to calibrate his weak radio with the Borkum Telefunken and the "gate ship" *Arkona*, an old minelayer, bobbing endlessly as a sentry before Wilhelmshaven Roads. Soon only the gray waters lay ahead.

He ran mostly on the surface, scanning the horizon with binoculars until his eyes watered and were temporarily blinded.

Inside his oil-reeking uncomfortable steel coffin there was always a background of clangor. If someone of the crew of twenty-five was not working on the maze of machinery and instruments—as was usually the case—he was surely bumping into them. At night it was quieter, through deadly necessity. The purr of the engines, at idling, found a chorus only in occasional tinny strains from the U-boat's gramophone, or from an accordion as the ever-lonesome sailors hummed sad *Lieder*.

At times, Weddigen allowed the *U-9* to rest on the surface, with engines cut, listening through hydrophones for the sound of approaching propellers. As infrequently as possible, he cruised, submerged a few feet, using his electric motors. It required several hours to recharge the batteries and replenish the foul air below.

As hints of dawn appeared through the swirling mists, that Tuesday, the *U-9* was barely under water, showing five feet of periscope. More than 200 miles had been logged on this maiden war patrol and it was time to put back to Wilhelmshaven or Emden for refueling. Weddigen had been watching the familiar glow and wink of the Maas lightship when he detected shadows moving near it on the horizon. The hour was 6:10 A.M.

He shot up at once, to see better. The conning tower was still swirling with salty foam and reeking with its familiar pungency as he climbed up into it. He steadied himself. The little craft was pitching sickeningly.

One shadow, magically, grew into three. He shouted down through the voice tube:

"*Raus! Raus!*"

Off went the gramophone and down on the bunks went two or three guitars as the crew tumbled to action stations. The boredom and the weary discomfiture of U-boat patrol had been ended with the abruptness of a dashing of cold water into one's face. Later, Weddigen reported:

". . . I submerged completely and laid my course so as to bring up the center of the trio which held a sort of triangular formation. I could see their gray-black sides riding high over the water."

Although he believed the procession was near enough for "torpedo work," he maneuvered in a little closer, he said, "to make my aim sure."

As unbelievable as it was, Weddigen could not dispute his own eyes. ". . . I soon reached a good shooting point," he said, and the command rang out: " '*Los!*'

". . . I was then about twelve feet underwater and got the shot off in good shape, my men handling the boat as if she had been a skiff." It was exactly 6:30 A.M.

Within seconds, Weddigen watched an awesome sight: "A fountain of water, a burst of smoke, a flash of fire, and part of the cruiser rose in the air." Next he "heard a roar and felt reverberations sent through the water by the detonation. She had been broken apart and sank in a few minutes . . . ."

Submarines had to be carefully loaded for long trips away from port. Inside, the U-boats were crowded with men, food, machinery, and torpedoes.

On the *Hogue*, those who had been sleeping were awakened by a spurt of speed as Captain Nicholson, incredulous, watching the destruction of the *U-9*'s first victim, loped to his sister's aid. Within the minute the heavy ship had heeled over on her port side so that the starboard plates were plainly visible, glistening red in the brightening morning. Those on the upper decks were projected almost at once into the water. One boat was lowered from the badly listing vessel, then stopped halfway down, like a game bird caught in the branches of a high tree.

Captain Drummond, thinking his ship had struck a mine, signaled the other two cruisers to come closer, presumably to pick up survivors. He ordered starboard wing compartments

Disaster on the Broad Fourteens • 49

flooded in an effort to right her. But the old and tired *Aboukir* appeared to welcome execution. She was going down fast.

"Abandon ship!" Drummond ordered.

The *Cressy* stopped and lowered every one of her boats.

Weddigen, entranced at the sight through his periscope, was impressed with the "brave" sailors of the sinking ship. Many seemed to be at gun stations, even though she was listing at an angle impossible for shooting. However, fully aware that the other two cruisers were hurrying to the assistance of the third, he let go another torpedo. "I had scarcely to move out of my position," he said, "which was a great aid since it helped to keep me from detection."

On the *Hogue*, those not lowering boats or manning guns, continued to be transfixed at the spectacle of a mighty ship in her death agonies. One young reserve officer, noting that the *Aboukir* was sinking by the bow, watched "the sun shining on pink, naked men walking down her sides inch by inch as she heeled over, some standing, others sitting down and sliding into the water, which was soon dotted with heads."

It now registered on him that survivors would shortly be coming aboard. He put on his shoes, and still clad in pajamas raced down to sick bay and reminded the stewards to have blankets and hot coffee ready. Running back to his cabin for his clothes, he was halted by "a terrific crash . . . the ship lifted up, quivering all over . . . a second or two later another and duller crash and a great cloud of smoke, followed by a torrent of water, came pouring in through my open scuttle. The noise for a second or two was deafening. . . ." In the background was the sound of breaking, crashing, and splintering as though every piece of glass and crockery, every chair and table, anything that wasn't riveted to the bulkheads was being fragmented.

The executive officer, Commander Reginald A. Norton, noted, "The *Hogue* was struck on the starboard side amidships by two torpedoes at intervals of ten to twenty seconds. The ship at once began to heel to starboard. . . ."

If the personnel of the three cruisers were stunned, however, the Admiralty in London was struck dumb when it intercepted this wireless message, "*Aboukir, Hogue* sinking . . . !" followed by the position, then repeated.

Of course, as the radio duty officers this early morning observed to one another, it wouldn't have come as such a shock "if we'd had some warning there was anything wrong with the old girls in the first place."

Commodore Tyrwhitt, picking up the distress signal, ordered his destroyer flotilla full speed ahead. He was still fifty miles distant from the Broad Fourteens. In his heart was the sick dread that he could not possibly get there in time.

On the *Cressy*, which no longer had as much as one lifeboat suspended from her davits, there persisted a firm belief that the cruisers had been surrounded by a squadron of five submarines. She opened fire. Albert Dougherty, a chief warrant gunner, was certain that, on his third or fourth shot with a 12-pounder, he "hit one of 'em."

"Every man for himself!" Captain Drummond shouted in the dying minutes of the *Aboukir*.

"What about yourself, Captain?" more than one of the handful left aboard asked.

"You look to yourself, my boy, never mind me," he counseled, assisting several crewmen into the water, which now lapped over the bridge.

Less than twenty minutes after she had been struck, the *Aboukir* turned turtle. For a while she floated upward, tempting those in the water to struggle upward onto her slimy, red-leaded keel. Few succeeded. The climb was too steep, too slippery. Those who somehow clawed their way to relatively level footing were cut, begrimed, exhausted, and choking from the water, oil and lead paint they had inhaled and absorbed. The *Aboukir* soon vanished altogether, taking with her most of the wild-eyed derelicts who had clung to her keel.

The *Hogue* opened fire—at nothing more substantial than shadows and hallucinations. Captain Nicholson ordered all water-tight doors, deadlights, and scuttles closed. Mess stools, tables, any timber or, indeed, anything which floated was thrown over the side—for the saving of life. Boats were swung out on their booms. Excited bos'ns ordered the men variously to strip down and to provide themselves with wool clothing as well as their hammocks.

For a time it seemed as though the *Hogue* was going to make it in spite of her wound, but within five minutes the quarterdeck was awash. The cruiser heeled dizzily to starboard, throwing men against the bulkheads, breaking their arms and legs, cracking their skulls. An explosion deep below added to their misery. Not until the doomed *Hogue* lay almost on beam ends did the gunners reluctantly cease their futile firing. Captain Nicholson now was compelled to repeat the final orders of Drummond, of the *Aboukir*: "Abandon ship!"

She sank at 7:15 A.M., just ten minutes after the torpedo had driven home. One seaman, trapped below decks, was spewed out in a cascade of water through an opened hatch by the very momentum of the plunging cruiser. He lived to tell of his uncanny deliverance.

The *Cressy* with all her boats away and her guns still hotly in action commenced to zigzag. Thereby, unintentionally, she was menacing anew the sea of bobbing men from the sunken *Aboukir* and *Hogue*. Already, in the oil-filmed and debris-cluttered water, they were ducking the caroming shells and machine-gun fusillade.

Weddigen, emboldened by his spectacular success, surfaced and took aim: ". . . within suitable range I sent away my third attack. This time I sent a second torpedo after the first to make the strike doubly certain. My crew were aiming like sharpshooters and both torpedoes went to their bull's-eye."

The *Cressy's* boiler room ruptured and was at once enveloped in a scalding miasma of steam. The "black gang," blinded, screaming with pain, clawed toward the ladders.

The cruiser, halted like a charging rhinoceros hit by a high-velocity bullet, dipped her bow deep. An angry cascade of water foamed over her fo'c'sle. *Cressy* was stopped dead. Those in the water saw the torpedoing as "a sudden explosion and a great column of smoke black as ink" which "flew up as high as the *Cressy's* funnels."

She heeled, momentarily righted herself, and as with the

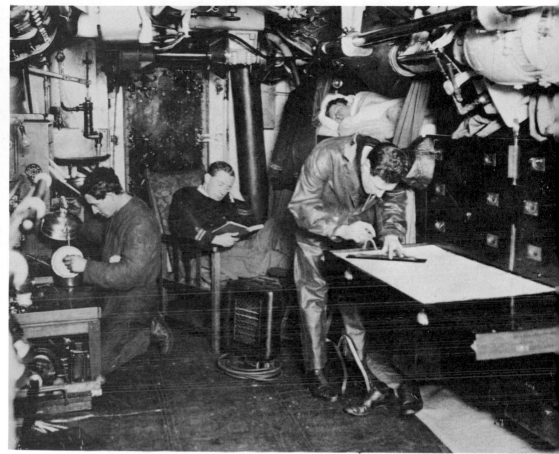

Submarine interiors were a crowded maze of men and machinery. Here, four crewmen occupy limited space in wardroom.

Aboukir and *Hogue* the same dismal, taunting sequence was repeated. "Our decks slipped beneath our feet," one gunner noted, "but the good old tub recovered." It seemed as though "the good old tub" could be saved, as engineers and their helpers rushed about, steadying themselves against the slant of the decks, to close doors and scuttles. Like her sisters, unhappily, she had been designed without consideration of ways to check flooding after torpedo hits.

Disaster on the Broad Fourteens • 53

The *Cressy* was sinking fast, like a heavy oil drum which had been split in target practice. "She careened far over," Weddigen continued, "but all the while her men stayed at the guns, looking for their invisible foe. They were brave and true to their country's sea traditions."

Captain Johnson, walking calmly among his men, clucked in fatherly tones, "Keep cool, my lads, keep cool! Pick up a spar, my lads, and put it under your arm. That'll help you keep afloat until the destroyers pick you up." He even instructed them how to inhale " . . . mouth closed . . . breathe through the nose."

At 7:30 A.M., just one hour after the *Aboukir* had been struck, the remaining boilers of the *Cressy* tore loose in one deafening, devastating explosion. Like the *Aboukir*, she turned turtle and floated keel up for a few minutes before taking her final plunge to the silent depths of the North Sea.

While Weddigen, jubilant, set course for Wilhelmshaven, nearly 1,000 men who so far had survived the torpedoing thrashed amid flotsam on the littered surface. They cried or shouted, prayed, or simply moaned like hurt, uncomprehending children. The most chilling sounds were the piercing screams of the truly terrified.

Since the *Aboukir* and *Hogue* had sunk without launching more than a boat or two, the survivors struggled to climb aboard the *Cressy*'s lifeboats, rafts, wreckage, anything that was substantial and floated. Twenty-four found a lattice target bobbing about and clung to it, others clutched fenders of twigs (used to keep the ships from scraping against docks), and as many as five sailors were clinging to each of the larger life buoys. One officer, pinioned around the neck in a death grasp by a drowning man, quickly tore off his own life jacket in order to escape and left it to his panicked shipmate.

Dr. Gerald Noel Martin, a temporary surgeon aboard the *Cressy*, reported the experience of many when he described what happened to him in the water:

"As the vessel went over I was washed off by a big wave. Before this I had stripped. I saw the *Cressy*, keel upwards; there were perhaps fifty men clinging to her, and when she finally went down I was surprised to find that there was only a little bit of suction. Luckily I am a good swimmer, and after I had gone 100 yards I came across a long plank to which half a dozen men were clinging. They were men I knew and they asked me to share it with them, which I did, with the object of giving them some directions. I told them to hold on with one hand and move their legs about.

"After I had been hanging on to the plank for a quarter of an hour, some of the men were giving out and began to sit on the wood, forcing it under the water. Leaving the plank, I struck out on my own and swam on for some time till I came across a man who beckoned to me. I got to him and found he had a table under one arm and a piece of wood under the other. He gave up the table to me. The top was fifteen inches square and the legs were very stout. I looked round for something to swim to, and caught sight of a fishing smack to the windward. After a long swim I found it was getting nearer and nearer, and I began to shout to it. All this time I had been swimming on my own. The only human forms I came across were two or three dead bodies— men who were bent over the wood or wreckage to which they had clung.

"As I got nearer to the smack I shouted for all I was worth. I would shout, swim a hundred yards, and shout again. At last the crew spotted me and sent their small boat, which picked me up."

Not until 8:30 A.M., one hour later, did two small Dutch steamers, first the *Flora*, then the *Titan*, and finally the English trawler *Corianda* arrive at the scene of the triple disaster. Bravely pushing into risky waters which were demonstrably the haunt of submarines as well as mines, their crews began bringing the dead and the dying on deck.

"It was a very difficult undertaking," recalled Captain Voorham, of the *Flora*, "as the survivors were exhausted and we were rolling heavily. All were practically naked and some were so exhausted that they had to be hauled aboard with tackle."

The Reverend G. H. Collier, chaplain of the *Cressy*, who had made last-minute checks in the darkened cabins and fo'c'sles, could not swim. He clung gamely to one side of a bobbing life buoy. Beside him was Engineer-Commander Stokes, an expert

The submarine quickly proved its effectiveness in naval warfare. Here a German U-boat torpedoes a British merchant ship.

swimmer who nonetheless was helpless. His legs were broken. Both were rescued by the *Corianda*, whose skipper managed to find room for 120 other survivors in his small craft.

With all their suffering and the depletion of their stamina and nervous energy, the survivors were philosophical: "Hard luck, but it's in the day's work . . . !" A few professed admiration for their vanquisher: "A fine piece of work, a gallant piece of work!" The two captains who had survived, Drummond and Nicholson, were unstinting in praise of the "splendid discipline" evinced to the end by the plucky reservists.

The destroyer flotilla of Commodore Tyrwhitt arrived at 10:30 A.M., too late to more than carry groups of survivors back to England. They were a pathetic sight as they disembarked at Harwich. Most of them were shoeless and some were still clad in their pajamas, with blankets or sacking clutched about them.

Others were wearing white trousers and heavy, navy-issue sweaters. The officer survivors had generally come off with their thick llama watch coats—though many wore nothing beneath.

The Great Eastern Hotel had been commandeered and here those who could stand and walk lined up, first for steaming baths. Outside the building and in the lobby, often weeping, but sometimes frozen-faced, families waited for loved ones.

In more than 1,400 homes it was as though the lights had all at once been switched off, the coal hearths gone abruptly cold. Almost all the families were civilian and they had not given especial thought to "the forces" except on drill nights, when "daddy," "junior," or "hubby" donned his uniform and strode out of the front door. Now, in its early weeks, the Great War had come shatteringly home to the little people of Great Britain. Time would dull the ache in their hearts, it would never altogether remove it. Only 837 men had been saved, making the catastrophe almost of a magnitude of the *Titanic*.

The British, weaned on the exploits of Drake and Nelson, were not prepared for an unrelieved defeat of the Royal Navy, certainly not one of stunning proportions. Nor was it enough that the reservists "died like Englishmen." They were expected to do that and to keep cool to the last, as Captain Johnson had exhorted in the last instructions he would ever give.

The loss, wrote the London *Chronicle* in requiem, was "a disaster the meaning of which it would be foolish to minimize." A marine authority asserted, "Nothing that had yet occurred had so emphatically proclaimed the change that had come over naval warfare, and never perhaps had so great a result been obtained by means relatively so small." Almost at once, the Admiralty laid down the stern dictum:

. . . natural promptings of humanity have in this case led to heavy losses, which would have been avoided by a strict adhesion to military consideration . . . . it has become necessary to point out for the future guidance of His Majesty's ships that the conditions which prevail when one vessel of a squadron is injured in the mine field, or is exposed to submarine attack, are analogous to those which occur in action, and that the rule of leaving ships to their own resources is applicable so far, at any rate, as large vessels are concerned.

More than 1,400 lives were lost in the sinking of the *Aboukir, Cressy,* and *Hogue* by the German *U-9.* Above, men climb to *Aboukir's* starboard side as port side goes under.

The cheers still echoed in Germany for their newest hero, Otto Weddigen,* and the tears still welled in the eyes of those who had known and loved the lost sailors of the *Aboukir*, *Cressy*, and *Hogue* as naval designers bent anew over their drawing boards. Neither Admiral von Tirpitz, the British Admiralty, nor even the neutral United States Navy could afford to overlook, in future planning, the deadly submarines.

Hitherto, its potential had been merely suspected, and only by the most visionary. The submarine, in moments of terrible truth, had now been unmasked as a modern David—"the chief weapon," according to Admiral Hugo von Pohl, then chief of staff for the High Seas Fleet.

And across the world's oceans and along the ravished, contested lands of France where the Germans were pulling back after nearly taking Paris, the war in all its insane hates and cruelty raged on. Only dichards closed their eyes, covered their ears, and pretended that the world of yesterday had really not ended during that August.

The Paris *Herald*, for example, could report that "Riviera visitors find it sunny and tranquil," despite the war. The late autumn season along the Côte d'Azur, at the spas of Nice, Antibes, Cannes, and Juan les Pins was accelerating to its customary fragile tenor.

For that matter, the same society columns also noted that there was "excellent attendance" at the horse races in Birmingham, England. The results of these and other sporting events were often printed in British and Continental newspapers in columns alongside the casualty lists, now swollen with the names of those who had marched so jauntily up the gangplanks of the *Aboukir*, *Cressy*, and *Hogue*.

---

*Awarded the Iron Cross for sinking the *Aboukir*, *Cressy*, and *Hogue*, Otto Weddigen wrote in January, 1915, to his sister of his "lust for life." The next month he proved that he had, as well, a lust and an aptitude for war when, commanding the *U-29*, he sank six merchant ships on one patrol. Now dubbed a "polite pirate," because of his gentlemanly attitude toward his victims, he slashed out boldly on his next patrol, March 18, against the Grand Fleet, off Moray Firth. He was rammed by the 17,900-ton *Dreadnought*. The battleship's captain glimpsed the numerals "29" on his smashed victim's prow before the U-boat and all aboard her sank into oblivion. A "meteor," grieved the official German obituary of Weddigen, "has disappeared."

(3)

Revenge at the Falklands

⊕ Early in December, 1914, one of the most savage battles of naval history was fought off the remote Falklands, at the gateway to the Antarctic.

The Coronel engagement came about as a result of Germany's stubborn but forlorn hope of maintaining trade with South America, a continent which could supply her with nitrates and other raw materials needed for war, in addition to beef and other food. The task of attempting to protect these sea-lanes had fallen to Count Maximilian von Spee, who brought a sizable squadron all the way across the Pacific from Tsingtao, the German colony on the China coast. His ships included the 11,000-ton heavy cruiser *Scharnhorst*, flying his flag, her sister, the *Gneisenau*, and three 3,300-ton light cruisers, the *Leipzig*, *Dresden*, and *Nürnberg*. These were augmented from time to time by whatever colliers he could fall in with.

When von Spee struck, he struck hard—and unexpectedly. The news of his first encounter had reached England four days late, on November 5, a drizzly dull day which would ever after be thought of as "Black Thursday." The Admiralty received its first official word of the attack from a British consul-agent in Valparaíso:

Have just learnt from Chilean admiral that German admiral says that on Sunday at sunset in thick and wicked weather his ships met *Good Hope, Glasgow, Monmouth* and *Otranto*. Action was joined and *Monmouth* turned over and sank after about an hour's fighting. *Good Hope* and *Glasgow* and *Otranto* drew off into the darkness. *Good Hope* was on fire, an explosion was heard and she is believed to have sunk. *Gneisenau, Scharnhorst* and *Nürnberg* were the only German ships engaged.

It was all too true. On November 1, Admiral Sir Christopher Cradock's two cruisers, the 14,000-ton *Good Hope* and the 10,000-ton *Monmouth*, had been sunk, with no survivors. Hopelessly outgunned, silhouetted against the evening glow on the western horizon, Cradock and 1,600 men perished in their exploding warships.

The *Glasgow*, 4,800 tons and lightly armed, was able to escape because of her speed. The *Otranto* (a 12,000-ton Peninsula and Oriental liner used as an armed auxiliary) had been forced to keep at a safe distance during the debacle since she was more defenseless even than the *Glasgow*. The obsolete battleship *Canopus*, mounting 12-inch guns, was fighting a gale, accompanied by two colliers, 120 miles to the south, when she intercepted the last radio message from Admiral Cradock, "I am about to attack enemy now . . . !"

The effect in London was pall-like. Utter strangers stopped one another to ask, "Have you heard?" Coming after the loss of the *Aboukir*, *Cressy*, and *Hogue*, this latest disaster was almost too much to bear.

The war, of course, had to be put up with. Was the leadership faulty? The controversial Prince Louis of Battenberg had already been replaced by Admiral Sir John Fisher, seventy-four years old, who had fathered the "all big gun" ship concept and always defended the role of the submarine. First Lord of the Admiralty Winston Churchill, lauding Fisher's "genius . . . originality," thought him "the most distinguished British naval officer since Nelson."

The team, Churchill and Fisher, while they did not always agree between themselves, was deemed worthy of certainly a few more tries at their luck. Certainly, vacillation on basic strategy had already been too protracted: was it enough to keep the German sea wolves (from battleships to submarines) within their lairs, or should every one of them be flushed out?

Emotional involvements complicated this seemingly elementary problem. The officers of the German and British fleets had always been friendly. They had exchanged official visits and entertained each other lavishly at Kiel and Cowes, manifesting both respect and warmth. Indeed, British ships had been saluted by the kaiser himself at Kiel during the week of the archduke's assassination.

The Germans spoke Oxford English. Many of the German and English officers were related. Indeed, King George V and Kaiser Wilhelm II were first cousins.

Sentiment, however, could not stand in the way of Lord Fisher's decision. A man of proven fiery temper, who once had cried, "war is violence and moderation is imbecility!" added a postscript to suit the needs of the moment: "destroy with overwhelming force . . . annihilate!" As a colleague observed, the two chief pilots of the Royal Navy became like "twin thunderbolts of war." As an instrument of retribution, they chose square-jawed Vice Admiral Sir Frederick Charles Doveton Sturdee, a man who appeared to be an embodiment of the tradition and the great names of the Royal Navy. Now in his fifty-sixth year, he had served His or Her Majesty all his adult life, and had risen to the command of cruiser and dreadnought squadrons.

Sturdee had been knighted in 1913 and had been brought into the Admiralty as chief of the war staff. He concerned himself mainly with tactical and intelligence matters. Now, at news of the loss of the *Good Hope* and the *Monmouth*, Fisher barked challengingly at Sturdee, "You made all these plans, Sturdee; now go and carry them out yourself!"

In no way responsible for Sturdee's appointment, Fisher nonetheless was anxious to see what he could do outside of Whitehall.

Sturdee was directed to proceed to Devonport, near Plymouth, on the southwest tip of England, take command of a special squadron, and sail on November 11. It was pointed out to him that November 11 did not mean November 12. He was told that if the ships were not fully ready for sea he was to take the workmen aboard and put them off later in small boats—or do whatever he wanted with them. And Fisher was not bantering; the ghost of Captain Bligh echoed in "Jacky" Fisher's angry footsteps. As a final broadside, he bade Sturdee not to come

At seventy-four, Sir John Fisher was appointed admiral of the British Fleet after the disaster in the Falklands. Father of the "all big gun" concept, he proposed total annihilation of the German fleet. First Lord of the Admiralty Winston Churchill, praising Fisher's genius, called him the "most distinguished British naval officer since Nelson."

home until his orders had been carried out "to the letter!" . . . that is, until von Spee and his squadron had been wiped off the face of the earth.

Sturdee understood this blunt, salty talk and was not at all dismayed. There was yet ample time for a spot of tea and phlegmatic good-byes to most of his friends before packing and entraining for Devonport.

More distressed as to timetables, however, were the commanders of the two mighty battle cruisers on which Sturdee was to hoist his admiral's flag. They were Captain Percy T. H. Beamish, of the *Invincible*, and Captain Richard F. Phillimore, of the *Inflexible*. Each warship displaced 17,000 tons, could make twenty-seven knots when urged, and mounted a main battery of 12-inch guns.

One of the lieutenant commanders aboard the *Invincible* was thirty-three-year-old Edward Barry Bingham, Ireland-born, captain of the polo team when he was attached to the Malta station, and an amateur jockey of note. The genial, athletic Bingham had helped recommission the five-year-old *Invincible* at the outbreak of war. The vessel had suffered deplorably from her lay-up. "A more hopeless looking ship . . . " he wrote later, "I never wish to behold or to commission again."

However, by November, the twin cruisers already had sparred in the North Sea with their counterparts of the High Seas Fleet. They weren't first-line fighters, but they were 5,000 tons heavier than anything von Spee commanded, and they decisively outgunned his main battery of 8-inch cannons on his flagship, the *Scharnhorst*, as well as the batteries on the *Gneisenau*.

The *Invincible* and *Inflexible,* with no advance warning or explanation, were ordered to cast off at once from Cromarty, the Moray Firth naval base on the northeast Scottish coast, and steam at flank speed to Devonport. There was no time to bother even with the recall whistle. It would summon only those in the closest waterfront pubs, and they would be too full of 'alf-an'-'alf to respond. Sailors ashore, along with their wives and sweethearts, could buy third-class tickets for the long uncomfortable rail journey to Devon.

A raw southwest wind was whipping the English Channel

when the big cruisers slipped into Devonport before dawn, on Sunday, November 8. They were rushed into drydock to have their bottoms scraped and painted, even while stores enough for six months at sea were trundled aboard, and workmen with a hundred different marine specialties crawled in and out of them. Officers rolled up their sleeves and worked around the clock beside their men, hoisting coal, ammunition, and provisions in order to meet the Wednesday sailing date.

On that same Sunday afternoon, Sturdee arrived and his pennant was quickly unfurled above the *Invincible*. Before him were a "begrimed, haggard, and weary" group of salts, nearly 1,000 on each ship, "staggering around like flies." But Sturdee couldn't have cared less. He knew they were getting his command ready for sea at breakneck speed.

So efficient were the men that his two captains, Phillimore and Beamish, were able to report to him at midmorning on Tuesday, a day early, that their cruisers were ready for sea.

"Very well," he told them laconically, "we sail at 4 P.M."

Sailors aboard the Australian cruiser *Sydney* cheer their victory over the German raider *Emden*.

At noon, Lady Sturdee and her daughter were piped on for a farewell dinner that should have taxed the admiral's renowned capacity for masking his emotions. Just before four o'clock, eight breathless midshipmen heaved their seabags and lockers onto the fantails of the two warships and leaped aboard to the cheers of their shipmates and the strains of "Rule, Britannia" from the *Invincible*'s band. The gangplanks had been removed, black clouds were boiling out of the funnels, and tugs strained at the hawsers.

The group of eight young naval men had learned in Exeter, forty miles distant, of the early sailing. They had taken taxis in the race to keep their first date in the war at sea.

The shipyard superintendent fared less well. Especially disturbed about the "impossibility" of bricking-up fireboxes in so "ridiculously" short a time, he had entrained for London, where he argued and blustered his way into the offices of the great man himself—Lord Fisher—who brusquely informed the unhappy superintendent that the cruisers had already sailed. The shock was nearly overpowering. The man had visions of that crazy admiral dumping his workmen—their services completed—into the cold Atlantic one by one.

As this temporary command, known as the South Atlantic and South Pacific Fleet, butted southwestward into the wintry ocean, Sturdee's quarry was resting in the sunshine of Valparaíso. Von Spee, two years Sturdee's junior, had been strangely saddened by his defeat of Cradock. The two officers, of the same vintage and the same general naval schooling, had become friends while serving together on the China station. They evinced much the same personality, the same professional reserve, and also— unlike Lord Fisher—were distinguished by a soft approach and kindly nature. With their heavy beards, they even looked alike. They could without detection have switched uniforms and commands.

At one of the functions tendered the victor of Coronel by Chilean naval officials and members of the large German colony in Valparaíso, von Spee declined to drink a toast to the "damnation of the British Navy." Later, he refused a spray of flowers thrust into his hands by a German woman.

"Keep them for my funeral," he observed gloomily.

Von Spee had cause to be gloomy. Tsingtao had fallen to the Japanese and its loss meant the crumbling of Kaiser Wilhelm's Asian and Pacific empire. The fabulous *Emden* had been destroyed by the Australian cruiser *Sydney,* south of Sumatra, and the new cruiser *Karlsruhe* had blown up mysteriously off Barbados. Those two raiders, in a short wartime career, had sunk forty-one merchant ships.

Writing to his wife about the quick victory over the *Good Hope* and *Monmouth,* von Spee said: ". . . it may not mean much on the whole and in view of the enormous number of British ships." The German admiral was far from home. Could he possibly continue to find enough coal, enough food? When his gunners had discharged their last rounds, where would be obtain fresh ammunition?

Indeed, von Spee had reason for his almost Wagnerian presentiment of doom when he cleared Valparaíso. His visions of wandering the world's seas, a hunted creature, were solidly founded.

By only a few hours he had missed a cable received in Valparaíso from Berlin: "You are ordered to attempt to break through with all ships and return to Germany." In other words, it had been decided that his squadron was needed in the High Seas Fleet, which one day might grow so bold as to challenge the juggernaut which was Britain's Grand Fleet.

More than 1,000 miles south and east of von Spee's waifs of the war—250 miles from Patagonia on the east coast of South America—the several hundred inhabitants of the Falkland Islands were taking fresh courage. The battleship *Canopus,* which had been unable to come to Cradock's assistance, had dropped anchor in Port Stanley, where almost all of the Falkland Islanders lived. The seas in the ever-unfriendly South Atlantic and the demands of war had all but put the old warship out of action. Her captain, Heathcote Grant, had cabled Portsmouth for new engine parts. However, his ship was separated from his supply base by more than 6,000 miles of uninterrupted ocean. He could guess that his visit to this most southerly of British colonies might be of considerable duration.

After gathering supplies, this landing party from the *Emden* found that their ship had been destroyed by an Australian warship.

Bleak and inhospitable, the Falklands knew almost no summer, were swept with wind and rain the year round. On the rugged terrain, the hardy descendants of Scottish settlers raised sheep, the islands' principal industry. For further companionship, they had the thousands of seals, sea lions, and penguins that multiplied on the rocky bastions of the coastline. The land was so bare of trees that it inspired the joke that the governors would surely have hanged themselves from utter despair had there been a stout limb to throw a rope over.

The Falklands marked the grave of 130 ships, mostly sailing

vessels that had foundered on offshore reefs. Because of the islands' remoteness, however, they offered sanctuary to British warships. For the same reason, along with the target presented by the islands' wireless station, the Falklands could be desirable also to the enemy.

Governor William Allerdyce was elated when Captain Grant speculated that his 12,000-ton juggernaut might be around for quite a while.* Between them, they then concocted an ingenious blueprint for defense of the islands. As a first step, the crew removed the topmost masts of the warship, then camouflaged her funnels and the exposed portions of her upper works with brown and green paint to help her blend with the landscape. From where she lay—behind the sand hills that separated Port Stanley from the outer bay, Port William—she was almost invisible from the sea to the east.

Next a range-finding station was erected on a promontory, Sapper Hill, and a telephone line run to the battleship fire-control station to direct her 12-inch guns. Her lighter cannons were removed and placed in rocky abutments on the island. Still not satisfied, Captain Grant loaded empty oil drums with explosives, sank them at the approaches to Port William, and ran electrical detonating lines from them to the *Canopus*. In order to be able to fire with some precision, the homemade mines were numbered, then plotted over the sea area already marked off in squares.

As a final touch, the captain's gig was converted to a picket boat, loaded with a torpedo and dispatched to prowl the outer reaches of the harbor.

In the town of Port Stanley itself, the Falklands' only "center" of habitation, Governor Allerdyce had, with incredible dispatch, organized a home guard of 300 males—old and young, tall and short, firm and infirm, shepherds, fishermen, such businessmen as the islands could support (including two undertakers), doctors and orderlies from the King Edward VII Memorial Hospital. Clutching obsolete rifles spared from the *Canopus,* the motley militia drilled with a Gilbert and Sullivan enthusiasm.

---

*Prodded by the Admiralty, the *Canopus'* engineers patched "the old girl" up the best they could. She left the Falklands early in 1915 to aid in the Dardanelles campaign.

At 10:30 A.M., Monday, December 7, Sturdee arrived—to the surprise, but relief, of all in Port Stanley, including Captain Grant of the *Canopus*. The vice admiral's orders to move with "extraordinary secrecy" had been carried out meticulously. Wireless transmitters had been shut down during the entire crossing from Devonport. The radio's garrulous days of September and October were belatedly passé in the Royal Navy.

The admiral's battle cruisers had paused at the Abrolhos Rocks off Brazil—recently a convalescent retreat for the *Carmania*—long enough only to coal and then rendezvous with the remainder of the special squadron. And it had grown, this squadron—like a magic beanstalk—into Britain's most powerful force outside of the Home Fleet.

Invincible and *Inflexible* were now joined by the 11,000-ton heavy cruiser *Carnarvon,* with 7.5-inch guns, the *Kent* and *Cornwall,* of 10,000 tons, plus the *Glasgow* (her wounds from Coronel patched up) and *Bristol,* sisters of 4,800 tons. The latter four mounted main 6-inch batteries. And just to be sure that nothing the Germans possessed could prevail against this newest British squadron, the armed liners *Otranto* and *Macedonia* were included, although they were not expected to trade haymakers with any but opposing auxiliary warships. The entire assemblage displaced nearly 100,000 tons, three times what the German admiral could possibly muster.

Sturdee, however, admitted to no intuition in steaming for Port Stanley. He was "completely in the dark," Lieutenant Commander Bingham had overheard him say, as to von Spee's whereabouts. It was like looking for a needle in a bundle of hay. The commander in chief's only purpose in putting in at the Falklands had been to coal—in twenty-four hours, if possible—and continue sniffing over the trackless infinity of the South Atlantic, to the Antarctic if necessary, for an elusive "needle" named von Spee.

As evening silhouetted the barren islands against an equally forlorn and foreboding sky, the squadron—except for the *Kent* and *Macedonia,* which were picketing offshore—was busy in its new refuge, preparing to return to the hunt. Coaling had started, or was about to start, on all the ships. The *Bristol* had extinguished her fires, preparatory to cleaning her boilers, and the *Cornwall* was dismantling one of her engines.

As a chill dawn touched Cape Pembroke Lighthouse and the swarming seabirds commenced their harsh morning matins, Sturdee's fleet redoubled its coaling efforts. Bingham on the *Invincible* was at his "third cup of coffee and marmalade stage" when a signalman dashed into the wardroom.

The island lookout had sighted, first, two spirals of smoke far out to sea, then, straining with his long glass, had been able to elaborate: "A four-funnel and a two-funnel man-of-war in sight from Sapper Hill, steering northward . . . !"

In the estimation of his critics, von Spee, after finally catching up with his orders to set course for home, had "dawdled" down the west coast of South America. His speed and even his direction dictated by his furnace's ravenous appetite for coal, he had steamed first to the Más Afuera rocks, west of Valparaíso, to rendezvous with colliers, then south to St. Quintin's Bay, on the south Chilean coast, for yet more fuel.

By the time he sailed from St. Quintin's, to round the Horn, his plans to return quietly to Germany had apparently been complicated by a last-minute desire to take another sideswipe at the British. He would stop by the Falklands, blow up the wireless tower, and destroy any patrol vessels he might catch in the harbor along with government buildings and wharves. Before coaling up for the long run home, he would take the governor aboard as his prisoner.

En route, von Spee had the luck to encounter the British full-rigged ship, *Drummuir,* rounding the Horn, bound for San Francisco and loaded almost to the gunwales with coal. The German squadron hove to long enough to complete the tedious operation of transferring her cargo and then opened the sea cocks of the luckless sailing vessel.

As Tuesday, December 8, brightened, the characteristic drab skies blossomed most unexpectedly into a clear morning. The wind died down; the waters flattened. Von Spee, then fifteen miles at sea, ordered the *Gneisenau* and *Nürnberg* to steam ahead until they hauled abeam of Pembroke Light at approximately 9:30 A.M. They were then to await further orders from the flagship.

Shortly after 8:30, the lookout on the *Nürnberg* picked up the land, still hazy in the morning mist. In a few minutes more the wireless tower of Port Stanley could be recognized, smoke spirals, then, then . . . the masts of a ship, another, and yet another. Excitedly, he reported to the officer of the deck, who, peering through a telescope, fancied he saw not only what had been reported but at least one telltale tripod mast, the distinguishing mark of a battle cruiser or modern battleship. He signaled by blinker back to the *Scharnhorst*.

Not only was it at first impossible to convince von Spee of the probable size of the leashed enemy, but his officers—even when they were certain that two battle cruisers were waiting in the Falklands trap—admitted that they tried not to believe it! However, when at 9:20 the *Canopus* opened fire with her 12-inchers, at an absolute maximum range of nearly six miles, there could be no doubt that *"schwerste Artillerie"* (big guns) was at hand.

The fifth shot came very close to the *Gneisenau* when von Spee signaled her and the *Nürnberg,* now within six miles of Cape Pembroke, to swing around and race, behind the *Scharnhorst* and the *Leipzig,* for the open sea. There was nothing in his orders, in the dictates of common sense, or even in valor that compelled him to give battle to an overwhelming enemy squadron, built around two glowering battle cruisers.

The twin U wakes of the curving warships glittered momentarily in the rising sun and then flattened. Engineers opened up the steam lines as wide as the valves could be turned; pistons strained. Every joint and rivet shook, each bit of tableware and crockery danced and rattled as the German cruisers fled a peril that was all too likely to overwhelm and (as Lord Fisher willed) annihilate them.

Action off the Falklands, December 8, 1914. Three charts showing the location of the battle and the relative positions of the British and German fleets.

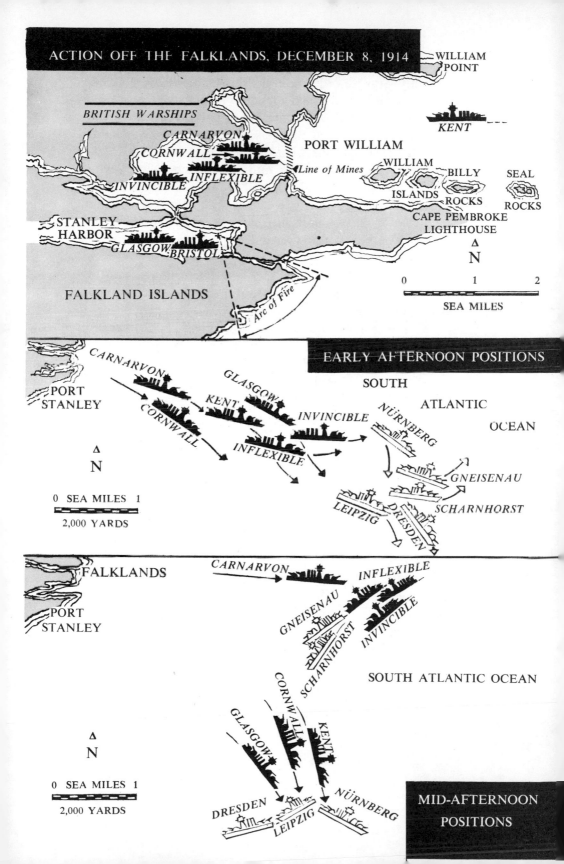

ACTION OFF THE FALKLANDS, DECEMBER 8, 1914

WILLIAM POINT

BRITISH WARSHIPS

CARNARVON

CORNWALL

INVINCIBLE

INFLEXIBLE

KENT

PORT WILLIAM

Line of Mines

WILLIAM ISLANDS

BILLY ROCKS

SEAL ROCKS

CAPE PEMBROKE
LIGHTHOUSE

Δ
N

STANLEY HARBOR

GLASGOW

BRISTOL

FALKLAND ISLANDS

Arc of Fire

0   1   2

SEA MILES

EARLY AFTERNOON POSITIONS

CARNARVON

PORT STANLEY

CORNWALL

GLASGOW

KENT

INVINCIBLE

INFLEXIBLE

SOUTH

ATLANTIC

OCEAN

NÜRNBERG

GNEISENAU

SCHARNHORST

LEIPZIG

DRESDEN

Δ
N

0   SEA MILES   1

2,000 YARDS

FALKLANDS

CARNARVON

INFLEXIBLE

PORT STANLEY

GNEISENAU

SCHARNHORST

INVINCIBLE

SOUTH ATLANTIC OCEAN

CORNWALL

GLASGOW

KENT

Δ
N

0   SEA MILES   1

2,000 YARDS

DRESDEN

LEIPZIG

NÜRNBERG

MID-AFTERNOON POSITIONS

Calmly, Sturdee ordered all his ships under way. The *Kent*, already patrolling, had taken off after the intruders as fast as she could go, laying down a thick black curtain of smoke while her stokers strove to feed the fiery furnaces below. The *Glasgow* was the first out. She went over the minefields, picking up speed like a greyhound racing into the stretch—past William Islands, Billy Rock, and Seal Rocks. The armed liner *Macedonia*, big and slow, was a vulnerable target, with guns of indifferent range. However, she gamely sought to keep up with the pack, even though her blunt prow tended to push the sea before her instead of cleaving it cleanly.

"He [von Spee] came at a very convenient hour," the English admiral was to recall with splendid nonchalance, "because I had just about finished dressing and was able to give orders to raise steam at full speed and to go down to a good breakfast."

The imperturbable Sturdee was enjoying his porridge, tea, and kippers when *Invincible*, at 9:45 A.M., pounded out of the harbor. She was followed closely by the *Inflexible*, *Carnarvon*, and *Cornwall*. By 10:30 A.M., in record time, the squadron had fired boilers and upped anchors to respond to the most exciting of all flags, now unfurled on *Invincible*'s halyards: "General chase!"

There was cheering on the warships—all except the *Bristol* which couldn't possibly fill and heat her boilers in less than six hours. The *Cornwall*, in a remarkable exhibition of seamanship, was forging ahead on available power while engineers raced to reassemble the engine which had been under repair.

So bright was the morning that the mast tips of the *Scharnhorst* and *Gneisenau* were visible at twenty-two miles when the pursuit began. The battle cruisers kept increasing speed until they were boiling southward through the South Atlantic at twenty-five knots with indications that they would soon be bettering that high rate. Obviously, neither the *Glasgow*, *Cornwall*, *Kent*, nor even the larger *Carnarvon*, could keep up. Little by little, they commenced to drop astern.

Sturdee, closing on his adversaries despite their desperate course-changing, now followed tradition. He ordered his men, who were already dressed in clean uniforms, to eat dinner.

Shortly after 1 P.M., at approximately eight miles, Sturdee opened fire on the *Leipzig*, the nearest of the German warships, with a "ranging" shot. After about fifteen minutes of ineffectual firing back and forth between the opposing juggernauts, the battle—by the strangely simultaneous decisions of both Sturdee and von Spee—was divided into two distinctly separate fights.

The *Invincible* and *Inflexible*, backed by *Carnarvon* to the rear, would take on the *Scharnhorst* and *Gneisenau*, while the lighter cruisers would battle it out among themselves. The *Leipzig* and *Nürnberg*, at von Spee's orders, tried once more, without success, to elude their pursuers and race for the South American coast.

To one of the German officers, at least, the opening of this engagement was exhilarating. Captain Hans Pochhammer, first officer of the *Gneisenau*, wrote later:

"Again the trains of ammunition groaned in the well-rooms leading past the central station, and overhead sounded the dull tramp of munition men securing shells and cartridges, placing them on trucks and sending them off to distribute amongst the guns. Orders re-echoed in the block house and reached us below. The transmitter shrieked, speaking tubes blew and were shouted through. The floor of the central station shook and vibrated to every salvo that rolled from the ship. The finest music, the music of battle. It soothed the nerves after the anxious wait of the long morning. . . ."

Because of their superior speed and firepower, the British battle cruisers could pick their targets, one at a time, and hold off the next one until they were ready. The *Scharnhorst*, being the flagship, was logically marked first for annihilation. As the two British warships concentrated on their 12,000-ton opponent, the gunners warmed to an executioner's task, with a peculiarly personal venom.

"Give 'em one for the *Monmouth*!" they would cry, as the firing button was pushed, or "Go on, boys, give 'em hell—let the blighter feel what it's like!"

Before 3:30 P.M., in mist and beginning rain, the *Scharnhorst* was learning what it was like. And the "music" of this battle, in spite of Captain Pochhammer's giddy lyricizing, was far

Admiral Fisher sent Vice Admiral Frederick Sturdee (left) to the Falklands with orders not to return until he had destroyed von Spee's fleet. Sturdee carried out the orders: the British lost 10 men, against German losses of 2,300 men, four warships, and two colliers.

from "the finest." The flagship was afire, she had lost two of her four funnels, and was now being pummeled by murderous lyddite shells, which exploded in yellow smoke, instead of emitting the more familiar angry red glow, and wreaked appalling carnage among crewmen.

Still about six miles apart, the two Germans and the two Britishers continued to slug it out. The *Invincible*, however, had to break off the action for a few minutes to rid her decks of a blinding miasma of coal and gun smoke. She herself had been hit twenty-two times. Her tripod mast had lost one of its legs. One shot, piercing the armor beneath the waterline, had flooded a coal bunker, necessitating counter-flooding on the opposite side to keep the ship on an even keel. Everything, including the piano in the officers' wardroom, had been reduced to matchwood. A dud shell had slid gently to rest in the admiral's pantry and came to a stop on a shelf of marmalade jars. But, surprisingly, no one on the big warship had even been scratched.

At 4 P.M. the *Scharnhorst* signaled the *Gneisenau*: "If your engines are still intact, try to get away."

Ten minutes later, according to Lieutenant Commander

Bingham on the *Invincible*, von Spee's flagship, "looking pretty sickly," stopped dead in the water, her funnels and masts gone, and fire billowing red and angry from her entire length. In the next moment, "she rolled quietly over on one side, lay on her beam ends, and then took a headlong dive, bow first, at 4:17 P.M." Her flags flew at their staffs until they were engulfed by the waters as the torn hulk of the warship, which had fought so courageously, sank beneath the waves.

Aboard the *Invincible*, there was elation amid the weariness, as "echoes of the cheering rose from the bowels of the ship."

The *Scharnhorst* carried with her to the depths of the South Atlantic more than 750 men, thousands of miles from home and those they knew or loved. Von Spee and his entire complement succumbed during those three hours of December 8, 1914. Not one survivor, nor even one floating body, from the *Scharnhorst* was ever found, so fast was her death plunge. It seemed as if the stricken vessel could not wait to quench her fires.

The two battle cruisers now concentrated their fury on the already bloodied *Gneisenau*. She also was afire, her internal communications disrupted, and all electrical circuits shorted out. Ammunition was hand-carried, orders—even those to aim and fire the guns—were conveyed by messenger.

The decks were awash with debris, ranging from splintered jagged metal to parts of bodies which had become a ghoulish testimony to the blasting power of the lyddite shells. In the kitchen and mess halls, a clattering chaos of broken crockery, pans, and assorted cooking and eating utensils was augmented and made all the more macabre by the loosening of hundreds of chickens, geese, and pigeons from their crates. The terrified poultry, which normally would have found its way to the tables, flew, fluttered, cackled, and screeched in a feathery, blinding pandemonium. The squeals of a wounded pig were finally silenced by a pistol shot.

The sounds of battle aboard the *Gneisenau* had become something less than "the finest music." As the flagship was turning on her side, the shell-shocked human beings aboard her lost touch with reality. Another officer asked Pochhammer, "*What* is the *Scharnhorst* doing?"

"She is sinking," Pochhammer flatly replied.

The cruiser's "resistance capacity," Pochhammer was also to note, "was slowly diminishing as I ascertained from an inspection of the lower compartments which I made at this time. Debris and corpses were accumulating, icy water dripped in one place, and in another gushed in streams through panels and shell holes, extinguishing fires and drenching the men to the bone . . . ammunition was passed from hand to hand when wagons were lacking."

When the *Carnarvon* joined the melee at 5 P.M., the *Gneisenau* was finished. Her colors were shot or burned away repeatedly only to be replaced by courageous crewmen.

At about 5:30 P.M. "Cease fire!" was ordered aboard the three British ships, as Sturdee, by blinker, asked the *Gneisenau* to surrender. Either the German ship did not receive the request because of the thickening rain and evening dusk, the blinding smoke and flames, or Captain Maerker stubbornly refused to comply. Shelling was resumed.

"At this moment," Pochhammer continued, "the *Gneisenau*, whose damaged engines were no longer capable of much speed, began to turn slowly over on her starboard, owing to a shattered helm . . . so silence fell upon the ship. . . ."

At 6 P.M., Captain Maerker rasped the order, "Abandon ship."

Sea cocks were opened and the nearest remaining piece of ammunition—a torpedo—was exploded. This scuttling, however, was entirely unnecessary. The pummeled warship, a handsome creation by the measure of those who had known and loved her, was sinking quite determinedly, without any nudging.

The crew sang "Deutschland über Alles" as they began to jump into the water to escape the licking flames, then struck out to be ahead of the suction which was sure to follow the death plunge of 12,000 tons of stricken steel. Many of the men froze to death within minutes.

"I felt the ship giving way under me," Pochhammer wrote, "I heard the roaring and surging of the water come nearer and nearer. . . ."

From the *Invincible*, Bingham recorded these last moments

of a dying battler: "Almost on the stroke of 6 o'clock the *Gneisenau* rolled over and dived down in precisely the same way as her sisters before her," her propellers turning grotesquely in the air before she vanished in a vortex of froth, steam, smoke, and debris.

Nearly 200 were saved by the *Gneisenau*'s three conquerors. The British tars worked not only against darkness and the thrashings of drowning men but against peculiar new antagonists—the thousands of seabirds, from small gulls to huge albatrosses, that had been attracted from the Falklands' rocks by the hours-long sound of battle. They dove for the bodies which littered the water.

But none, in that hushed twilight, could lift voice to accuse the birds of cruelty.

To the southwest, meanwhile, two equally violent battles were raging. The burly *Kent* was gunning the *Nürnberg*, a mere third the size of her opponent, while *Cornwall* and *Glasgow* were attacking the *Leipzig*.

During this engagement, all combatants were amazed at the sight of a large unidentified schooner moving between the antagonists, as though unaware of the battle. As one of the officers on the *Kent* said, "Out of the mist loomed a great four-masted barque under full canvas. A great ghostship, she seemed. Slowly, majestically, she sailed by and vanished in the night."

The gunners could accord only momentary attention to this distracting sight, not uncommon near Cape Horn. The fighting continued and the luckless *Nürnberg* was next to go. Her final moments were dramatically described by the English cruiser's commander, Captain John D. Allen:

"It was hard to understand how the *Nürnberg* could survive so long. At times she was completely obscured by smoke and we thought she must have sunk, but as soon as the smoke cleared away, there she was, looking much the same as ever and still firing her guns. She now turned away from us, as if unable to face such a heavy fire. Her fore topmast was shot away, her funnels riddled with holes, her speed reduced, and only two of her port guns were firing. At 6:10 [P.M.] she turned towards us, steaming very slowly, and we crossed her bow, raking her with all our starboard guns as she came end on. Two of our 6-inch shells burst together on her forecastle, destroying her forecastle guns.

"After crossing her bow, we turned to port till we were nearly on parallel courses again, firing at her with all the port guns. This was a great joy to the crews of our port broadside guns, as up till now they had not had a chance to fire. It was the port guns' turn now, and well they availed themselves of the chance, simply raining shells on the *Nürnberg*. At last, at 6:36, the *Nürnberg* ceased firing and, immediately, we ceased firing too. There was the *Nürnberg* about 5,000 yards away, stopped, and burning gloriously.

"We steamed slowly towards her, taking care to keep well before her beam, so that she could not hit us with a torpedo. As we got nearer to her we could see that her colours were still flying, and she showed no sign of sinking. We had to sink her, there could be no doubt about that, so at 6:45 we opened fire again. After five minutes, during which time she was repeatedly struck, she hauled down her colours. We immediately ceased firing. We could see now that she was sinking. Orders were given to get the boats ready for lowering, but when the men went to lower the boats they found them riddled with holes. The carpenters then collected all the necessary materials, and set to work to patch the holes in the two boats which were least damaged—the second cutter and the galley.

"The men had now left their action stations and were all on the upper deck watching the *Nürnberg*. Ropes' ends, heaving lines, lifebuoys, and life belts were got ready to save life. We could now see some of the men leaving the *Nürnberg*, jumping into the sea and swimming towards the *Kent*. At 7:26 she heeled right over on her starboard side, lay there for a few seconds, then slowly turned over and quietly disappeared under the water. Just before she turned over we saw a group of men on her quarterdeck waving a German ensign attached to a staff. As soon as she had gone, we steamed slowly ahead towards the spot where she had gone down, so as to try and pick up as many men as we could from the ship while the boats were being patched. The sea was covered with bits of wreckage, oars, hammocks, chairs, and a considerable number of men were holding on to them or swimming in the sea. It was a ghastly sight. There was so little that we could do.

"Our sailors were shouting to them, trying to encourage them, telling them to hang on, etc. Directly our two boats were sufficiently patched up to float, they were lowered and pulled about, picking up men in the water. Only twelve men were picked up altogether, and out of these only seven survived.

"A northwest wind had sprung up during the afternoon, the surface of the sea was rough, and the water very cold. The two boats we lowered had only been patched up very hurriedly, and were leaking badly. In fact, when they returned to the ship they were full of water, and on the point of sinking: we just hoisted them up in time."

The engagement of the *Glasgow* and the *Cornwall* against the *Leipzig* was marked by a comparative degree of solicitude. The German ship, now 200 miles south of the Falklands, was burning fiercely by 7 P.M. and appeared to be in such a shambles that Captain John Luce of the *Glasgow* held his fire for more than half an hour while he repeatedly signaled: "Am anxious to save life. Do you surrender?"

Captain Haun, strangely avoiding a direct decision, looked at those standing nearest him and pointed to the flag, saying, "There is the ensign, and any man who wishes may go and haul it down but I will not do so."

Luce, worried about a desperate torpedo attack from his opponent, unloosed another broadside. The results on the helpless *Leipzig* were gruesome. Finally, someone found a flare pistol and fired two green rockets above the flaming cruiser: surrender.

The *Glasgow*'s captain, turning his searchlights on the water, sent boats toward the *Leipzig*. About 9:20 P.M., a junior officer saw Captain Haun light a cigar and walk toward the crumbling holocaust of his bridge. In the next moment, the cruiser turned over and disappeared in a requiem eruption of flames, a shower of sparks, and a billowing cloud of oily black smoke.

The number of men rescued was as small as from the *Nürnberg*: five officers and thirteen men.

That day, on the perimeter of the Antarctic, in the most

southerly naval engagement ever fought, the kaiser's sea arm lost 2,300 men, along with four warships and two colliers which could not be casually spared. Only the speedy *Dresden** escaped, assisted by night and thickening rain.

The Royal Navy's price for this stunning victory was ten killed and fifteen wounded. More than half of the casualties were on the *Kent*, which had been hit thirty-eight times and damaged more than any of the other British vessels. Nonetheless, she had fought determinedly on, even obtaining extra speed from her straining engines.

After three days, Sturdee abandoned his search for the *Dresden* and brought his squadron triumphantly back to Port Stanley. Frustrated at being left out of the battle, but nonetheless exultant, the militia fired their old guns in salute, while other citizens, "jubilant with joy," lavished flowers and fruit upon the conquerors. The wounded were treated at the King Edward VII Memorial Hospital. The dead had already been accorded the ultimate a sailor could desire: burial at sea.

Crewmen from the *Invincible* proudly lugged the shattered column from the tripod mast ashore and mounted it high on Sapper Hill so future generations would always be reminded of a December day in 1914.

*See Appendix 1.

(4)

On Safari for
the *Königsberg*

⊕ In the summer of 1915, the 3,350-ton *Königsberg* was
hunted down. She was the last of the German light cruisers which
had been running amuck. The search involved improvisations
never dreamed of by Captain Sydney R. Drury-Lowe, of the new
5,400-ton cruiser *Chatham*. He had vainly sought the *Königsberg* in her hunting grounds—the Indian Ocean off German
East Africa. The very names of the places where she had called
or been sighted read like an exotic travelog: Zanzibar, Dar es
Salaam, Kilwa Kivinje, the Mozambique Channel, Madagascar.

Captain Max Looff, the German cruiser's commander, had
not been as successful as Captain von Mueller of the *Emden*, but
he was a threat to the shipping lanes and to the convoy route from
Australia. He succeeded in tying down an ever-increasing fleet,
commencing with Captain Drury-Lowe's cruisers, the *Dartmouth*
and *Weymouth*, in addition to his flagship. Moreover, the English captain had a score of his own to settle. His command had
been represented in the "watchdog" Mediterranean fleet during
the opening days of the war, when the important German battle
cruiser *Goeben* and the light cruiser *Breslau* had slipped through
the Dardanelles and into Turkish sanctuary. The government
of Turkey had then claimed it had "bought" them.

The *Königsberg* had chalked up two sinkings: the steamer
City of Winchester and the old British cruiser *Pegasus*. Then,
elusively, the fast German cruiser had vanished.

During the winter and spring of 1915, the tides of battle swirled back and forth, alternately infusing hope in one side and despair in the other. There were those who could say with some justification that the gods of war smiled upon the Royal Navy, allowing it time and again to make amends for its repeated incredible mistakes. The loss of the *Aboukir*, *Cressy*, and *Hogue* still had not taught the Admiralty that heavy ships had mortal need of a destroyer screen against U-boats.

On New Year's night, bathed in brilliant moonlight, moving majestically across the North Sea, the British battleship *Formidable* was struck by two torpedoes and went down. Only 201 of her crew of 800 were saved, and those by a trawler which happened to come by.

Three weeks later, off an English east coast fishing grounds, the Dogger Bank, the German battle cruiser *Blücher* was sunk during a series of High Seas Fleet sorties against the British coast.

Members of the crew scramble to the topside as their ship, the German battle cruiser *Blücher*, sinks into the North Sea. Photo was taken from the British cruiser *Arethusa*.

A spectacular photograph of the *Blücher* sinking, her crew clambering for their lives over the keel, was printed widely in England. It had the doubtlessly unintended effect of imbuing the public with a false sense of confidence in the Royal Navy's ability to sink enemy ships on sight. This impression was also unfair to the courageous seamen who could not be expected to perform miracles.

Certainly, in hard truth, the navy was having as rough a time of it as the army was in France. The attempt that winter to force the Dardanelles had resulted in an Allied disaster of unrivaled magnitude. The main object of the action had been to relieve the sagging Russian lines by establishing a front against Turkey.

Then, in March, Great Britain paid with three warships and France one in trying to transit the heavily defended straits. The *Inflexible*, fresh from the Falklands, was beached after striking a mine.* The battleships *Majestic* and *Triumph* would be sacrificed to an ill if not stupidly conceived operation, both victims of the same submarine, the *U-21*. In the Mediterranean, the French cruiser *Provence* was among other shocking losses. She carried to the bottom 930 men.

During this spring of 1915, however, the most fateful decisions would not be so much concerned with the Dardanelles and running fights in the North Sea, as with a German proclamation attempting to establish a "War Zone" around the British Isles:

All the waters surrounding Great Britain and Ireland, including the whole of the English Channel, are hereby declared a war zone . . . every merchant ship found within this war zone will be destroyed without it being always possible to avoid danger to the crews and passengers . . . . It is impossible to avoid attacks being made on neutral vessels in mistake for those of the enemy.

President Woodrow Wilson, through Secretary of State William Jennings Bryan, immediately warned Chancellor Theobald von Bethmann-Hollweg that Germany would be held strictly accountable for loss of American ships or, more impor-

---

*The *Inflexible* was ultimately refloated.

tant, the lives of United States citizens. The warning was disregarded.

Yes, Germany meant what she said. Von Tirpitz could not keep more than fifteen U-boats at sea simultaneously, but the underseas fleet was still building and technical developments were being perfected to increase the range of the small, sensitive craft. She would lash out pugnaciously and cause all the damage she could. Norway was the first neutral to lose a merchantman without warning. In March, the English steamer *Falaba* was sunk with the loss of 104 lives. Among them was a thirty-one-year-old American, Leon Thrasher. He was the first citizen of the United States to die in the war at sea. Increasingly bold challenges to America's insistence on "freedom of the seas" followed Thrasher's drowning. On May 1, the *Gulflight* was torpedoed with the loss of three more Americans, including her captain, Alfred Gunter, of Texas. The tanker was the first ship flying the United States flag to be violated in Germany's proscribed zone. She was salvaged later, but irreparable damage to international relations had been inflicted.

Diplomatic protests came angrily from the Department of State and the recall of Count Johann von Bernstorff, the German Ambassador, was considered.

However, the death of Mr. Thrasher and the other United States citizens aboard the *Gulflight* were minor incidents compared with a greater one that took place on a sunny afternoon, May 7, in sight of the Irish coast. The largest liner remaining in transatlantic service, the 32,000-ton Cunarder *Lusitania*, was torpedoed by the *U-20* with the loss of 1,198 lives including 124 Americans. Names such as Alfred Gwynne Vanderbilt, the multimillionaire sportsman; Elbert Hubbard, the writer; and Charles Frohman, the theatrical producer, were included in the seemingly endless casualty lists. But as well known as these men and other passengers were, it was the "murder" of so many women and children in the sudden attack that aroused the United States and all but sent her marching at once toward France.

"For the German Navy," editorialized the Frankfurt *Zeitung*, "the sinking of the *Lusitania* means an extraordinary success." *Lusitania* medals were struck and commemorative post-

At 32,000 tons, Cunard's ill-fated luxury liner, the *Lusitania*, was the largest passenger ship remaining in transatlantic service.

cards were printed in Germany to celebrate the "extraordinary success." But in months to come, Berlin would be obliged to regard the "success" in quite a different light.

Von Bernstorff called at the White House to express his "deep regrets." His avowal was sincere because, for all his moustached Prussian formidability, the count was personally a peace-loving man of artistic temperament. "Regrets" would not, however, bring back the 124 Americans. The strongly pacifistic William Jennings Bryan was replaced as secretary of state by Robert Lansing—and the United States was that much closer to war with Germany.

However, in spite of the *Lusitania* tragedy and the ever-

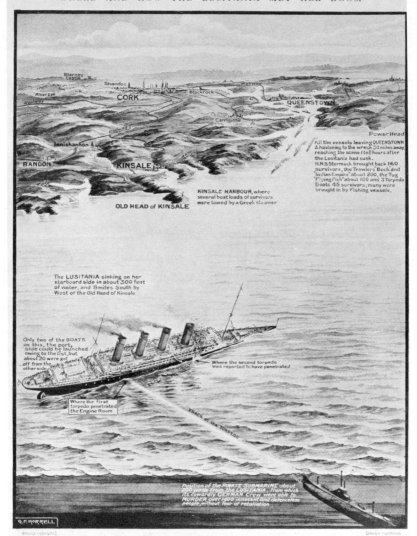

Blarney Castle

Shandon

Blackrock

Glanmire

River Lee

Railway

CORK

QUEENSTOWN

Carrigaline

Power Head

All the vessels leaving QUEENSTOWN & hastening to the wreck 30 miles away, reaching the scene 1 to 2 hours after the Lusitania had sunk. H.M.S Stormock brought back 160 survivors, the Trawlers Bock and Indian Empire about 200, the Tug "Flying Fish" about 100 and 3 Torpedo Boats 45 survivors; many were brought in by Fishing vessels.

Innishannon

BANDON

KINSALE

KINSALE HARBOUR, where several boat loads of survivors were towed by a Greek steamer

OLD HEAD of KINSALE

The LUSITANIA sinking on her starboard side in about 300 feet of water, and 8 miles South by West of the Old Head of Kinsale

Only two of the BOATS on this, the port, side could be launched owing to the list, but about 20 were got off from the other side

Where the second torpedo was reported to have penetrated

Where the first torpedo penetrated the Engine Room

TRACK of the TORPEDO

Position of the PIRATE SUBMARINE about 200 yards from the LUSITANIA, from which its cowardly GERMAN Crew were able to MURDER over 1400 innocent and defenceless people, without fear of retaliation

G. F. MORRELL

Hailed by a chorus of horror from the whole civilised world, and by jubilation throughout Germany, the sinking of the Lusitania is not merely a crime, but will go down to posterity as a blunder of the first magnitude, serving the cause of the Allies better than a great victory, as a Brazilian paper puts it. That Germany should find it necessary to resort to such dastardly methods is interpreted by the world at large as an evidence of despair, while the fact that the enemy praise the "pluck and daring" of the submarine and claim that the deed is the German answer to the destruction of von Spee's squadron seems to suggest that the Germans are bereft of their senses.

Illustrated London News

Chart showing relative positions of the *Lusitania*, the *U-20*, and the Irish coast. At the time of the attack the liner was eight miles from shore, thirty miles from the British fleet at Queenstown. The torpedo penetrated her broadside, and she sank twenty minutes later.

A MASSACRE OF THE INNOCENTS: THE SCENE AFTER THE DISAPPEARANCE OF THE LUSITANIA

The scene after the Lusitania went down is thus described by one of the survivors: "Above the spot where she had been serenely afloat less than twenty minutes before was nothing but a nondescript mass of floating wreckage. Everywhere one looked, one saw a sea of waving hands and arms belonging to struggling men and frantic women and children in agonising efforts to keep afloat." Every available boat put out from Queenstown, Kinsale, and other harbours along the coast, but it was an hour before the first of them could reach the scene, and by that time two-thirds of the ship's company had disappeared, while many of the rescued died from shock and exposure before they reached land.

Illustrated London News

Survivors cling to lifeboats and floating debris after the *Lusitania* is sunk. The severe list to starboard had prevented launching most of the port life-boats, and 1,198 men, women, and children lost their lives.

89

In this famous cartoon of German barbarity, the U-boat crew stands idly by the struggling survivors from the sunken *Lusitania*. Actually, the *U-20* never surfaced at all.

increasing rate of torpedoings, Britain seemed to be winning the naval phase of the Great War. Germany's raiders, one by one, were being knocked off the seas or compelled to give themselves up because their supply lines had been cut.

The *Kronprinz Wilhelm*, for example, arrived in Newport News in April, after sinking fifteen merchant ships, aggregating 58,000 tons. Unable to continue her patrols without fuel or ammunition, she was interned beside another, but less successful, armed liner, the *Prinz Eitel Friedrich*. Captain Paul Thierfelder, who had been given permission to "lay up the ship" after a remarkable 250-day cruise, could for the remainder of the war devote his crew's energies to the oft-interrupted rat hunt.

On board were a number of small English sports cars that had been removed from the holds of one of his victims, sunk by the clumsy method of ramming, one of his favorite tactics. On calm, quiet days, he had allowed his men to race the little cars around the broad promenade deck of the spacious Hamburg-American liner. Now, he took them ashore for less restricted courses.

Not until the end of October was the *Königsberg* located—seven miles up the steaming Rufiji River, in Tanganyika. For Captain Drury-Lowe, on the *Chatham*, even a peek at the enemy's mast tips was a triumph. His success in finding the cruiser was due to the fact that his intelligence officers had broken the German naval code in spite of vexing language difficulties. The first clue, handed to Drury-Lowe half apologetically, advised that the *Königsberg* was "somewhere spelled with six letters."

The enterprising captain hired African and Arab guides as well as informers and, like Lawrence of Arabia, went ashore in disguise to search native villages for clues of the missing ship and its crew. Working in the heart of what was still the kaiser's East African empire, the Briton's life was in daily peril. More than once he fled into the bush, firing from the two pistols he always carried.

It was not easy to recognize the cruiser even when they found it. Her masts and superstructure had been painted green and covered with shrubbery so that it blended into the jungle. Her lighter cannons and Maxims had been removed and set in breastworks on a full perimeter to guard the *Königsberg*. Thus the cruiser had become the center of a strange seagoing fort, temporarily at anchor.

Captain Thierfelder, of the raider *Kronprinz Wilhelm*, made up in enthusiasm what he lacked in finesse. On a 250-day cruise, he sank 15 merchant ships by the unconventional method of ramming. In this photograph by one of the auxiliary cruiser's officers, the French cargo vessel *Mont Agel* is rammed. This method, while economical in ammunition, was hard on the bow plates.

It was almost impossible to get to her—by land or by sea. The Rufiji, except at flood, was so shallow that only flat-bottomed monitors could transit her perilous channels. The cruiser had reached her hideaway only by unbunkering her burden of coal and lightening herself of other removable cargo and equipment.

Now that the *Königsberg* had been discovered, what should be done about her?

Lord Fisher had already demonstrated his espousal of overwhelming superiority, then "annihilation." However, for a single enemy cruiser, even a first-rate one like the *Königsberg*, he surely was not going to send in anything like the *Invincible*.

Thus, day by day and week by week, a most incredible, overage, half-obsolete tatterdemalion squadron churned toward the Rufiji delta in the hope that even graying, lame watchdogs would cause the adversary concern. The strange fleet suggested a Gilbert and Sullivan opera, or the hastily improvised backwater squadrons of the American Civil War. In some ways the most pathetic—even if the largest—of its members was the 12,950-ton *Goliath*, launched before the turn of the century, prior to the Boer War. This ancient battleship had little to offer except the power of her 12-inch guns, Her engines were a mechanic's nightmare; her furnaces were gluttons for coal.

Another remarkable addition to the blockaders was the well-used postal and telegraph steamer *Duplex*, which had laid tens of thousands of miles of cables for the Empire. She had commenced service for the far-reaching Royal Post Office system when Queen Victoria still reigned. The *Duplex* had chugged along coasts in the Near and Middle East and transited many tangents of the Indian Ocean, the Red Sea, Persian Gulf, Arabian Sea, and the Bay of Bengal, speeding overseas communications for at least two generations of Britons. Many of her crewmen had grown old with her.

There arrived, too, the *Fox* and the *Hyacinth* (a misnomer of misnomers), light cruisers as ancient as the *Goliath*. A kind of mother ship was needed, to provide storage space, hospital wards, and recreational facilities, including a gymnasium, for the ever-increasing number of tars that were congregating in this God-forsaken reach of East Africa. The answer to this need was found in the old Union Castle liner, the *Kinfauns Castle*, which clanked down her rusted, barnacled anchor chain one December morning in the Rufiji delta. She brought, if not speed or flash, a great deal of comfort.

A windfall came in the capture of two German seagoing tugs, the *Adjutant* and the *Helmuth*. The former's career under the Union Jack was nonetheless short-lived. She ventured too far up the Rufiji one day, her steam line was pierced by a well-aimed projectile from a shore battery, and she surrendered. Her former owners recovered her, along with her British crew.

And, just to top off the wondrous assortment of besieging ships, four steam whalers were rushed south. Their shallow draft, like that of the *Duplex*, was calculated to be a real advantage in a river studded with sandbars. The *Chatham*, drawing fifteen and one half feet, could navigate only modest distances from the sea. She was the only first-class, fully modern ship of the squadron, the *Dartmouth* and the *Weymouth* having been summoned to duties more in line with their capabilities.

When this almost comic-opera navy had been assembled, the question still persisted: what shall we do about the *Königsberg?* Her crew existed in conditions far from comfortable or healthy. Millions of mosquitoes hummed in the jungle and malaria and dysentery were regular visitors. Quinine had become more valuable than silver—certainly than shells. Nonetheless, the men could probably endure. Nor would they easily starve as long as they were able to hunt hippos and other bountiful wild game.

While the Germans held on, they tied up many of His Majesty's men-of-war and, still more important, several thousand skilled sailors who would soon be needed in the new warships being spawned on England's ways.

However, the Britons could make life less and less pleasant for their enemy, while tightening the net around the *Königsberg*. An obsolete collier, the *Newbridge*, was sunk midway in the principal channel that snaked through the Rufiji delta. The *Chatham* ranged the *Somali*, a German supply ship which had ventured too far down the river, and sank her with a few lucky shots. The Germans would face a lean winter.

Seaplanes arrived to scout the cruiser and keep tabs on her intentions. It was always possible that she could take advantage of the sudden rise in water level, following a jungle downpour, to escape through one of several secondary channels. Each reconnaissance, however, was a life-or-death gamble for the pilot. He could not fly high enough to keep out of range of the Germans' excellent rapid-firing guns. The planes, whatever had been in the manufacturer's mind, surely had not been designed for the tropical heat and humidity of East Africa. The glue melted

After vainly searching for the *Königsberg* in the Indian Ocean, Captain Sydney Drury-Lowe found her in Tanganyika—seven miles up the Rufiji River. His first clue, after he had broken the German code, was that she was "somewhere spelled with six letters."

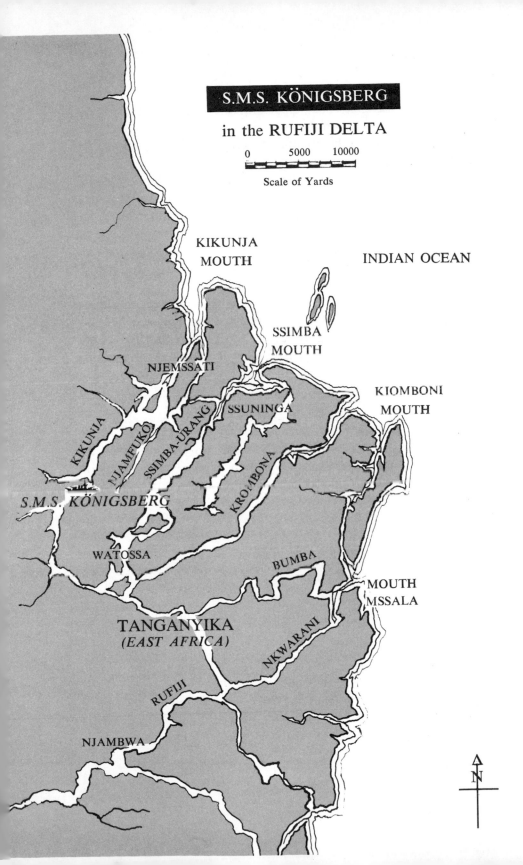

S.M.S. KÖNIGSBERG

in the RUFIJI DELTA

0   5000   10000

Scale of Yards

KIKUNJA
MOUTH

INDIAN OCEAN

SSIMBA
MOUTH

NJEMSSATI

KIOMBONI
MOUTH

SSUNINGA

KIKUNJA

NJAMFUKO

SSIMBA-URANG

KROMBONA

S.M.S. KÖNIGSBERG

WATOSSA

BUMBA

MOUTH
MSSALA

TANGANYIKA
(EAST AFRICA)

NKWARANI

RUFIJI

NJAMBWA

N

between propeller laminations, the rubber hosing used in many sections of the engine became perforated after a few hours' operation, the paint peeled off the pontoons, and not even an adequate gasoline supply could be obtained to keep the cylinders firing efficiently.

More often than not, the perspiring, harried pilots could not drag their lumbering planes higher than a few hundred feet over the treetops. Cruising at a torturous sixty miles an hour, they were an excellent target for the bored German gunners. Only a kindly providence, which manifestly looked with favor upon English aviators, kept those on duty above the Rufiji from being hit or killed.

By Christmas time, a martial camaraderie had developed between attacker and attacked, somewhat analagous to the exchange of pleasantries that occurred between the trenches of the western front. On Christmas Eve, one of the planes dropped a note near the *Königsberg*:

Koniy, we wish you the best of good cheer,
But blame you for stopping our Xmas beer.

The jingle, with more passion than poetry, no doubt alluded to the sailors' nostalgia for their familiar pubs. Captain Looff's reply, in the same spirit, was conveyed by a runner, brandishing a white towel:

Thanks. The same to you. If you want to see me I'm always at home. Looff, *Königsberg*

Winter in the Rufiji was passed in a state of apathetic siege, the opponents contenting themselves with minor annoyances. Marker buoys, for example, had been placed in many bends of the channels to aid the navigation of this large if unheroic fleet. In the night, native allies of the Germans would row out with muffled oars, cut the cables, then happily watch the buoys bob down toward the Indian Ocean.

The attackers, like naughty boys, would retaliate by severing chunks of the German telephone network that linked sentry posts with gun batteries. Or, if the seaplane pilots were especially daring, or even just bored, they would pepper the Germans with hand grenades or crude bombs, or even shoot signal flares at them.

By spring, the Admiralty's patience was exhausted. The affair on the Rufiji had degenerated into the counterpart of a sparring action between neighborhood gangs who are too wary to provoke a showdown fight. Something *had* to be done—and quickly.

There were surely enough warships, or makeshift warships, in the delta as well as in the vicinity along the East African coast —several dozen at least. Possibly, even so, there still was not a vessel for *every* conceivable purpose.

Someone remembered two monitors—ferryboat-like craft made famous by an ancestor's duel with the *Merrimac* in 1861. They had been built only in 1913—over the unremitting protests of the "battle-cruiser gang," who had insisted that the ten well-seasoned river gunboats in the Middle East and on the China station could serve the same purpose as monitors.

The monitors were rusting and barnacled, their engines were stiff and cranky. But now, the Royal Navy was happy to have the *Mersey* and *Severn*, grossing 1,260 tons apiece, 267 feet long, with a 49-foot beam, and a somewhat froglike outline. Carrying 6.1-inch and 4.7-inch cannons, their greatest bonus was their lightweight draft of only four feet, nine inches. "They could sail into Kensington Gardens!" boasted their designers.

Crews were tumbled aboard and fuel and provisions were poured into their holds. Indeed, these monitors were comprised largely of holds, with living accommodations provided, manifestly, only as a grudging afterthought. After all, naval architects didn't have to inhabit what they blueprinted.

However, in a last-minute pang of conscience, Whitehall sent along with them two grande dames of the sea-lanes, the liners *Laconia* and *Laurentic*, to brood over the ugly ducklings and take them under their wings should occasion arise.

For all their shallow draft and turtlelike speed of seven knots, the *Mersey* and *Severn* sailed like veterans through winter and spring storms on the long voyage by way of the Suez and Aden to Zanzibar. Only then did their crews really suffer. The heat rose to intolerable heights of 120 and even 135 degrees. Since the working areas of the monitors were all within decks and much of this was encumbered space below the waterline, there was little opportunity for escape into the fresh air.

When they arrived at Tirene Bay, a staging area off the delta, life became increasingly arduous. As a crewman recalled, "The men worked from sunrise to sunset." When they weren't busy with the machinery, they were hard at gunnery practice— shooting at a target they could not see—in preparation for their real mission. The wood target was towed to the other side of a small sand island and hits or misses were spotted by the seaplanes.

By May a climax was obviously building. From South Africa arrived the admiral himself, Herbert King-Hall, commander of the Cape of Good Hope Squadron and the senior naval officer in the area. The whole venture had become increasingly embarrassing. For more than half a year now, the German cruiser— and not too large a one at that—had been roosting in the admiral's back yard. In size, the blockading fleet was probably comparable to the one Lord Nelson pitted against the entire French Navy, and, some said, about as modern.

In June, the admiral took over immediate command from Drury-Lowe, hoisted his flag on the *Goliath*, and ordered: "Immediate attack!" However, after a few days on the creaking contrivance of bolts and museum-piece weapons, King-Hall decided that quite possibly his ship presented more of a threat to life and limb than the enemy did. Besides, she drew so much water that she could barely enter the outer reaches of the delta. He summarily hauled down his flag and moved aboard the old *Hyacinth*. The *Hyacinth* was feeling her quarter of a century of service, but she could probe farther up the Rufiji.

The *Goliath*, which had proved about as useful as a Percheron at Epsom Downs, was ordered to Gallipoli to do what she could. She waddled off and was sunk by a torpedo from a Turkish destroyer almost immediately upon arrival. Less than 200 of her crew made the shore.

Time was running out, too, on Admiral King-Hall. He did not wish to risk the hellfire of Lord "Jacky" Fisher's comments if the *Königsberg*'s destruction was postponed another week. Nervously, he transferred his flag once more—to the *Weymouth*, which had returned after southern patrol—and ordered the *Severn* and *Mersey* to move up the river. The *Weymouth* could toss some shells from a distance, while the steam whalers, shallow-going vessels, screened the ponderous monitors from shore fire.

Admiral King-Hall could not avoid one last addition to the *opéra bouffe* aspect of the operation. Aboard the *Laurentic* were a few companies of Indian troops which had embarked at Zanzibar for whatever use might be found for them. So far, there had been little for them to do but loll on the sizzling decks and eat themselves into torpor. On July 5, they were disembarked, with much commotion and loud playing of the ship's band, at Dar es Salaam—in the hope of giving the impression that a land expedition was being mounted against the *Königsberg*.

In the dusk of evening, minus shoes, they tiptoed back aboard, as bulldog-voiced top sergeants whispered orders. Even as the curtain was dropping on this last scene of the admiral's little play, the *Severn* and *Mersey* were pushing upriver.

At 5:20 A.M. Tuesday, July 6, the Royal Navy learned that the Germans had not been fooled. One of the "beastly field guns" hidden in the bordering jungle barked a surly matins at the monitors. The explosions sent a herd of crocodiles, which had been lazing through the tropical night on the riverbank, splashing vocally through the mud and into the dark waters.

But the sister craft chugged on, through machine-gun fire and dodging torpedo booms placed by the Germans. At 6:30 they were at anchor in a bend of the stream, four and one half miles below the German cruiser. The *Königsberg* had the draw on her attackers. For fifteen minutes there was the repeated "soft whistle of shells" overhead, then the detonation in the jungle, or sometimes a dirty geyser of river water as her gunners continued to straddle their target.

Remarkably, no blood was shed until 7:40 A.M. At that time, a salvo scored a direct hit on *Mersey*'s forward 6-inch gun, instantly killing three men and wounding many others. In moments, she was holed at the waterline. The rest of her crew were stunned, and the monitor was flooded.

There was nothing to do but withdraw, leaving the *Severn* to carry on alone. Her lookout thought he had finally discovered the reason for the *Königsberg*'s deadly accuracy against the *Mersey*. He spotted a khaki-clad figure in a treetop platform about half a mile distant in the jungle.

For several minutes, concentrated fire was directed at the observation post. Either it was wiped out, or the spotter decided that the area had become unhealthy. The *Königsberg*'s accuracy decreased.

By mid-afternoon, the two monitors had hurled a total of 635 shells at the cruiser and her elaborate gun emplacements about the Rufiji. The *Severn*'s crew had sweated in the unbearable heat for nine hours without respite. They were too exhausted to go on. The airplanes themselves had to return to base for repairs.

As the *Severn* withdrew, several more shells from the *Königsberg* cried their deadly *auf Wiedersehen*. The spotting pilots had reported six hits on the *Königsberg*, but little damage of consequence had been inflicted. The first assault on the German cruiser had ended decisively in her favor.

The German light cruiser *Königsberg* was destroyed by the British after a nine-month blockade in the Rufiji River.

On July 11, the repaired monitors came back and crept several hundred yards closer to their target. The Britons were out for blood this time, just as Sturdee had been in the Falklands. Flight Lieutenant J. T. Cull flew dangerously low to give exact locations of where the shells were dropping.

"Four hundred yards!" was his first visual signal, then "Two hundred!" and "One hundred!" The personnel of the *Mersey* and *Severn* were jumping up and down. The action was "frightfully exciting!" by the measure of one of the *Severn*'s officers.

Then all at once eight out of twelve hits scored bull's-eyes on the *Königsberg*. Smoke began to pour from the wounded cruiser and there was the sound of an explosion. Her firing slowed, was reduced to salvos of only three projectiles at a time.

Heartened, other Royal Navy ships joined in—the *Weymouth* from maximum range and a recently arrived Australian light cruiser, the *Pioneer*. They lobbed their shells high, hoping the trajectory would send them raining down on the burning enemy.

Shortly after 1 P.M., Lieutenant Cull signaled from his seaplane, "We are hit, send a boat for us!" Like a wounded duck, the plane hurtled down toward the river, hit the surface in a cascade of spray, somersaulted, and came to rest, a mass of splintered wood, shredded fabric, and twisted wires.

Motor launches from both monitors raced to the spot in the river, less than 200 yards distant, where the plane had crashed. The coxswain on the *Mersey*, who reached the wreckage first, found—instead of what he was grimly prepared for—both Lieutenant Cull and his observer perched on a half-awash pontoon, waving and as "merry as crickets."

By early afternoon, it was over. Captain Looff, himself twice wounded, ordered scuttling charges placed, then ignited. The blast shook the jungle for miles around. A tower of black smoke boiled high over the *Königsberg*'s broken masts, up, up above the mangrove swamps.

There was nothing left for the German naval commander to do but march his survivors inland to join Colonel von Lettow-Vorbeck's diminutive but gallant East African army (which would prove both elusive and unconquerable to the thoroughly frustrated British). Curiously enough, Looff's men would sail again—in a patched-up motorboat navy on Lake Tanganyika!

Admiral King-Hall could settle down now to more important operations in the broad South African theater. He had attained his objective—the destruction of an especially troublesome and intangible enemy cruiser—but the victory was without glory. The bludgeoning by the vast blockading fleet had been tantamount to shooting field mice with elephant guns.

Perhaps the sole contribution of this operation to naval science was its demonstration of the increasingly effective use of airplanes for spotting naval gunnery—without the aid of radio equipment.

The kaiser was losing his first-line surface ships, but his submarine fleet (numbering seventy-four by the end of 1915) was taking an ever-mounting toll of Allied merchantmen—more than 100,000 tons a month during this summer of 1915. The emperor's risk, while calculated, was far more mortal than he or the fire-breathing von Tirpitz could possibly have envisioned. In August, the White Star liner *Arabic* was sunk off the coast of Ireland, with the loss of four more Americans.

Like clay ducks in a shooting gallery, these seagoing mainstays of Britain's lifeline went under, one by one, even though many of them were now armed: liners, freighters, tankers, and even cross-channel steamers like the *Sussex*, on which still more United States citizens perished.

Names were being continually emblazoned in the public's glossary of the war, names of ships flying the United States flag or carrying her citizens—ships which had been sunk, damaged, or merely "roughed up" through being halted on the high seas. Added to the *Falaba, Gulflight, William P. Frye* (a sailing ship destroyed without injury to any persons or any loss of life), *Lusitania,* and *Arabic* were the *Nebraskan, Odenwald, Armenian, Hesperian.*

The names ticked on with the unmistakable ring of doom—names that were becoming gaunt milestones on America's road to war.

(5)

"...something wrong with our bloody ships!"

⊕ One spectacular climax of the Great War at sea was a battle which the Allies would label "Jutland" and the Central Powers "Skagerrak." It was the mightiest naval engagement in history, dwarfing the clashings of yesterday's armadas—an engagement in which the main fleets of Britain and Germany met head-on.

Singularly enough, the rendezvous was an accident, brought about through the independent inspiration of each combatant to lure his adversary into a contest. When it came about, the thunder, the fury, and the carnage were testimony to the fever of hate in 1916. Barbarity flourished unchecked.

One of the worst lapses into primitive conduct involved the Q-boat *Baralong*, a British tramp mounting hidden guns. Her holds were stuffed with lumber and buoyant material intended to keep her afloat if torpedoed. These Q-boats were decoys, or "pirates" as the enemy labeled them, infrequently effective against submarines.

Cruising on August 16 near the Scilly Islands, the *Baralong* sighted the 6,300-ton *Nicosian*, a Leyland Line freighter which was carrying a cargo of mules and fodder from New Orleans. The *Nicosian* signaled: "Captured by a submarine!" And her captor was plainly visible astern of the *Nicosian*.

The *Nicosian* crew commenced to abandon while the undersea craft—the *U-27*—drew near and opened fire. The *Baralong* was strangely ignored by the German gunners who apparently believed they could finish off the *Nicosian* at leisure. However, Lieutenant Commander Godfrey Herbert of the *Baralong* was in no mood to wait. He raised the naval white ensign, dropped the bulwark camouflage, and started shooting.

About a dozen of the German sailors jumped overboard before their riddled submarine sank, and swam toward the *Nicosian*. Not until the freighter's own crewmen were being helped onto the *Baralong* did Commander Herbert realize what the U-boat's survivors were doing. They were now on the *Nicosian*, with the apparent intention of getting her under way as a prize.

The Q-ship pushed alongside the *Nicosian* and a party of Royal Marines leapt aboard. The next few minutes were ones of slaughter; there would be no pride in this naval action. The marines scoured the *Nicosian* from engine room to chart house, shooting and bayoneting the unarmed enemy on sight, until all the German sailors were dying in darkening pools of blood.

Once ashore the marines boasted of their exploit. Soon Berlin heard, and the outcry was wild. Reprisals were not slow in coming. A German submarine machine-gunned the lifeboats from a torpedoed collier-transport, the *Ruel*, killing the captain and seriously injuring seven others.

Stranded off the Danish coast and helpless, the British submarine *E-13* was strafed by two German destroyers. The enemy did not permit the crew to surrender or even abandon their flaming derelict. Fifteen petty officers and sailors were shot or drowned before Danish torpedo boats could intervene in the line of fire and rescue the English submariners.

The United States, asked to arbitrate an increasing procession of atrocities, not surprisingly refused to pass judgment. However, in October, Edith Cavell, a fifty-year-old British nurse, the matron of a Belgian nursing school and clinic, was charged with assisting Allied soldiers to escape from the country and return to England or France. Her execution on October 12 by the German occupation authorities in Brussels rocked the sensibilities of Americans and almost all others of the civilized world.

The kaiser himself realized he had gone too far, especially

when 10,000 Britons enlisted during special "Who'll avenge Nurse Cavell?" recruiting rallies. This swelling of the forces came at a time when replacements were sorely needed in France for the wasting Somme battle, and Lord Kitchener, the gaunt formidable secretary of state for war, was gravely concerned over lagging enlistments.

The reaction in America was even more ominous for Kaiser Wilhelm. "German savagery" was denounced in pyramiding letters to the editors of the nation's press. Women's clubs passed resolutions calling for a break in diplomatic relations with Germany. "Preparedness Parades" marched ever more militantly from Manhattan to Main Street, in communities large and small.

Q-ship *Margaret Murray* looked like an innocent sailing vessel. But in reality she was an anti-submarine "pirate" ship. Her hidden guns were ready to strike at unsuspecting enemy raiders.

Imperial War Museum, London

The *New York Tribune* printed a cartoon captioned *"Gott Mit Uns!"* depicting a German officer, in spiked helmet, holding a smoking revolver as he stood over the bleeding form of a nurse. It symbolized the rising popular demand that the United States shed its neutrality.

This winter of 1915-1916, it appeared that the world's greatest navy was in need of assistance. The troops were evacuated from the Dardanelles, ending the most disastrous Allied expedition of the war. Churchill, who had fathered the campaign, was replaced as first lord of the Admiralty by Arthur J. Balfour. Fisher, who had never approved the operation in the first place, resigned as sea lord. He was succeeded by Admiral Sir Henry Jackson.

Germany's own nautical house was, at the same time, being put in ever more efficient shape. In January, 1916, a month before his death, Admiral Hugo von Pohl, commander in chief of the High Seas Fleet, was replaced by popular, dynamic Admiral Reinhard Scheer, a brilliant tactician. Scheer, who had been in command of the 3rd (Dreadnought) Squadron, had long and vocally chafed under Britain's "hunger blockade" of Germany. He could not meet Jellicoe's mighty fleet head-on; he knew that. He was outgunned in major weapons by a preponderance of 344 to 244. His largest cannons were but 13.5 caliber, while the British "heavies" mounted massive 15-inch guns, a crushing superiority.

However, Scheer reasoned that he could, by means of troublesome raids on the east coast, increase Britain's war weariness. In March and April the German admiral staged two fast bombardments, spearheaded by his battle cruisers and supported by zeppelins, which were employed primarily as fleet scouts.

During the second assault, two hundred houses were wrecked in the fishing town of Lowestoft, on the Norfolk coast, north of Harwich. Few lives were lost, and little damage done to military objectives. The spontaneous result of the raids was an uproar from Britons, criticizing the navy for letting these "insults" be repeated with relative impunity. *Why* didn't the mighty Grand Fleet do something?

Lord Balfour wrote heartening notes to the mayors of

Lowestoft and other coastal communities which had been "insulted," assuring them that it would prove "highly dangerous" for the enemy to try this sort of thing again. But more than penciled encouragement was demanded. The mayors, as indeed most subjects of the king, were calling for the extermination of the entire High Seas Fleet. The principle of a British "fleet in being" as a deterrent to the High Seas Fleet was proving more and more a myth.

Cautious, diminutive, plodding Sir John Jellicoe, admiral of the Grand Fleet, hardly seemed the officer to accomplish so vast, demanding, and final a task. He lacked the drive and daring of the recent first sea lord, Fisher. The Nelsonian qualities lacking in Jellicoe's mental complex were amply supplied, nonetheless, in Admiral Sir David Beatty, handsome commander of the Battle Cruiser Fleet, junior only to Jellicoe himself.

Actually, there was more of the swashbuckling Drake or Hawkins in this square-jawed, broad-shouldered vice admiral than of the tactician Nelson. Completely self-assured, he could meet the most acute challenges with a *sangfroid* that continually amazed his subordinates. When he worked he worked like no one human. When he played he played. If, in peacetime, for example, he had been off on a holiday to Antibes or Cyprus—he would return to his ship just at sailing time and not before.

Between them, however, goaded by the supreme War Council, Jellicoe and Beatty concocted a scheme to encourage the High Seas Fleet away from its bases and into battle. To accomplish this, light units would expose themselves off the Danish, Dutch, and German coasts, while the Grand Fleet almost in toto would be concentrated eastward of the "Long Forties" (stretching about one hundred miles east of the Aberdeen coast) or steaming from the three major anchorages: the northernmost Scapa Flow in the Orkneys, Cromarty about eighty-five miles farther south in Moray Firth, and Rosyth on the Firth of Forth leading into Edinburgh and neighboring ports and anchorages.

By an almost implausible coincidence, Scheer was scheming simultaneously along much identical lines. He would bombard the town of Sunderland, near Newcastle and south of the Firth of Forth, in the hope of luring the Battle Cruiser Fleet to its doom. Waiting for Beatty's vessels in the North Sea would be heavy units of the High Seas Fleet plus all the submarines—possibly as many as twenty—that could be called off distant patrol to be bunched in a single, relatively confined area.

If his bold venture met with success, and Scheer was confident it would in spite of past reverses (notably that in the Falklands), the victory might serve another purpose as well. It would perhaps give heart to the German people, sickened by the mounting toll at Verdun, a bottomless burial pit.

Scheer relied heavily on his airships. With their magnificent cruising radius and their ability to fly at altitudes beyond the accurate range of the enemy's guns, they were indeed the "eyes" of the fleet. The German admiral would attempt his Sunderland ruse only with intelligence from the zeppelins that Jellicoe was *not*, by chance, out in force sweeping the North Sea. Scheer was not prepared to take on the Grand Fleet. At least, he did not think he was.

Impatiently, he waited for the word. There could be none during the last days of May because the weather was so misty in Germany and in Belgium (where there also were hangars) that the big cigar-shaped aircraft could not climb aloft. His fleet was ready, straining at anchorage in the Jade Roads outside of Wilhelmshaven.

Finally, Scheer resolved to churn to sea with an alternate plan. On Tuesday, May 30, he ordered Vice Admiral Franz von Hipper, Beatty's counterpart as commander of the battle cruisers, to lead off past the Frisian Islands and Helgoland into the North Sea. Von Hipper, a strategist without peer—an officer in whom, it was said, "the spirit of the offensive burned strong"— would pound northward in his flagship, the 26,000-ton *Lützow*, newest and possibly the fastest of the Imperial battle cruisers. She would be attended by the court "ladies," the scouting force of light cruisers and destroyers. They would hug the Danish coast up to the Skagerrak, the seventy-five-mile-wide strait or "arm" of the North Sea that separates Norway from Denmark.

It was Scheer's intent to tip his hand deliberately to the British by having von Hipper steam into sight of the neutral coasts of Denmark and Norway, which he knew were studded

Sir John Jellicoe, admiral of the Grand Fleet, led the British forces at Jutland.

with observers for the Royal Navy. Just to be sure his presence was detected, the admiral in charge of the German battle cruisers planned to be indiscreet with radio transmission too.

By this plan, Scheer hoped to surprise with his heavy battle fleet any lighter British units which recklessly pounced on von Hipper's advance guard.

As a matter of fact, British torpedo boats and seaplanes, sniffing about the reaches of the North Sea, had already reached the conclusion that more submarines than usual were on patrol. Sightings of wakes and suspected wakes, periscopes, and flocks of gulls following a not fully visible underwater object (often a U-boat's giveaway) indicated this. However, there was no reason for the Admiralty to deduce any more from this tenuous evidence than that a new smash was being flexed against merchant shipping.

The German radio itself was to be its own giveaway to a greater degree than Scheer had intended. Captain J. H. Rounds, a communications expert, had established a series of secret radio direction-finding stations on the English coast. By means of them he could listen, not only to the large transmitters such as those at Nauen, near Berlin, or Wilhelmshaven, but also to high-power transmitters on enemy ships.

Rounds' electronic sleuths learned that the 28,000-ton battleship *Bayern* (first in the German Navy to mount 15-inch guns and so new that she had not yet formally joined a squadron) was a principal wireless unit of the High Seas Fleet, a virtual radio station afloat. He ordered a ceaseless watch on her traffic, and marshaled the best linguists and decoders available to listen around the clock to the unwittingly telltale voice of the mighty *Bayern*.

On May 30, direction-finding stations established that the *Bayern* and those answering her had moved one and one half degrees overnight. In other words, the High Seas Fleet had been shifted northward from berths in Wilhelmshaven into the Jade estuary, preparatory, beyond a doubt, to some new operation *zusammen!* (in mass).

"This movement," First Sea Lord Jackson recalled later,

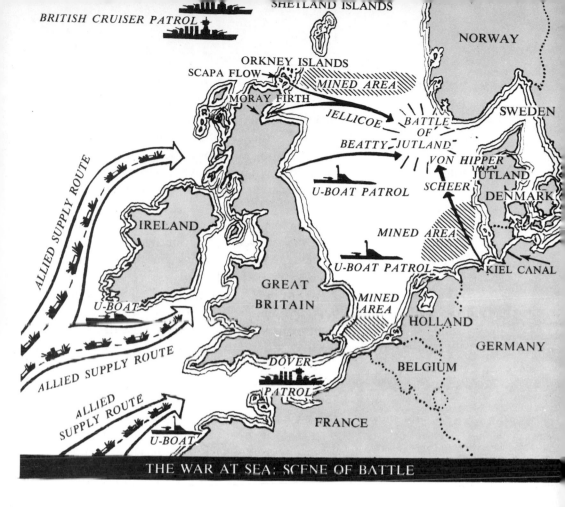

THE WAR AT SEA: SCENE OF BATTLE

Main area of the war at sea. Arrows indicate approach to action at Jutland.

"decided me to send our Grand Fleet to sea . . . to try to meet the German fleet and bring it to action."

And even as von Hipper's *Lützow* showed her broad stern to Wilhelmshaven, followed closely by other battle cruisers of the elite First Scouting Group, there was activity to the westward. In the wake of the *Lützow* were the *Derfflinger* and *Seydlitz* (slightly smaller, older sisters which nonetheless could hit better than twenty-seven knots), the *Moltke* and the *Von der Tann*. Every one was a winner of Imperial efficiency and gunnery awards. Across the North Sea in the Firth of Forth, at Cromarty, and also in the blustery, rocky expanses of Scapa Flow there had been so much secrecy surrounding the Royal Navy's intent that some commanding officers did not realize what was happening until that same Tuesday afternoon when the Grand Fleet was firing its boilers.

Commander Barry Bingham, for example, who had fought through the Falklands on the *Invincible*, had finished a game of golf with his first lieutenant, Maurice Bethel, on the Queensferry links, bordering the Firth of Forth, and was returning to his new command, the 1,000-ton, 35-knot destroyer *Nestor*. Now commanding the Second Division of the 13th Destroyer Flotilla, a blue-ribbon group composed of the best and newest destroyers, Bingham was surprised to read a signal hoist on Beatty's anchored flagship, the 30,000-ton battle cruiser *Lion*: "Raise steam for twenty-two knots and bank fires at half an hour's notice."

The evening lights still shone palely along the Firth of Forth and the fires for late tea glowed in waterside cottages as six battle cruisers, trailed by four dreadnoughts and attended by a swarm of destroyers (twenty-nine, in three flotillas) as well as the first seaplane carrier in any navy, the *Engadine*, swept eastward in the gathering dusk. Admiral Beatty's assemblage appeared to be unbeatable in its size and power.

And yet his was but one of three mighty fleets that were outbound from their yawning anchorages that fateful Tuesday evening. Mankind had never witnessed such a navy putting to sea.

Summer was almost at hand. The hours of darkness were ephemerally brief in these northern latitudes. Dawn was unveiling the Danish coast at about 4 A.M. Wednesday, May 31, when the twenty-year-old tramp, *N. J. Fjord*, out of Esbjerg, set a northerly course for the Skagerrak and Scandinavian ports of call. Like almost any coaster in these waters, she reeked of two decades of cargoes, mostly dried fish.

During the morning she passed the familiar Vyl lightship

west of Esbjerg and then, a few miles farther north, Horns Reef, an historic peril to mariners ten miles west of Blaavand Point on the Danish coast. By noon she was wallowing ahead over Jutland Bank,* about seventy miles off the Tyland shores of Denmark near the approaches to the Skagerrak.

N. J. Fjord was, for the moment, to steam no farther. Two German destroyers, racing in, signaled abruptly: "Heave to!"

Shortly after 2 P.M. the *Galatea*, flagship of the 1st Light Cruiser Squadron, was knifing through calm seas on the extreme eastern fringe of the battle cruisers' sweep area. The day had begun for the *Galatea* on a note of excitement. She had left the Firth of Forth at 3:15 A.M., pirouetting from the wake of a torpedo. Nothing, however, was ever seen of the presumed U-boat.

It was nearly time to turn helm for a more northerly course when the lookout spotted a column of steam drilling upward into the leaden atmosphere.

Commodore E. S. Alexander-Sinclair, squadron commander, studied the sighting for a few minutes. Then he ordered a message sent by light blinker via the chain of destroyers and cruisers which linked even picket vessels, like the *Galatea*, with the *Lion*: "Two-funnelled ship has stopped steamer bearing ESE eight miles, am closing."

Beatty at once ordered an alteration of course to investigate the sighting, while Jellicoe (with his portion of the Grand Fleet still two hours to the northwest) wirelessed further commands: "Raise steam for full speed with all dispatch!"

A German boarding party of two had barely set foot on the *N. J. Fjord* when a signal from one of the German destroyers began to wink, in frenzy. The two men paused, then snapped in German at the Danish merchant officer who had met them, "Stand by and await further orders!"

They were gone, leaving the coaster to roll gently in the swells moving ever outward from the shore. Thus, the obscure little tramp, *N. J. Fjord*, had brought together the outermost units of the Grand Fleet and the High Seas Fleet. Even as the

---

*Jutland Bank is an underwater plateau that rises to within 700 feet of the surface, in an area where depths otherwise average approximately 2,400 feet.

destroyers churned away at full speed, the light cruiser they were to screen, the *Elbing*—in turn protecting von Hipper's westernmost flank—had the *Galatea* in her sights.

"Raus! Raus! Raus!" rang the alarm through her fo'c'sles, magazines, gun positions, and down to the depths of her engine compartments. She was clearing for action.

At 2:20 P.M., the *Galatea* streamed the code flags out on her halyards: "Enemy in sight!"

Silence would, manifestly, serve no further purpose. The English fleet now opened up with a garrulous interchange by radio as well as flag and blinker communication, until, fifteen minutes later, *Galatea* wirelessed from her own transmitting station, called a rabbit hutch by its operators: "Have sighted large amount of smoke as though from a fleet. . . ."

Commodore Alexander-Sinclair then reported his own position and the bearing of the fleet. Eleven minutes later he added: "Smoke seems to be seven vessels besides destroyers and cruisers. They have turned north. . . ."

In another minute, he signaled that he was under fire. The time was 2:52 P.M., Wednesday, May 31, 1916. The *Elbing's* long, ranging shot at the *Galatea* had opened the battle of Jutland. Before dusk that afternoon, 265 major warships (149 British, 116 German), involving more than 100,000 men, would meet head-on, steel leviathans battling to the death in Mesozoic seas.

"Assume complete readiness for action in every respect!" Beatty ordered all ships.

From the *Engadine*, Flight Lieutenant F. J. Rutland was sent aloft in a seaplane equipped with one of the first air-to-ground wireless sets. Flying low in order to avoid patchy clouds, he steered his flimsy machine on a northeasterly course, expecting attack at any instant from a zeppelin with its machine-gun platform. About 3:20 P.M., a formidable sight began to take shape through the blur of Rutland's whirling propeller blade. Below and ahead of his aircraft lay the enemy fleet.

"It was very hard to tell what they were, and so I had to close to within a mile and a half at a height of 1,000 feet," Rutland reported afterward. "They then opened fire on me with antiaircraft and other guns, my height enabling them to use their antitorpedo armament. . . . I flew through several of the columns of smoke caused through bursting shrapnel."

But a defective fuel line, rather than enemy steel and lead, caused Rutland to descend after his reconnaissance.

At 3:25 P.M., Captain Alfred E. Chatfield of the *Lion* reported: "Enemy in sight on starboard bow!"

Within fifteen minutes, Admiral Beatty had made one of his dynamic if impulsive decisions. He ordered his six sleek battle cruisers to rev up to their full twenty-five knots and, leaving his four slower battleships behind, he took off after the five German battle cruisers led by von Hipper in his *Lützow*. This meant that he had, of his own choosing, deprived himself of a main fleet superiority of nearly two to one.

The two squadrons racing south on converging courses, Beatty's about two knots faster, were nearly twelve miles apart when von Hipper opened fire. Seeing the flash of the enemy's guns, the *Lion* returned fire within seconds. It was 3:47 P.M.

For fifteen minutes, the interchange was furious. The *Lion*, and the *Tiger* nearby, were hit several times, as the Germans proved once more their superb gunnery. At 4 P.M., a shell from the *Lützow* penetrated *Lion*'s Q turret and burst inside, killing the turret crew, including two volunteer ammunition passers who quite possibly should not have been there—the chaplain and an assistant surgeon. A powder fire flared ominously downward toward the magazine.

Yet, the commander of this turret, Major F. J. W. Harvey of the Royal Marines, dying, with both legs mangled, picked up the phone and ordered the magazine flooded. By this heroic act he saved the ship and was awarded a posthumous Victoria Cross, the Empire's highest honor.

From the nearby destroyer *Nicator*, the stark drama had been observed—"suddenly a large burst of flame shot up from her." For "one ghastly moment," the horrified spectators thought their flagship, Admiral Beatty, and all were gone, then, "as the smoke cleared away we saw the *Lion*'s remaining turrets fire together and everyone on board us burst into a cheer!"

For those not in turrets, or whose ships had not yet been hit, the engagement was an exhilarating affair, etched in a wild, fluid beauty. As the officer of another destroyer observed, "A magnificent sight . . . the sea became a continuous succession of water spouts, both ahead, astern and on the sides of us . . . !"

The Danish steamer *Naesborg*, en route from Sunderland to Copenhagen, got caught in the contested area. She lingered long enough to hear the opening salvos between the opposing fleets, then poured on the steam and raced for the coast as fast as her old pistons would pound just as the *N. J. Fjord* had done.

Minutes after the *Lion* had narrowly escaped annihilation, the *Indefatigable* began to stagger after a murderous bout with the *Von der Tann*, a battle cruiser of 21,000 tons that matched her quite evenly. The contest so far had been as orderly as mass mayhem can be.

"Two or three shots falling together hit *Indefatigable*," laconically reported Rear Admiral W. C. Pakenham of the 2nd Battle Cruiser Squadron, "about outer edge of upper deck in line with after turret. A small explosion followed and she swung out of line, sinking by the stern. Hit again almost instantly near 'A' turret by another salvo, she listed heavily to port, turned over and disappeared."

While not one member of her crew of 1,017 survived to explain just what had happened, the probability is that a magazine had blown up.

"From 4:15 to 4:43 P.M.," Jellicoe later reported, "the conflict between the opposing battle cruisers was of a very fierce and resolute character. The 5th Battle Squadron was engaging the enemy's rear ships, unfortunately at very long range. Our fire began to tell, the accuracy and rapidity of that of the enemy depreciating considerably. At 4:18 P.M., the third enemy ship was seen to be on fire. The visibility to the northeastward had become considerably reduced, and the outline of the ships very indistinct. This, no doubt, was largely due to the constant use of smoke balls or charges by the enemy, under cover of which they were continually altering course or zigzagging."

About 4:20 P.M., the *Queen Mary*, 30,000 tons, mounting 13.5-inch guns—the newest, and at thirty-two knots probably the fastest of the battle cruisers—was observed by nearby ships to be dueling heatedly and "splendidly" with two of the enemy.

All at once, buffeted by multiple salvos, there was an explosion and the warship was enveloped in clouds of gray smoke.

On board her, Gunner's Mate E. Francis, in X turret, would remember the first shock as "the big smash," after which, he said, "I was dangling in the air on a bowline, which saved me from being thrown down on the floor of the turret . . . everything in the ship went as quiet as a church. . . . One man turned to me and said, 'What do you think has happened?'"

Francis did not know. But he told his turret mates, "Steady, everyone . . . !"

Topside almost everything had been swept clean, and the big battle cruiser staggered with "an awful list." It was time to order the turret clear of personnel:

"I was halfway down the ladder at the back of the turret . . . men getting off the ladder went sliding down to port." He held on, watching others who were reluctant to make the final plunge into the cold, turbulent waters.

"Come on, you chaps!" Francis encouraged, "Who's coming in for a swim?"

Someone answered, "She will float for a long time yet!" Francis, not convinced, was aware that "something—I don't pretend to understand what it was—seemed to be urging me to get away, so I clambered up over the slimy bilge keel and fell off into the water, followed, I think, by about five other men.

"I struck away from the ship as hard as I could and must have covered nearly fifty yards when there was a final big smash . . . the air seemed full of fragments and flying pieces. A large piece seemed to be right above my head, and acting on impulse I dipped under to avoid being struck. . . . I stayed under as long as I could and then came on top again . . . coming behind me I heard a rush of water, which looked very much like surf on a beach, and I realized it was the suction or backwash from the ship which had just gone."

The *Queen Mary* was the sunken tomb of 1,266 officers and men—all but 18 of those who had sailed on her. As he watched her go down, Admiral Beatty turned to his flag captain and, muttered, "There seems to be something wrong with our bloody ships today, Chatfield." He didn't yet realize what an understatement that was.

In the view of the Germans, the *Queen Mary* and the *Indefatigable* had gone "like powder casks." They were blistering refutations of a naval architect's theory that big guns and speed were preferable to heavy armor plating. So far, the Germans had lost only the *Wiesbaden.*

This 400-square-mile segment of the North Sea continued to be torn by monsters of steel, battling for their survival. The area had become a kind of watery charnel house. One British tar recalled:

". . . the percussion shells striking the water exploded, and masses of the metal were hurling all over us. All naval shells striking the water exploded just as if they had hit a solid wall. Millions of dead fish were spread on the surface of the sea. We passed the bodies of mangled men from the ships ahead and wreckage blown out."

As the afternoon waned, the destroyers were far from idle. Commander Barry Bingham slashed ahead in the *Nestor*, followed by the *Nicator* and *Nomad*, of his flotilla. The little ships launched a torpedo attack at the suicidal range of 5,000 yards against the main line of von Hipper's battle cruisers. While it could not immediately be observed whether the torpedoes had struck home, the German ships swerved sharply off course.

One of the cruisers reacted with especial violence toward these snappy terriers. It opened up at point-blank range upon the *Nestor*, piercing her boiler room. At 5 P.M., the destroyer was dead in the water, as steam billowed upward.

"Though crippled," Bingham wrote, "we had guns that were still intact, and a hostile destroyer, swooping down on what she thought an easy prey, was greeted with volleys of salvos from our invaluable and semiautomatic weapons. After such a warm reception, the German destroyer sheered off posthaste."

Soon Bingham was "dumbfounded" to observe the main body of the German High Seas Fleet steaming in a northwest direction, in the wake of the battle cruisers, and "smothering" with broadsides the *Nomad*, which was also disabled. Preparing to give up the *Nestor*, Bingham got rid of charts, confidential

The Queen Mary, Britain's newest and fastest battle cruiser, going down under enemy fire.

books, and other printed matter, then put biscuits in boats and lowered Carley floats. He fired one last torpedo at the enemy, even as "the *Nestor*, enwrapped in a cloud of smoke and spray, the center of a whirlwind of shrieking shells, received not a few heavy and vital hits."

She began to "settle by the stern and then to take a heavy list to starboard. Her decks now showed the first signs of havoc amongst life and limb. It was obvious that the doomed *Nestor* was sinking rapidly."

Bingham gave his final order, "Abandon ship!" then stepped into the gig, or whaler, already half-awash from shrapnel punctures.

"Now where shall we go?" he asked First Lieutenant Bethel, his golf companion of the previous day.

"To Heaven, I trust, Sir," was Bethel's spontaneous reply.

Maurice Bethel had spoken his last words. Turning to aid a wounded signalman, he was hit full on by a shell, "and was seen no more amidst a cloud of fumes."

As the survivors watched the *Nestor* sink, they gave three cheers and sang "God Save the King!"

"Are we down 'arted?" one spluttered bravely.

"No!"

"Wot about 'Tipperary'?"

Soon the water-logged derelicts from the *Nestor* were picked up by a German destroyer. Commander Barry Bingham, whose stalwart humor had not been shaken by either the Falklands or Jutland, went on to prove his ebullience in a prisoner-of-war camp, where he was to be reunited with a great majority of his crew as well as the crew of the *Nomad*.

Bingham was among the Empire's fortunate. He lived to accept his Victoria Cross. All too often, a widow, a weeping mother, or a grim-faced sister had, of necessity, to receive this highest award. Major Harvey was but one of several from the hellfires of Jutland upon whom the Victoria Cross was bestowed posthumously.

John Travers Cornwell, sixteen, had interrupted his studies at the Walton Road School, London, to enlist as "Boy First Class." Serving a 5.5-inch gun aboard the light cruiser *Chester*, engaged by three enemy ships of similar size and firepower, he was the last survivor when a shell exploded close beside the muzzle. Bleeding, mortally wounded, Johnny managed to ram home one final projectile, slam the breech shut, then press the firing button. The shell arced across the seas and exploded on the *Wiesbaden*, augmenting the damage which finally sank her. Johnny Cornwell would not live to see his enemy sink in flames, but he had proved, as a recipient of the Victoria Cross, that he was in truth "Boy First Class."

The destroyer *Shark*, trying to assist the *Chester* (which somehow made it home, carrying fifty dead and wounded), was all but blasted out of the water by enemy cruisers. They tore along on either side of her, pumping devastating broadsides into her thin metal skin.

Her captain, Loftus W. Jones, was a fearless scrapper, a proven scourge of the High Seas Fleet in the North Sea. During the final salvos he lost a leg. Nonetheless, bleeding to death, he was still complaining that the flag was not hanging properly when the North Sea closed over the *Shark*'s bridge.

All but six of her crew of ninety-one went down with the *Shark*. Monk, the destroyer's chimpanzee mascot, was last seen chattering wildly in the rigging. On a raft, the survivors tried to shout "Nearer My God to Thee" above the din of battle.*

Shortly before 5 P.M., Beatty learned with some shock that Scheer's High Seas Fleet was thundering toward him. He relayed a message to Jellicoe via a sister of the lost *Queen Mary*, the *Princess Royal*: "Urgent. Priority. Have sighted enemy's battlefleet bearing SE. . . ." The communications officer of the *Princess Royal* added, "probably hostile."

Beatty, whose fleet had been hammering south, roughly parallel but never closer than nine miles to the German cruisers steaming on an opposite course, now ordered a radical alteration. He turned to the starboard and kept going until he was headed in exactly the opposite direction. He explained, "I pro-

---

*The six were on hand later to see Loftus Jones's widow receive his Victoria Cross.

ceeded on a northerly course to lead them [the German battle-ships] towards the Battle Fleet."

It was a dangerous maneuver, pivoting while under fire, but the battle cruisers' great speed enabled them to accomplish the 180-degree turn with no serious consequences. While his cruisers fought a rear-guard action for the first forty-five minutes, they soon drew out of range of Scheer's "heavies," even though "general chase!" had been hoisted on all of the High Seas Fleet's foretops.

The German commander had reason to think that his opponents were fleeing, in fact "succeeding in getting away." However, Beatty, gradually veering more and more to the eastward, would be in a position, when he met the Grand Fleet, to describe an arc ahead of the pursuing German warships—in other words to "cross the 'T'" of the enemy. The Royal Navy then would be so situated as to pour fire from both sides on the leading vessels of the High Seas Fleet.

About 6 P.M., the Grand Fleet dramatically began to take shape through the late afternoon light on the northwest horizon.

Since most of the airships were still grounded by the poor weather which prevailed in their hangar areas, Scheer was deprived of his eyes. Only a few zeppelins had even a glimpse of the Skagerrak fight. Hence the Germans were as stunned to sight Jellicoe's ships as Beatty had been when he was confronted with Scheer's main battle force.

"We had no intimation," noted Commander Erich Raeder,* von Hipper's staff officer aboard the *Lützow*, "that the British Grand Fleet was also on the scene!" And from the perspective of a member of the Grand Fleet:

". . . the spectacle of seven or more miles of ships, at fairly close range and all fresh to the fight must have stricken terror into the heart of many a superman. Within the space of a few minutes the tables had been absolutely turned."

However, it wasn't quite that simple. With the arrival of

---

*As a grand admiral, Raeder later headed Hitler's navy, and ultimately was sentenced to prison as a war criminal (a punishment that senior officers in the British and United States navies denounced as unjust).

The master strategist—Grand Admiral Scheer (left)—sets trap for British off Danish coast.

more than a hundred additional warships, the jockeying for position and picking a target out of the hazy, fast-moving multitude was complex and confusing. The crisscross of communications between the members of the English fleet attested to this nightmare:

"Firing reported off starboard bow."

"Battle fleet sighted."

"What can you see?"

"Open fire and engage the enemy!"

"Remember traditions of glorious first of June and avenge Belgium!" [This was sent in a burst of enthusiasm from Vice

"... something wrong with our bloody ships!"   •   123

Admiral Sir Cecil Burney on the *Marlborough*, commanding the newly arrived 1st Battle Squadron.]

"*Where* is enemy . . . ?"

"I was told to keep touch with battle cruisers. It seems to be getting a bit thick this end. *What* had we better do?"

"*Urgent!* Have lost sight of enemy's battle fleet. . . ."

"Disregard the Admiral's motions . . . !"

"Whole Hun battle fleet coming up, steering North by East."

"Cease fire."

"Altered course to avoid torpedo."

". . . large explosion seen in enemy's line!"

"Open fire and engage the enemy!"

"Can you see any enemy battleships?"

"*Urgent*. Have been struck by a mine or torpedo, but not certain which. . . ."

"*Urgent*. Have been struck by a torpedo . . . !"

"There is a submarine ahead of you."

Jellicoe kept asking Beatty for course, bearing, and speed of Scheer's battle fleet. But Beatty could convey only the momentary flickerings of a fluid kaleidoscope. It was frustrating to both admirals, a deadly game of blindman's buff.

Some ships fell victim to chaos. It was a product not only of the engagement's magnitude and the heat and fast pace of the battle, but of communications which were not the best. Flag signals, obscured by smoke, were almost incomprehensible even in the daylight hours.

The 14,000-ton *Defence*, aging flagship of Rear Admiral Sir Robert Arbuthnot who commanded the 1st Cruiser Squadron, somehow came within a deadly two-mile range of the German battle cruisers as it was going into battle. Bravely, if foolishly, Admiral Arbuthnot held to his course and attacked. Blanketed by salvos, he lost his life, his ship, and all the remaining 907 men aboard the lightly guarded *Defence* in a towering rush of flames.

Less than fifteen minutes later, the *Invincible* was scoring on the *Derfflinger*, hoping to avenge the destruction of the

124 • ". . . something wrong with our bloody ships!"

Queen Mary. Aboard her, Rear Admiral Horace L. A. Hood, commanding the 3rd Battle Cruiser Squadron, was increasingly pleased with his men's marksmanship. Phoning the *Invincible*'s gunnery officer, Commander H. E. Dannreuther, in the control top, Hood complimented him: "Your firing is very good. Keep at it as quickly as you can. Every shot is telling!"

On the *Derfflinger*, reeling from the fury of the British cruiser's assault, Dannreuther's counterpart, Commander Georg von Hase, marked in dismay the number of shells which "pierced our ship with a terrific force and exploded with a tremendous roar which shook every seam and rivet."

Thus no one, especially those in the crew of the beleaguered *Derfflinger*, was prepared for the spectacle suddenly presented by the *Invincible*. In the words of one who had fought aboard her at the Falklands, now watching in horror from the deck of another vessel:

". . . a great crimson rose of flame 100 feet high and perhaps 200 broad that rose leisurely, contemptuously, with an awful majestic dignity to a good 400 feet—at its very top an immense baulk of ship's plating and many lesser bits. Then the deep red faded out and there remained only a black pall below, merging in the general pall that the many ships' smoke at full speed was creating; and, above, a new billowy cloud added to the others in the sky. . . ."

Minutes later, "a gentle shower, like the first snowfall, of ashes fell or rather came drifting down about us. . . ." This was what remained of 18,000 tons of warship—the final amen to a mass cremation and the death of the battle cruiser. Dannreuther, the gunnery officer to whom Hood had spoken what were probably his last words, was among the six who miraculously lived to tell how they were "blown up" on the *Invincible*.

The battle of Jutland indicated that there *was* indeed "something wrong," not necessarily with the Grand Fleet as a whole, but with the battle cruisers. There was insufficient armor atop the turrets, and no flash control to protect the magazines from blowing up. German gunnery was superior, too, even with the disadvantage of lighter calibers. The *Lion* and *Princess Royal*, for example, scored only three times during the entire battle; they were struck a total of twelve times. Nearly every hit from the High Seas Fleet produced terrible devastation.

The war, as Churchill had augured, could be lost "in an afternoon." Jellicoe was in a position to "lose" it, or at least be saddled with the responsibility. Beatty, having witnessed more than 70,000 tons of his beautiful ships hissing to the bottom in a relatively few minutes, could wonder on his own score if this were not indeed *that* afternoon?

The commander in chief of the battle cruisers was not one, however, to brood for long, even when faced by the spectacle of a disaster unparalleled in the Empire's marine annals. Drake, Hawkins, Nelson, and surely those Americans, John Paul Jones, Davy Farragut, Dewey and Sampson must have been somewhere looking over Beatty's shoulder as he scribbled an almost imperious dispatch to Jellicoe: "Urgent. Submit van of battleships follow battle cruisers. We can then cut off whole of enemy's battle fleet."

A subordinate, even the second in command, telling the leader of the Grand Fleet what to do and stamping it "Urgent!" was far from customary. But, then, this was not an ordinary battle.

Jellicoe would have gone along with most any constructive suggestion, even one originating from a junior admiral. However, he still kept asking, "Where is enemy's B.F. [battle fleet]?"

It did nothing to restore the commander of the Grand Fleet's peace of mind to receive replies such as that from the *Southampton,* flying the flag of Commodore W. E. Goodenough, leading the 2nd Light Cruiser Squadron: "Have lost sight of enemy's battle fleet . . ."

Jellicoe, however, admitted, "At this stage it was not clear whether the enemy battle fleet was ahead of our battle fleet or on the starboard beam, as heavy firing was proceeding from ahead to the starboard beam, and the cruiser ahead was seen to be hotly engaged."

The death struggle appeared less confusing to Commodore G. von Schoultz than to the average participant. The head of Finland's tiny navy, von Schoultz was temporarily acting as an observer for the czar of Russia. On board the 20,000-ton battleship *Hercules* of Jellicoe's main fleet (commanded by Captain Lewis Clinton-Baker), he presented an especially lucid picture of the early evening's action, beginning at about 6:30 P.M. when he was "lifted . . . involuntarily into the air," from the commencing fire of the battleship's 12-inch guns, an ear-punishment which nonetheless caused him "a thrill of joy." In his book, *With the British Battle Fleet,* the Finnish observer wrote:

". . . my attention is distracted by enemy shells shrieking over the ship. I see a splash very close to our port side which gives me a thorough shower bath. Other shells are falling to starboard of us. The salvo is straddling us, and that at the very beginning: the German gunnery must be particularly good. While waiting for our second salvo I ask the foretop whether the enemy is in sight. They reply that for the moment he is hidden in dense smoke, but that the fall of our first salvo has been observed. It was *over* a battle cruiser of the *Derfflinger* class which had been sighted for a few minutes.

"Just then our second salvo is fired and the voice-pipe gives me a heavy blow on the ear. I seize my marine glasses, look towards the direction of the salvo, and can vaguely distinguish the silhouettes of two or three enemy battle cruisers. Again I am unable to observe the falling of our salvo, for again I am deluged by a splash, and the gunner in charge of the range-finder tells me that the latter has been torn from its fastenings. I have just asked him our distance from the enemy, but the instrument is now useless, as it has been thrown out of gear by the last shock. The bridge is very sensitive to the shock of our guns, and after the first few salvos the prisms seem to have been jolted from their fittings. I tell the petty officer to try to put the gear in order and spend a few minutes myself trying to do so. I notice, however, that one of the screws of the mounting has been broken off. I therefore send the men away from the bridge, wet through by the splashes of the enemy shells. A few splinters from German shells exploding in the water fall on the bridge. I pick one up, but drop it at once; it is as hot as if it had just come out of a furnace.

"The Grand Fleet has now formed a line of battle, but the intervals are uneven and for the most part too close. Some of the ships are firing tentatively to starboard, others have completely ceased fire. On our starboard beam are the *Barham* and two other ships of Admiral Evan Thomas's [Fifth Battle] Squadron. They are firing regular but infrequent salvos from their heavy guns. To all appearances the bad visibility is hampering them as much as us.

"A fresh douche of water nearly washes me off the bridge, but I succeed in finding better shelter on the lower bridge of the conning tower. It occurs to me that the enemy can see us better than we can see him.

"A few minutes later the smoke lifts and I think I can make out the enemy again in the haze. Owing to the smoke from our guns, however, they are difficult to see, as the guns are on roughly the same level as my position. It is lucky for us that our director firing control is fitted in the foretop, as fire control from the forward conning tower or from the gun turrets would have offered no hope of success.

"I decide to go up to the upper bridge again, and there find our bugler, a youth of fifteen. When I ask him what he is doing there I notice tears in his eyes and realize that the poor lad, whose duty it is to pass on signals, is terrified by the gunfire and probably more still by the loneliness, for not a soul is to be seen on deck.

"I take him with me to the upper bridge and put him at the voice-pipe connecting with the foretop. Our gunnery officer, Lieutenant Commander Dewar, has just reported that a German battleship of the *König* class, and therefore in the van of the enemy Battle Fleet, has just been sighted. I can see the ship with the naked eye and through my glasses can distinguish the characteristics of the class. But much nearer to us, not more than a mile to starboard, is the damaged cruiser *Warrior,* so straddled by enemy salvos that the water round her looks as though it were boiling. Astern of her is the battleship *Warspite* which has fallen far behind her squadron. Both ships are obviously in a dangerous situation, and their crews going through a critical time, while they try to find cover behind the Grand Fleet. The *Warrior* is constantly altering course and is badly on fire, apparently, however, only in her superstructure. The *Warspite* is much farther away from us and only comes into sight now and again for a short time out of the smoke and haze. . . .

"Our battle formation has now developed itself into a long column in line ahead, with *Hercules* among the rearmost ships. At 6:45 P.M. the van of our Battle Fleet begins to turn to starboard. Only the ships in the centre and rear of the line are firing; the van apparently cannot see the enemy.

"At 6:47 I enter in my diary that a burning cruiser is in sight on the starboard beam. I am told from the foretop that she belongs to the enemy. We do not engage her however and, owing to the great distance, I cannot distinguish her class. The sun is now almost directly behind us and our course E.S.E.

"The enemy splashes are nowhere near us. I speak to the bugler, who has now grown accustomed to the firing and regained control of himself. I send him back to his action station near the forward conning tower.

"Once more I am alone on the bridge. Around me all is deserted, astonishingly deserted; I cannot see a single man. Meanwhile the ship drives forward as though propelled by some supernatural force, trembling and quivering under the shock of her own salvos, while fire, smoke, and steel are belched from her guns. . . .

"Looking ahead I see a British destroyer on the *Marlborough's* [1st Battle Squadron flagship] beam. She is stopped, and is flying a signal from her mast. She is apparently severely damaged; bridge, funnels, and superstructure completely shot away.

"Whilst I am watching her through my glasses the *Marlborough* comes into my field of vision as she passes the destroyer, and suddenly I see on the starboard side of our Flagship a high, dense column of water. My first thought is: Mine or torpedo? The second: Enemy submarine or destroyer? The column of water still hangs in the air as I pull out my watch, look at the second-finger and say to myself: The *Marlborough's* fate will be decided in the next minute.

"Racked with anxiety, I again look through my glass towards our flagship. She seems to have a slight list to starboard and has ceased fire. I glance at my watch and note that it is only half a minute since the explosion. So far I have heard no explosion, and so all depends on the development of the list. The minute seems strangely long. The list seems to become more pronounced and can be seen with the naked eye. Then a load falls from my heart. From every turret of the *Marlborough* the flashes of the next salvo spurt out, followed by the thick clouds from the 'smokeless' powder, the characteristic red smoke of cordite. I see from my watch that the minute is not yet up. I report the damage to the *Marlborough* to Clinton Baker and reassure him at the same time by pointing out that the ship is firing.

"In reply to my question, the fore-top reports that from there they have seen neither the track of the torpedo which has struck the *Marlborough* nor the periscope of an enemy submarine. . . .

"According to my reckoning, the explosion occurred at 6:55 P.M. Five minutes later we pass a heavily damaged destroyer. I hear from the fore-top that she is the *Acasia*. For some reason she reminds me of a winged bird, still alive but unable to rise.

"At 7:05 P.M. the order comes from the *Marlborough* that our division is to turn three points to starboard. This is to guard against enemy submarines; for in the smoke and haze which cover the enemy, destroyers cannot be seen. I can only guess at the enemy's course from the flashes constantly illumining the mist.

"The German ships cannot be seen any better from the fore-top, and the fire is now trained upon the flashes. For this reason there are long intervals between our salvos.

"I suddenly remember the effect upon me of our first salvos and am surprised that they no longer disturb me. I wait for the next and notice that I am still thrown a few inches into the air, as was the case with the first. The force of the concussion is in no way diminished and the whole hull of the ship is shaken as by internal convulsions. The salvos and concussions, however, have now ceased to worry me, as also the shrieking of the enemy's shells overhead and the great volumes of water which continually wash over the bridge. . . .

"At 7:10 P.M. we come up close to a ship, apparently a cruiser [the light cruiser *Wiesbaden*]. She is about two or three miles away on our starboard beam, with her bows towards us so that her class is difficult to determine. I can only see her hull and three funnels. She is heavily on fire and stopped, reminding me again of a winged duck.

"Then Clinton Baker comes out of the conning tower on to the bridge, followed by the Chief Yeoman of Signals. He thinks the ship has four funnels. In this case she may equally well be British. I am convinced that she is an enemy cruiser and the Yeoman of Signals is of the same opinion. I say nothing, however, for I feel sorry for her, and in any case she is in no way dangerous to us. I delay my answer, as just at that moment the burning cruiser opens fire from one or two guns. This seals her fate. Clinton Baker goes to the voice-pipe and orders the fore-top to fire on the ship. We fire one salvo, and she is at once enveloped in water and the smoke of the bursting shells.

"Since we altered course to starboard our distance from the enemy is decreasing, and once more the splashes from the enemy guns are closer round us.

"According to my notes, the *Hercules* was straddled by an enemy salvo at 7:20 P.M. and this was followed by a second and third. There is a regular hail of splinters on the bridge and upper deck, which, however, no longer disturbs me. I am only wondering from exactly where the enemy fire is coming. I cannot see the enemy and from the fore-top only the gun-flashes can be distinguished. As range-measuring with the instrument is impossible, I take out my watch and try to determine the enemy's range by the interval between the flash from the muzzles and the fall of the shells. By multiplying this by a shell's average rate of flight I get a range of seven miles. I ask the fore-top for the range. They too do not know but reckon it at about six miles. . . .

"At 7:30 P.M. I am told from the fore-top that we are passing floating wreckage of a large ship [the *Invincible*]. Looking over the port side, I see through my glasses two objects like sailing boats. They are very close together, and apparently are the stern and bow of a ship whose middle part is below the surface. English or German? The fore-top cannot answer and we sweep past with the riddle unsolved. We notice one of our destroyers making for the wreckage.

"At this moment the fore-top reports that light enemy cruisers and torpedo craft are approaching on the starboard hand.

I cross to the starboard side of the ship. The bridge is still deserted, and the ship drives forward in uncanny silence. Our giant guns stretch far over the side towards the enemy. A dense veil of smoke drifts towards us from ahead. A destroyer attack! It looks innocent enough but may easily cost us our lives.

"Through my excellent marine glasses I can just make out four destroyers in the smoke, and upon these our quick-firing guns open rapid fire. The ships near us also fire with frenzied rapidity.

"How long can the enemy destroyers hold out under such fire? As they are steaming 30 knots, they cover a mile in two minutes. The success of the attack depends as much on the endurance of the destroyers as on the accuracy of our gunnery. We are firing at random, however, for there is no time for range finding and the smoke prevents observation of the splashes. . . .

"My watch points to 7:38 P.M. Now our heavy guns join in the bombardment of the destroyers, chiefly for the sake of the morale effect. This seems to be successful, for the destroyers turn about and send out a heavy smoke cloud behind them. The foretop reports that one of the destroyers has been sunk by our gunfire. For the moment, however, that is of minor interest. The important thing is to keep a sharp look-out through the glasses for the enemy torpedoes which have assuredly been fired.

"So far no trace is to be seen on the glassy surface, for at long range torpedoes are set at low speed, and therefore run not much faster than the destroyers themselves. Then I discover through my glasses, in the distance, a slight ruffling of the surface which reminds me of the streaks which extreme cold produces on smooth ice. It is coming towards us from the direction in which the destroyers have just disappeared. . . .

"In such moments the brain works with immeasurable speed; otherwise the necessary measures would have been taken too late. The torpedo is coming ahead of our beam so I do not hesitate, but shout at once: 'Hard to starboard!'

"I at once feel a certain relief, although Clinton Baker has still to repeat my words and the man at the wheel to put down the helm, after which a short time must elapse before the ship, with her speed of 20 knots, responds. I had, however, fulfilled this

John Travers Cornwell left school at sixteen to serve aboard the *Chester*. Mortally wounded, he fired the shot which sank the *Wiesbaden*. He was awarded the Victoria Cross, posthumously.

task which chance had thrown upon me, and I felt the relief a satisfactory answer in an examination might give.

"The ship swings sharply to starboard. I lose sight of both the torpedoes astern and see only the third, now approaching us at an acute angle and very close. A short moment later it has passed. . . .

"After we had beaten off the attack we ceased fire for a short time and cocoa was served to the men at their action stations."

The excitement in the easterly reaches of the North Sea had spread back to the British Isles, wherever anyone possessed a powerful wireless receiver. One who became frantic with a desire to participate was Commodore Tyrwhitt and his Harwich Force, who had arrived too late to help the *Aboukir, Cressy* and *Hogue*. His smarting for another chance at the enemy had been irritated further during the Lowestoft raid. Then the only demonstrable result of his foray against the invaders was a disabling hit upon one of his own destroyers, the *Laertes*.

In these early evening hours, Tyrwhitt could endure it no longer. With his sixteen destroyers, recently strengthened by the addition of five light cruisers, he put to sea on his own say-so, though he had the good sense to radio his *fait accompli* to the Admiralty.

At 6 P.M., the abashed operations officers at the Admiralty crackled back at Tyrwhitt, "Return at once and await orders!" They had no desire to leave East Anglia and the Thames estuary, at the approaches to London, unguarded. After all, if Scheer was winning—and from the garble of dispatches so far intercepted he might well be—nothing was to prevent him from sailing on westward and pasting the east coast in a kind of victory salute.

"Tyrwhitt's Navy," as the people about Harwich had begun to call the commodore's burgeoning conglomeration (which included fishing smacks used for scouts) turned back to its base. It was a dismal anticlimax. The dejected commodore, wracked with aspirations, wondered if he would *ever* be allowed a more dynamic role in the war.

Meanwhile, as the late northern twilight darkened, smoke screens augmented the billowings from the furnaces of many ships and blended with the evening mist to form a miasma that was penetrated only by the somewhat more spasmodic flashes from the guns. Perversely, however, this accumulating duskiness of the approaching night served as a revelation to Scheer.

". . . the entire arc stretching from north to east was a sea of fire," the High Seas Fleet's leader reported. "The flash from the muzzles of the guns was distinctly seen through the mist and smoke on the horizon, though the ships themselves were not distinguishable."

Scheer, in his slow but comfortable flagship, the 24,700-ton dreadnought *Friedrich der Grosse*, was much alone. He knew that he was confronted with a decision that could save, or sink, his fleet. The enemy had crossed his T, as though spreading an umbrella before his advancing column. That is, the British ships were now so situated that they could pick off his lead vessels, or stream down either or both sides of the T, pouring broadsides at all his ships.

He theorized further that the enemy was fully intending "to

force us over to the west in order to open battle with us when it was light."

Von Hipper himself, studying the smoky dusk to the northwest, observed to the captain of the *Lützow*, "Mark my word, Harder, there's something nasty brewing. It would be better not to get ourselves in too deep."

The character of the battle, which had begun in such a routine manner that a staff officer had observed to Commander Raeder, "Why it's as calm as if it were nothing but a drill," suddenly changed.

Scheer was not one to tarry over a decision. He quickly demonstrated why he had risen to the fatherland's highest seagoing command. He would allow the British to *think* he was being forced farther and farther west. He would keep veering off for a little longer, then: a lightning battle-wheelaround toward starboard, for home. When the enemy blinked their eyes and looked around, the High Seas Fleet would be gone—or so Scheer hoped.

The plan was uncommonly bold.

Commander von Hase, the *Derfflinger's* gunnery officer, gave an especially vivid description of what was happening and about to happen:

"Meanwhile the commander in chief had realized the danger to which our fleet was exposed. The van of our fleet was shut in by the semicircle of the enemy. We were in a regular deathtrap. There was only one way of escape from this unfavorable tactical situation: to turn the line about and withdraw on the opposite course. Before everything we must get out of this dangerous enemy envelopment. But this maneuver had to be carried out unnoticed and unhindered. The battle cruisers and the destroyers had to cover the movements of the fleet.

"At about 9:12 P.M. the commander in chief gave the fleet the signal to turn about on the opposite course and almost at the same time sent by wireless to the battle cruisers and destroyers the historic order: 'Close the enemy!' The signal man on our bridge read the message aloud, adding the words, which stood against it in the signal book: 'And ram! The ships will fight to the death.' Without moving an eyelid the captain gave the order:

" 'Full speed ahead. Course southeast.'

"Followed by the *Seydlitz, Moltke,* and *Von der Tann,* we altered course south at 9:15 P.M. and headed straight for the enemy's van. The *Derfflinger,* as leading ship, now came under a particularly deadly fire. Several ships were engaging us at the same time.

"I could feel that our fire soothed the nerves of the ship's company. If we had ceased fire at this time the whole ship's company would have been overwhelmed by despair."

Further confusion was injected into the battle cruisers' maneuver since Admiral von Hipper was moving to another ship. His beautiful *Lützow,* smashed like an eggshell and aflame, was slowly, determinedly sinking. Meanwhile, Captain Hartog, of the *Derfflinger,* was acting as a stand-in for von Hipper, an old friend.

"Salvo after salvo fell around us," von Hase continued, "hit after hit struck our ship. They were stirring minutes. My communication with Lieutenant-Commander von Stosch was now cut off, the telephones and speaking tubes running to the fore-top having been shot away. I was now left to rely entirely on my own observation of the splashes to control the gun-fire. Hitherto I had continued to fire with all four heavy turrets, but at 9:13 P.M. a serious catastrophe occurred. A 38-cm. [15-in.] shell pierced the armor of the 'Caesar' turret and exploded inside. . . . The shell set on fire two shell-cases in the turret. The flames from the burning cases spread to the transfer chamber, where it set fire to four more cases, and from there to the case-chamber, where four more were ignited. The burning cartridge-cases emitted great tongues of flame which shot up out of the turrets as high as a house; but they only blazed; they did not explode as had been the case with the enemy. This saved the ship, but the result of the fire was catastrophic.

"The huge tapering flames killed everyone within their reach. Of the seventy-eight men inside the turret only five managed to save themselves through the hole provided for throwing out empty shell-cases, and of these several were severely injured. The other seventy-three men died together like heroes in the fierce fever of battle, loyally obeying the orders of their turret officer.

Shell hole in port side of the British light cruiser *Chester*. Carrying fifty dead and wounded, she somehow made it home.

Deck damage aboard the British light cruiser *Chester*.

"A few moments later this catastrophe was followed by a second. A 38-cm. shell pierced the roof of the 'Dora' turret, and here, too, exploded inside the turret. The same horrors ensued. With the exception of one man, who was thrown by the concussion through the turret entrance, the whole turret crew of eighty men, including all the magazine men, were killed instantly. The crew of the turret, under the leadership of their brave turret officer, Stückmeister Arndt, had fought heroically up to the last second. Here, too, the flames spread to the cartridge-chamber and set fire to all the cases which had been removed from their protective packing. From both after-turrets great flames were now spurting, mingled with clouds of yellow smoke, two ghastly pyres.

"At 9:15 P.M. I received a message from the transmitting station: 'Gas danger in the heavy gun transmitting station. Station must be abandoned.'

"Suddenly, we seemed to hear the crack of doom. A terrific roar, a tremendous explosion and then darkness, in which we felt a colossal blow. The whole conning tower seemed to be hurled into the air as though by the hands of some portentous giant, and then to flutter trembling into its former position. A heavy shell had struck the fore-control about 50 cm. in front of me. The shell exploded, but failed to pierce the thick armour, which it had struck at an unfavourable angle, though huge pieces had been torn out. Poisonous greenish-yellow gases poured through the apertures into our control.

"I called out: 'Down gas-masks!' and immediately every man pulled down his gas-mask over his face. I went on controlling the fire with my gas-mask on, which made it very difficult to make myself understood. But the gases soon dissipated, and we cautiously took off the masks. We assured ourselves that the gunnery apparatus was still in order. Nothing had been disturbed. Even the delicate mechanism of the sighting apparatus was, strange to say, still in order. Some splinters had been flung through the aperture onto the bridge, where they had wounded several men, including the navigating officer.

"The terrific blow had burst open the heavy armoured door of the tower, which now stood wide open. Two men strove in vain to force it back, but it was jammed too tight. Then came unexpected assistance. Once more we heard a colossal roar and crash and with the noise of a bursting thunderbolt a 38-cm. shell exploded under the bridge. Whole sheets of the deck were hurled through the air, a tremendous concussion threw overboard everything that could be moved. Amongst other things, the chart house, with all the charts and other gear, and—last but not least—my good overcoat, which I had left hanging in the chart house, vanished from the scene forever. And one extraordinary thing happened: the terrific concussion of the bursting 38-cm. shell shut the armoured door of the fore-control. A polite race, the English! They had opened the door for us and it was they who shut it again. I wonder if they meant to? In any case it amused us a good deal.

"I looked towards the enemy through my periscope. Their salvos were still bursting round us, but we could scarcely see anything of the enemy, who were disposed in a great semicircle round us. All we could see was the great reddish-gold flames spurting from the guns. . . ."

From the other side, the wild canvas of battle possessed much the same aspect. One Royal Navy officer wrote:

". . . the night was almost more exciting than the day. . . . All of a sudden the darkness would be interrupted by a glare of light as a searchlight was switched on . . . then would come the rattle and booming of guns fired at great speed, with red flashes stabbing the darkness. . . . Frequently there would be an explosion as some ship met her doom. The sky would become lighted with the flickering of fires started aboard some of the engaged ships. Suddenly, as though by a prearranged signal the firing would cease, the searchlights go out, and peace and darkness reign once more."

What was actually happening during this "rattle and booming" and the "red flashes" was that the High Seas Fleet was pounding and butting through the middle of the Grand Fleet. In audacity and brilliance of execution there had been nothing like it in naval history.

The destroyer action itself during these waning minutes of the battle was especially furious, reminding one Royal Navy officer of "infantry following an artillery preparation." He added of this "weird" aspect: "The German destroyers made attack after attack . . . on our big ships; but these onslaughts were singularly futile, not a single torpedo launched by them getting home. . . ."

The "infantry" of the sea nonetheless did greatly aid the escape of the High Seas Fleet, if only through the wild confusion it caused.

At 10:41 P.M., the wireless operator on the *Iron Duke* received a message from the Admiralty of unusual portent:

German battlefleet ordered home at 9:14 P.M. Battle cruisers in rear Course SSE. 3/4 E. Speed 16 knots.

If true, this revealed that the Germans were steaming about one knot slower than the Grand Fleet, that the two opposing assemblages had been converging for the past two hours, and that some units might even *still* be converging. Spasmodic gunfire, the fireworks display of star shells, the stabbings of searchlights —especially from the destroyers—all should have hinted that the enemy was up to something radically dramatic.

Jellicoe, however, did *not* act. He was distrustful of the Admiralty's intelligence, its communications, and quite conceivably he had not even been told of those radio direction stations. Certainly, signaling between his own fleet members had been confused and imperfect enough this day, to say nothing of interception and interpretation of the enemy's wireless traffic.

Now, wasn't it all too likely that the Germans were up to their old tricks, assuming that the Admiralty had actually succeeded in breaking an enemy message? Indeed, *why* should Scheer be steaming for Wilhelmshaven when he, Admiral Jellicoe, was quite prepared to tussle with him again in the morning? This surely wasn't the old cricket way of doing things.

The possibility that the dispatch meant just what it said appeared so preposterous to Jellicoe that he finally dismissed it from his mind. Besides, he was becoming increasingly worried over torpedo attacks in the night together with mine and submarine traps "on a large scale." In fact, he was to admit that the Royal Navy had a good deal to learn from the Germans when it came to fighting in darkness.

Admiral David Beatty, commander of the British cruiser squadron, crossed Scheer's "T" so he could fire from both sides.

There was also another factor—the admiral's loss of confidence in the resilience of his ships. In the United States Navy, the capacity of a warship to absorb pummelling was called "lifing." Jellicoe had reason to wonder if his beautiful vessels were not proving to be pugilists with glass jaws.

So, far from wishing to pursue the enemy, Jellicoe commenced giving instructions for his ships to close up and turn north—*away* from Horns Reef to the east, the Frisians to the south. In either direction the Grand Fleet would necessarily have encountered whole groups of the enemy.

Jellicoe abandoned his plan to force the High Seas Fleet to the west where Scheer would be entirely at his mercy. At least this had appeared to be the case to the German commander in chief, and he had taken desperate measures to extricate his ships. Nevertheless, Jellicoe determined to avoid further encounters. He even ignored a subsequent message from the Admiralty giving the position of "a damaged enemy ship, probably *Lützow*."

However, another part of the same wireless indicating that

U-boats "were apparently coming out from German ports" only strengthened his determination to have no more part of the fight. Jellicoe crackled out orders for his ships to "close up!" and turn north!*

At midnight, the sky lit up for miles. The old, 13,000-ton *Black Prince,* member of Arbuthnot's luckless 1st Cruiser Squadron, had strayed into the very center of the retreating German fleet. In the merciless glare of searchlights, including those of Scheer's flagship, she was torn apart. The *Black Prince* literally disappeared in a roar of shells.

A third member of the squadron, the *Warrior,* half-awash from earlier damage, was struggling toward Scotland.

The fortunes of war were not, however, entirely one-sided. At 2:05 A.M. the nine ships of the 12th Destroyer Flotilla charged bravely to within 2,000 yards of a line of enemy dreadnoughts and cruisers. Led by the *Faulknor,* the little terriers sent off their torpedoes, then wheeled away under a rain of shellfire. They singled out the 13,000-ton *Pommern,* an aging battleship, for the concentrated fury of their assault.

"Right amidships," reported one of the officers on the *Obedient,* "on the waterline of the ship that we had fired at—the *Pommern,* now on our port quarter—appeared a dull-red ball of fire. Quicker than one can imagine it spread fore and aft until, reaching the foremast and mainmast, it flared upwards, up the masts in the biggest tongues of flame, uniting beneath the mastheads in a big black cloud of smoke and sparks. Then one saw the ends of the ship come up as though her back was broken—before the mist shut her out from view."

In the very early dawn of these northerly latitudes, *Pom-*

---

*The order was to puzzle naval strategists for decades and divide them into two principal camps: those favoring the reluctant tactics of Jellicoe or the far more headlong tactics of Beatty. Churchill, the former first lord of the Admiralty, would shrug, "It is difficult to penetrate his [Jellicoe's] mind."

Another naval leader, a captain fresh from duty at the Dardanelles at the time of Jutland, Sir Roger Keyes, had asked Jellicoe's chief of staff, Vice Admiral Sir Charles Madden, why the fleet did not sweep toward Horns Reef at daylight on the first of June. He replied that that was the Admiralty's fault; if they had only sent Tyrwhitt's (Destroyer) Force to join them at daylight, the commander-in-chief would have given this order. But the Admiralty kept Tyrwhitt standing by at Harwich in case the enemy raided the coast . . . the fleet could not risk going into submarine-infested waters without a destroyer screen.

mern, with all 844 souls aboard her, was stricken from the list of effectives of the High Seas Fleet.

At 4 A.M., Thursday, June 1, Jellicoe delivered his "amen," though it hardly seemed necessary: "Cease fire!"

A few hours later, the Grand Fleet was heading for home on a northwest course, through waters strewn with fantastic debris.

The battle of Jutland was over. As dawn broke over the Frisian Islands, the first units of Scheer's yet unbeaten fleet were streaming into the Jade River, headed for Wilhelmshaven, safety, and the ovation of their countrymen.

Many of the ships should never have made home port. The *Seydlitz,* for example, burdened by 5,000 tons of water "swallowed" through jagged shell holes, sloshed homeward with an eight-degree list. She grounded at 2 A.M. on Horns Reef. Moving at a snail's pace when free, she became fast again in shoal waters that same evening, a helpless target for two hours. On June 2, when she struggled into the Jade River, more awash than otherwise, she was drawing forty-two feet of water, nearly twice her normal draft. For the third time she went aground.

Her crew, in the sporting estimation of her enemy, had performed "indomitably" in docking a warship that had been in imminent danger of sinking or being sunk for forty-eight hours. The *Derfflinger's* plight had been almost as dire. Both battle cruisers would have been easy targets *if* units of the Grand Fleet had possessed the daring and imagination to track them down.

Royal Navy captains were also heroically navigating their crippled ships home. Those worst hurt were the battleships *Marlborough* and *Warspite,* the cruiser *Chester* and the destroyers *Acasia, Broke, Defender, Nonsuch, Onslow,* and *Sparrowhawk.*

Lost sight of in the overriding sound and drama of battle was the role of the surgeons. The scenes in the medical fo'c'sles of the floundering *Warrior,* as pictured in the following contemporary newspaper account, were all too typical:

". . . a shell crashed into the ship and destroyed utterly the after dressing station; other shells followed, and finally a fire broke out resulting in many casualties. As soon as possible, and while firing was in progress, one of the surgeons went along the upper deck and the after part of the ship and rendered first aid, and in this he was assisted by the doctor in charge of the wrecked station who had escaped miraculously. The wounded were carried along the decks from the scene of the disaster to the forward station . . . then, to add to the terrible character of the situation, the electric lights went out and gas and smoke began to fill the mess decks and especially the forward dressing station. . . . Although candles and an electric torch had been provided it was very difficult to see owing to the dense smoke and consequently irritation of the eyes.

"These various circumstances rendered the dressing station a kind of inferno. But courage and devotion discounted even such great troubles. As soon as the watertight doors, which shut off one part of the ship from the other parts, were opened, the doctors went forth again with their stretcher parties to collect wounded from the various parts of the ship and to carry them to the sick bay and forecastle mess deck, which were still intact. Mess tables were rapidly cleared away and the wounded brought to a place of comfort with all speed."

In the forward dressing station, gas and smoke became so thick that doctors and attendants fainted, only to be revived and continue their feverish treatments. They worked so skillfully, sutured so rapidly, that not one casualty succumbed from bleeding.

"A bathroom forward of the sick bay was selected as an operating theater. As soon as it was ready the surgeons set to work. . . . All through the long hours they toiled, knowing little or nothing of what passed upon the seas about them, of the position of their ship, of the chances of personal safety. . . . The work went on without a break and by the light of candles, till 4 A.M., June 1, when all the wounded had been attended to and made comfortable. . . .

"The injuries received . . . were of the most terrible kind. Several bodies were rent in pieces; many limbs were torn from bodies; some men were stripped naked. Among the operations performed by the light of the guttering candles, upon a sinking ship in a gale of wind, were amputations, ligaturing of bleeding vessels, and removal of shell splinters."

Repeated many times during the morning after Jutland was the operation of transferring the wounded, via cargo hoist litter, from men-of-war to tugs and tenders.

Less than four hours after "all the wounded had been attended to and made comfortable" on the *Warrior*, she sank. In short minutes before her crew had given up the struggle to keep her afloat, the carrier *Engadine* came alongside. Surgeons, medical service ratings, and sick-berth stewards hastily organized stretcher parties. However, there was no time to transfer the patients onto litters.

Those who could sit or recline were wrapped in lifebelts. Then the cots were picked up and carried through the darkened passageways of the listing ship to the decks, now awash. The ship's band, ordered to "jog up the spirits!" added its own touch to the final bizarre moments of the *Warrior* as its surviving members played "Keep the Home Fires Burning."

When the North Sea claimed the *Warrior* a few minutes before 8 A.M., June 1, all but one of the one hundred cot cases had been safely transferred. This man, who slipped into the sea, was rescued by one of the *Engadine*'s officers.

All through that strange, hushed Thursday, the Grand Fleet streamed back to its bases—missing, however, the *Warrior* and thirteen other of its components. While many of the fleet's 149 principal warships showed scars, there were many others who sailed through Jutland wholly unblemished. The battleships, having little part in the battle, were ready and fresh to fight another day. Of the four cruisers which put out from Invergordon with Rear Admiral Arbuthnot, only one, the *Duke of Edinburgh*, returned. Of the 3,600 officers and men who had sailed with the 1st Cruiser Squadron, less than half came home. Sturdee on the *Benbow*, commanding the 4th Battle Squadron, was as lucky as he had been in the Falklands. He reported no hits on any of his four dreadnoughts. Indeed no one could doubt the observation in his report, "No apprehension was shown."

By 9:45 P.M. that Thursday, Jellicoe reported to the Admiralty that the battlefleet was "again ready for action and at four hours' notice." But his assurance was anticlimactic. Who was there to fight?

Friday passed without a murmur from the Admiralty that anything unusual had happened during the week, but the German press was already beginning to crow about a "great victory" at the Skagerrak. "Crushing defeat!" boasted the *Neues Wiener Journal,* while the *Leipziger Neueste Nachrichten* was more verbose: "England's invincibility on the seas is broken. The German fleet has torn the venerable Trafalgar legend into shreds. . . ."

All too late, and obsessed by the specious reasoning that vagueness and double-talk was the only antidote for the enemy's announcements, the Admiralty issued its first communique: "The German fleet, aided by low visibility, avoided prolonged action with our main forces, and soon after these appeared on the scene the enemy returned to port, though not before receiving severe damage from our battleships. . . ."

This at first caused a wave of optimism to roll through the British Isles. One paper, for example, set a forty-point boldface head that mirrored the giddiness of the moment:

GLORIOUS END OF OUR CRUISERS

Souvenir booklets were rushed into print with such incredible speed that their dazed editors could not possibly have taken the time to learn what had really happened, much less to assess the results or the implications.

One newspaper, shamelessly using the occasion to lure sponsors, mingled advertising copy with photographs of naval officers or artist's sketches. Admiral Jellicoe himself seemingly endorsed Swan fountain pens, while readers were led to believe that "Bird's Custard," Mackintosh's "Toffee de Luxe," and certainly "Ficolax, the Fruit Laxative" played a measurable if nonetheless self-effacing role in the assumed victory.

However, when the casualties were announced—more than 6,000 dead, twice the Germans' losses—one wondered if there was much to celebrate. The toll of fourteen sunken warships, grossing 114,000 tons, was approximately double that sustained by the foe (eleven ships, 63,015 tons).

In Portsmouth alone, where the publishing of the casualty tolls hit "like a thunderclap," lived the families of the men assigned to six of the lost ships: *Invincible, Queen Mary,* the cruiser *Black Prince,* and the destroyers *Ardent, Fortune,* and *Sparrowhawk.*

The Admiralty drew a storm of protest for the losses to British lives and ships and the inconclusiveness of the battle at Jutland. The man held responsible was First Sea Lord Sir Henry Jackson.

National Archives

Other lost ships were *Indefatigable, Defence, Warrior,* and the destroyers *Tipperary, Turbulent, Shark, Nomad,* and *Nestor.* In addition to the *Lützow,* the Germans lost the battleship *Pommern,* the cruisers *Wiesbaden, Frauenlob, Elbing,* and *Rostock,* and five destroyers.

Grief had come to roost upon households in every section

"... something wrong with our bloody ships!" • 149

of the United Kingdom. Fathers, sons, brothers, other relatives, and close friends had suddenly been snatched away from those who loved them in an overnight cataclysm not approximated in magnitude even in the day-by-day slaughter on the western front. There at least the wounded and prisoners of war were in a far more compassionate ratio to the slain. The cruel war at sea was the exact reverse.

In all too few homes was mourning turned to unexpected joy when it was learned that the missing were prisoners of war, or alive in remote Norwegian and Danish coastal villages after being hauled out of the sea by fishermen. Commander Barry Bingham, whose "death" was being mourned nationally for the gallant fight he had made, was among those located.

It was not long before the British press was excoriating the Admiralty for "making excuses," something it had never been accused of before. Even the most fair-minded agreed that the outcome of the battle was "disappointing." Others said that the German Navy had won the assurance that it could "cross swords" with the British Navy—and survive.

Now, the plaguing question publicly asked was: Was the battle of Jutland a defeat or a victory? In some respects, the riddle would never be resolved. At best, certain extenuating circumstances could be considered. For example, the Royal Navy had plowed into the great battle with cruisers of vulnerable design, generally poor communications, and gunnery that left much to be desired. On the other hand, the High Seas Fleet excelled in each of these areas. Furthermore, the daring of Scheer and von Hipper, while easily matched by the dashing Beatty, found no comparable challenge in the cautious Jellicoe.

Most fatal of all, perhaps, the British commander in chief was dominated by a "fleet in being" philosophy. Von Hase, the *Derfflinger*'s highly proficient gunnery officer and a man of reasoned objectivity, conceded that Jellicoe had wisely sailed his fleet home to maintain it in that very "being."

A man of equal intelligence, Scheer, in his formal report to the kaiser, soberly stated: "It may be possible for us to inflict appreciable damage on the enemy, but there can be no doubt that even the most favorable issue of a battle on the high seas will not compel England to make peace in this war. The disadvantages of our geographical position, compared with that of the Island Empire and her great material superiority, cannot be compensated for by our fleet."

He then added that resumption of unrestricted submarine warfare— "even at the risk of war with America"—was the only possible means of attaining "a victorious conclusion of the war within measurable time."

In just one, but incomparably major, consideration, Scheer, while not in error, was too casual. When he mentioned "even at the risk of war with America," he was making the unpardonable military blunder of downgrading a potential adversary.

The meaning of Jutland, *if* it had a meaning, quite possibly transcended the loss of ships and men and the "assurance" with which it had imbued the German Navy. It could indeed be found in that unfortunately casual statement by Admiral Scheer when he alluded to the United States.

(6)

"Make way for Lord Kitchener!"

The Secretary of the Admiralty announces that the following telegram has been received from the Commander-in-Chief of the Grand Fleet at 10:30 (B.S.T.) this morning: "I have to report with deep regret that His Majesty's ship *Hampshire* (Captain Herbert J. Savill, R.N.), with Lord Kitchener and his Staff on board, was sunk last night about 8:00 P.M. to the west of the Orkneys, either by a mine or torpedo. The wind was NNW and heavy seas were running. Patrol vessels and destroyers at once proceeded to the spot, and a party was sent along the coast to search; but only some bodies and a capsized boat have been found up to the present.

"As the whole shore has been searched from the seaward I greatly fear there is little hope of there being survivors. No report has yet been received from the search party on shore."

⊕ In London, the placards hit the streets at noon, on Tuesday, June 6, 1916. Diners dumbly left their tables to buy newspapers. They read and reread the brief announcement of Lord Kitchener's death. It was somehow less credible than the mass deaths at Jutland, more personalized and therefore of greater impact.

Flags everywhere were half-staffed. Curtains were drawn at almost every office in Whitehall's baroque buildings. Theaters were darkened and even some of the pubs were locked up. The Corn Exchange in Liverpool and the Glasgow Stock Exchange closed immediately.

Street placard announcing the drowning of Lord Kitchener. Flags were lowered, pubs closed, and London became a city in mourning.

153

Everyone felt he knew Kitchener personally, irrespective of his feelings toward the towering, unapproachable figure. After all, there was the glowing face on the recruiting posters everywhere: "Your Country Needs *You!*"

It was difficult for his countrymen to accept the obvious explanation of Lord Kitchener's violent end. He had embarked on a secret trip to Russia, and people wanted to believe that advance information had leaked to the enemy. The *Daily Mail*, for one, thought of "mystery" in its literal sense. On Wednesday, the editors flaunted a provocative banner: "Who Spied on Lord Kitchener?"

The German press took advantage of this climate of national delusion, unable to resist an opportunity to bluff about their intelligence arrangements.

The *Leipziger Neueste Nachrichten* prefaced an obituary of the earl of Khartoum with the comment that it had been written previously, "on receipt of information that Kitchener was going to Russia."

This was nonsense—just another gambit in the unending war of wits, the byplay of deception and subterfuge, filling in the gaps where machine-gun fire, artillery, torpedoes, and aerial bombs left off. No one, not even Jellicoe, had known Kitchener's west channel route until the afternoon he sailed.

On June 4, a foggy Sunday night, Londoners could think of little but the battle of Jutland. The papers were still asking pointed questions and printing recriminations alongside of incredibly long casualty lists. " 'ow many columns of type to print six thousand names?" the compositors could well ask.

In Victoria Station, the first survivors were arriving, some wearing oil-stained uniforms, shrunken by the salt water. Their welcome was subdued. Only a few kid brothers or little sisters broke from the waiting crowds with shrill greetings, with "Tipperary" or some other song.

On the other side of the city, at King's Cross Station, there were scenes equally muted. People with sad reflective countenances stood and waited. Unnoticed on one of the platforms in the gloomy preoccupation of the moment was a tall, gaunt, fore-

Through the efforts of Field Marshal, Lord Kitchener, England had raised an army of five million volunteers. Every Englishman had seen recruitment posters bearing his picture and the inscription, "Your country needs You!"

boding figure: the secretary of state for war, Horatio Herbert, Lord Kitchener, earl of Khartoum, bound on a secret mission of momentous import. Czar Nicholas had invited Kitchener to St. Petersburg to discuss munitions supplies and other critical matters concerning Imperial Russia's sagging role in the war. The spectre of a separate peace loomed all too large over this inadequate ally of Great Britain and France.

Kitchener, an unlikable sort of miracle man, had raised an army of 5,000,000 volunteers—the first 1,000,000 in the opening months of the great conflict—a feat all others in the government had scoffed at as impossible. Even so, among the other leaders of Empire, Kitchener, at sixty-six, was aging, tired, fractious, and intolerant of conflicting viewpoints. With the exception of Prime Minister Herbert Asquith and an ever-loyal King George, Great Britain's statesmen had become disenchanted with the veteran army officer. They were increasingly convinced that he had outlived his usefulness.

What success he had enjoyed in the past had been in spite of his autocratic methods. And while even his swelling multitude of opponents grudgingly conceded that Kitchener could probably make constructive suggestions to the Russians, they also were glad to see him out of London.

The train rolled out of King's Cross and hammered away toward the northwest Highlands of Scotland. Two of the most powerful locomotives had been overhauled and oiled in the roundhouses of the Midland Railway to make the 700-mile run to Thurso, across Pentland Firth from Scapa Flow. Kitchener had insisted that he must be there early Monday.

From the misty night of the London area, the crack train slapped into increasingly bad weather until, by midnight, it was pounding head-on into gale winds and driving rain. The secretary of state for war was the last man to suggest that the engineers slow down. It would have been entirely out of character in the ascetic Lord Kitchener, who stoically accepted alike the vicissitudes of nature and the opposition of his fellow men.

Like a good soldier, he settled back phlegmatically in his red-plush compartment and immersed himself in paperwork.

Occasionally he called in one of his official party of thirteen, with questions, requests, or flat orders.

And even as the express wailed through the stormy Midlands, there was activity on two vessels of war, whose destiny would be interlocked closely with that of the earl of Khartoum. Aboard one, events were approaching a crescendo; on the other, they were quite the opposite.

Back in her Scapa Flow anchorage, the 10,850-ton armored cruiser *Hampshire*, of the 1903 *Devonshire* class, was being hosed down and scrubbed up after the battle. As a liaison unit between other cruisers, she had done little firing at Jutland. However, it was believed that she had rammed and sunk a submarine toward the close of the engagement.

Jellicoe, advised four days before Jutland of the coming Russian mission, had chosen the *Hampshire* as a fast and comfortable ship for transporting Kitchener to Archangel. She could make twenty-one knots (though earlier the cruiser had not been fast enough to catch the *Emden*), and her 6-inch armor belt at the waterline and main battery of 7.5-inchers seemed to ensure her safety against enemy mines, torpedoes, and shellfire.

One reason for choosing her had been the *Hampshire*'s captain, Herbert Savill, good-looking one-time commander of the Royal Naval College at Greenwich, an officer who could be depended upon to pilot his ship by regulations. Jellicoe, with so important a charge as Kitchener, felt that he could rest easier knowing that Savill was at the helm. The *Hampshire* was not unfamiliar to Kitchener. He had traveled aboard her from Alexandria to Malta and back four years previously, when he had been consul-general to Egypt.

Not until Sunday afternoon, as Kitchener's servants were completing their master's packing, was Captain Savill summoned to the *Iron Duke*, lying at anchor a few hundred yards from the *Hampshire*. Only then, after crossing the choppy waters of Scapa Flow in a gig, did Savill learn of his mission.

He must be ready to sail at 4:30 P.M. the next day, Monday, June 5. He would depart by the principal east channel. Even as the two officers conferred, the route was being swept and reswept for mines. *Hampshire* must maintain a speed of at least eighteen knots for the first twelve hours, or until she was well past the Shetland Islands, following a north-northeasterly course which would keep the cruiser abeam of Norway but well at sea. During that first 200 miles, *Hampshire* would be escorted by two destroyers. Captain Savill had less than twenty-four hours to provision and fuel his ship.

This same Sunday afternoon, Kapitänleutnant Kurt Beitzen was conning his *U-75* down the Jade Channel into Wilhelmshaven. Like some giant reptile, the big submarine was fresh from sowing twenty-two contact mines off the west coast of the Orkneys. Working about two miles offshore, she had dumped her cargo between two rocky promontories, Marwick Head and the Brough of Birsay to the north, four miles apart.

Curiously enough, High Seas Fleet intelligence officers, in determining upon this minefield, were proving quite the opposite of their nominal classification. They had "ascertained" that the route planted was one "used by warships." Therefore, the mines were moored by chains at a "large vessel" depth, twenty-one feet below high water. The German officers had been misinformed; the west channel was traversed only by fleet auxiliaries and various craft which drew considerably less than twenty-one feet of water.

The Midland Railway engineers had kept the throttles hard down. Early Monday morning, on schedule, the locomotives ground into the pier-side station at bleak little Thurso. The village seemed all the more desolate this Monday as "the foulest weather ever known in that region" was sweeping out of the northeast in ever-mounting fury. There Kitchener was met by the destroyer *Oak* and hastened across squally Pentland Firth to the *Iron Duke*. The Grand Fleet flagship rode majestically at anchor as though the gale were but a figment of inferior imaginations.

At lunch, the two ranking officers, navy and army, chatted briefly. Jellicoe found his guest tired, verging on exhaustion. Kitchener, with unusual candor, contemplated the journey as "a real holiday," and confessed he could "not have gone on without the break." Even so, he emphasized to Jellicoe that he was "working on a timetable" and had "not a day to lose." Kitchener gave himself three weeks in which to complete his mission and return, though he said he was not "sanguine" at prospects of materially improving the czar's deteriorating position.

Jellicoe expressed his astonishment at the breakneck schedule the secretary of state for war had set himself.

The barometer continued to tumble. Spindrift smashed against every port of the big battleship as an endless succession of gray combers tumbled in along the eastern portals of the fleet anchorage. Most disquieting of all was the report that a submarine had just been sighted in the frothing waters off the east channels. In fact, the east side of Scapa Flow was frequently visited by attacking, rather than minelaying, U-boats. Only a week before, one had surfaced and loosed a torpedo at a mine-sweeper.

Jellicoe was now faced with yet another major decision. By the law of averages, it seemed that the battle-wearied Grand Fleet commander should make an exceptionally good one this time. He quickly weighed three factors as Kitchener finished his late lunch. With the northeast wind blowing, the destroyers would have a difficult time keeping up with the *Hampshire* in the eastern channels. Too, a submarine might be lurking out there.

The west channel, however, would present a lee from the gale. Further, it was practically impossible that a U-boat could have mined any route undetected, owing to the short summer nights. Therefore, on the basis of this partly fallacious reasoning, Jellicoe changed the *Hampshire*'s original orders.

He observed that he "should not have hesitated, if need had arisen, to take the Grand Fleet to sea on the same night and by the same route." On the other hand, there were those this same afternoon who elected not even to cross rough Pentland Firth to the mainland. Commodore G. von Schoultz, the Finnish navy observer, decided to enjoy one more night aboard the *Hercules*, snugly at anchor. He would set out in the morning for London, where he rented an apartment in the Whitehall Hotel, off Russell Square.

At 4:30 P.M., Kitchener was piped aboard the *Hampshire*. At 4:45 the bells jangled deep in her engine compartments and she slipped her mooring buoy. Two destroyers, *Victor* and *Unity*, took up escort just ahead of her bows.

Her stokers bent to their task, heaving in coal until the *Hampshire*'s furnaces glowed with a fury of creation. In minutes, she was clocking fourteen, then sixteen knots . . . finally eighteen, just as ordered.

The storm was braying a throaty bass as the cruiser rounded Tor Ness headlands at 5:45 P.M. and commenced to turn northward up the coast. It was then that Captain Savill realized that the worst had happened. The wind, blowing fifty knots or even more, had hauled around to the northwest and was buffeting the ship from dead-ahead.

The little destroyers, all but submerged by monstrous seas and blinded by spray, began to drop behind. They had neither the strength nor the engine power to keep up with the big *Hampshire* which could slug into a head-on sea simply by "pouring on the steam." A few minutes after 6 P.M., *Victor* signaled to *Unity*: "Can only make fifteen knots."

Captain Savill, a practical man, then ordered *Victor* to return to base. He had no sooner finished instructing *Unity* to accompany him alone when that destroyer began blinking through the gray scud: "Unable to maintain more than twelve knots."

Now loping into the Atlantic Ocean, less than 100 miles east of Cape Wrath where submarines were reported to be prowling, the *Hampshire* was suddenly in extreme peril. Britain had already sacrificed far too much to the illusion that capital ships do not need to be escorted. Savill hastily signaled to *Victor*: "Cancel order. Resume escort. I am only going fifteen knots. Can you keep up?"

Meantime, the disheartening word winked hazily back from *Unity*: "Only making ten knots."

As for *Victor*, she had already vanished in the swirling mists. Unbelievable as it seemed, the storm was still picking up velocity. Savill, despairing, knew he'd have to go it alone. He signaled to *Unity* at 6:20 P.M.: "Destroyers return to base!"

The *Hampshire* settled down to the routine of any ship at sea. Those who could eat groped their unsteady way to chow. Kitchener and his official party were served in the captain's suite which had been assigned to them. The earl of Khartoum, however, had no appetite; in fact, he was observed to be quite green from the quick rolls, plunges, and other contortions of this agonized cruiser.

Most crewmen, on or off duty, stayed where they were and, like Chief Shipwright Charles Phillips, hung on like grim death.

"It was," said Petty Officer Wilfred Wesson, "the most terrific gale in my experience."

Dusk was coming early because of the storm.

In the innate drama of understatement, the Admiralty's report (published ten years later) laconically summed up the climactic events of the next hour:

> Commanding Officer no doubt felt satisfied that the storm then raging practically precluded the possibility of successful submarine attack, which, as has been seen, was at the date the more probable danger to be apprehended.
>
> The *Hampshire* went on alone, and at 7:40 or 7:45 P.M. was in a position about a mile and a half from the shore between the Brough of Birsay and Marwick Head, shaping a course N 30° E. This position was somewhat inside the usual course steered by auxiliaries using the route, but there was very deep water—more than thirty fathoms—and no navigational risk whatever was involved in coming in thus, no doubt with the object of trying to get any shelter afforded by the shore from a wind that was still probably shifting about between NNE and NNW. From the accounts of survivors it appears that the ship had reduced speed to thirteen and one-half knots, had all but one of her hatches battened down and secured with shores, and was taking heavy seas all over her. Everything, however, on board was proceeding normally. The Captain was on the bridge. The routine order to "Stand by Hammocks" had just been piped. At this moment an explosion occurred.

There was scant agreement on the intensity of the explosion or even what it sounded like. It was, variously, "rumbling," "loud," "not loud," "like a big sea hit the ship," and "similar to one or two electric globes being broken."

Petty Officer Wesson associated the explosion with the immediate extinguishing of all lights and "a terrible draft of air"

Berliner Illustrirte Zeitung

British intelligence officers were aware of German minelaying activity off the west coast of the Orkneys, but they misjudged the depth at which the mines were placed. A submarine (similar to the one pictured) had sown twenty-two contact mines on the day before the *Hampshire* left Scapa Flow.

which "came rushing along the mess deck, blowing all the men's caps off." Still not knowing what had happened, he started aft to inspect the opened hatch.

Since the *Hampshire* had at once become heavy by the bow, there was little doubt as to the location of the blast, or the likelihood that she had plowed into a mine. From the devastating effect, it was also probable that the foremost boiler room had in turn blown up, tearing out a section of the cruiser's bottom.

Not only was the stricken *Hampshire* without lights, but the wireless would not function. Steam lines must have been cracked wide open, since the rudder would not respond to the helm. Fumes of high explosives penetrated acridly to the stokers' mess deck and then to the uppermost compartments of the ship.

The *Hampshire* settled lower and lower.

On the bridge there was certainty now that "the center part of her" had been ripped right out, and that she was "going right away." Orders were passed with the utmost urgency: "Abandon!"

While there was a surge into all the companionways and up the ladders, there was a surprising lack of crowding. Discipline, in the best traditions of the Royal Navy, was miraculously maintained for the most part, although a number of the younger sailors seemed on the verge of making a dash for it—where, of course, they did not know.

Captain Savill had been hugging the shore partly for the comfort of his distinguished passenger. It hadn't helped. Kitchener, sick, was lying down when the explosion came. However, he summoned his iron willpower, left his cabin, and was seen to walk calmly down a passageway toward the stern. Monolithic, impassive as though he were inspecting troops on the western front or in the Sudan, he climbed a ladder and emerged onto the gale-swept quarterdeck.

As he abruptly appeared, he was first spotted by the cruiser's gunnery officer, Lieutenant Humphrey Matthews, who breathed deeply, then barked: "Make way for Lord Kitchener!"

Wesson, one of those who made way, detected no outward sign of nervousness in Kitchener. He said, "He just looked very ill."

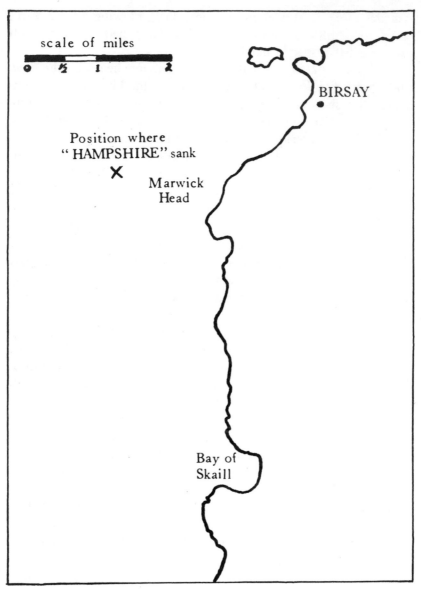

scale of miles

0 ½ 1 2

BIRSAY

Position where
"HAMPSHIRE" sank
X
Marwick
Head

Bay of
Skaill

Another crewman standing close by, Leading Seaman Charles W. Rogerson, observed with disbelief the majestic spectacle of poise: ". . . the captain at this time was calling to Lord Kitchener to go to the boat but owing to the noise of the wind and the sea Lord Kitchener could not hear him."

164 • "Make Way for Lord Kitchener!"

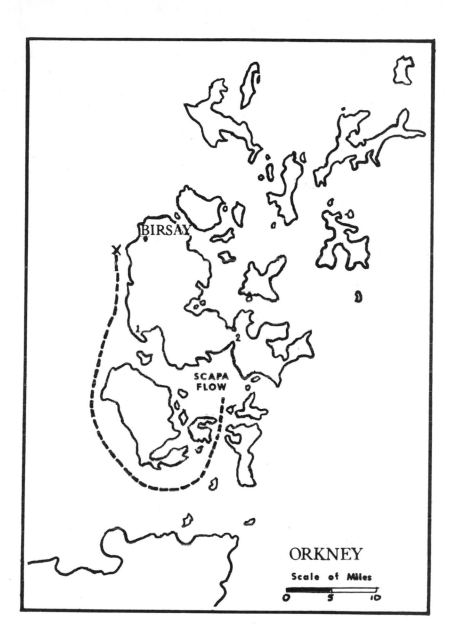

BIRSAY

SCAPA
FLOW

ORKNEY

Scale of Miles

0　　　5　　　10

(Left) Position where the *Hampshire* sank, one and a half miles off the coast of the Orkney Islands, Scotland. (Above) Course ship had followed from Scapa Flow to near Birsay, where she hit a German mine.

"Make Way for Lord Kitchener!" • 165

Young Rogerson then watched the tall, moustached figure "walking quite coolly and collected up and down talking to two of his officers. All three were wearing khaki without overcoats. In fact, they were dressed just as they were when they boarded the ship."

Kitchener did not seem "in the least perturbed but calmly waited the preparations for abandoning the ship which were going on in a quiet, steady, and orderly way. The crew went to their stations, obeying orders steadily, and did their best to get out the boats, but that proved impossible."

Apparently, Captain Savill was becoming aware that he would not succeed in launching any lifeboats. During these final frustrating moments, some thought they heard him calling to Lord Kitchener to go below again and wait in the warmth of the galley. No one, however, was able to hear with clarity anything that was shouted in this doomsday din.

In spite of the rain and wind, there were a few people out that evening on the Orkneys' rocky shores. They saw the *Hampshire* suddenly stop dead. Only a mile and a half offshore, she was readily discernible through the thick weather. Among the witnesses was Joe Angus, a lookout with the Orkney Royal Garrison Artillery stationed at the little hamlet of Birsay. He was absently watching the shadowy silhouette of the *Hampshire* butting through the maelstrom just offshore. He had seen so many ships come and go. Then, suddenly he was shaken into full alertness by the abrupt spectacle of "a cloud of smoke and a burst of flame from behind the bridge." He observed the ship seemingly change course and head for land.

That was enough. Angus raced the few yards to his billet and reported "ship in distress!" to Corporal James Drever of the Territorial forces. Drever took a look for himself and noted that the cruiser was "well down by the bows." He raced 200 yards along the high ground to Birsay's only link with the outer world, its post office.

Since there was no telephone, Drever scribbled a telegram and handed it to Miss Jessie Comloquoy, a subpostmistress. She was herself agitated, since she too had witnessed the disaster.

"Battle cruiser seems in distress between Marwick Head

and the Brough Birsay," the telegram read. It was addressed both to the naval and army commands in the area: to the Commander, Western Patrol, Stromness, about twenty miles down the coast, and to the Royal Garrison Artillery headquarters at Kirkwall, the same distance to the east on the shores of the Grand Fleet's anchorage.

While Miss Comloquoy worked the telegraph key, Drever hurried outside again to the bluffs.

Offshore, the *Hampshire* was going fast. Petty Officer Wesson began tearing away wooden hatch covers and throwing them into the waters, hoping they would keep some of the men afloat. He thought only three or four circular floats had been launched when the cruiser ducked her prow under the water and slid gradually downward. Her stern came up.

Wesson jumped off, plunged under the water, and came up beside one of the rafts. Gasping for breath, nearly paralyzed with cold, he saw Kitchener "still on the starboard side of the quarterdeck, talking to his officers." As the petty officer's raft, now refuge to nearly eighty half-frozen, terrified men, swirled and bobbed off into the mists, Wesson was afforded a final glimpse—or was it impression?—of Kitchener standing unbelievably erect, phlegmatic, riding the doomed cruiser down. Others stared at the propellers, that were sticking up, motionless. Rogerson thought the *Hampshire* at the last moment executed "a somersault forward," projecting into the water, like so many toys, all on her decks.

In moments there was nothing more to be seen but debris and the bobbing heads of a pitiful few of the warship's crew of 655. The large cruiser had sunk at about 8 P.M., no more than fifteen minutes after the explosion.

Corporal Drever, seeing the *Hampshire* disappear, ran back into the telegraph office. Wiping rivulets of water from his face, he gasped at the subpostmistress, "Can you add: 'ship sunk'?"

Almost hysterical, Miss Comloquoy tapped to a surprised receiver at the Kirkwall end of the wire: "Oh, the ship has sunk! Can that be added to the telegram?"

Now, equally in shock, the Kirkwall telegraphist clicked back: "That is all right."

Fifteen minutes later, about 8:20 P.M., the subpostmistress dispatched another telegram to Stromness and to Kirkwall: "Vessel down!" Then, at 8:35 P.M., she and Corporal Drever, calmer, prepared and transmitted a third message: "Four-funnel cruiser sunk twenty minutes ago. No assistance arrived yet. Send ships to pick up bodies."

It was not until 10:30 P.M. that the first rescue vessels arrived at the approximate position of the sinking. Among them were the destroyers *Victor* and *Unity* which had turned back, together with tugs, patrol yachts, and other craft. They might as well have stayed at dock. As the last telegram from the postmistress had augured, there were only bodies to be picked up.

All who would survive had already struggled ashore and flopped, barely alive, on the rocks. There were only twelve, including Rogerson and Wesson. Not one officer lived.

Farmers and fishermen of Birsay stripped the sodden clothes from the nearly blue bodies of the survivors, warmed them by coal fires, beat the circulation back into their limbs, and poured great quantities of hot tea and brandy into them. Seaman Richard Simpson revived so quickly that he made his way to the telegraph office and gave Miss Comloquoy a further message to transmit. It was to his mother in London and it read: "All right. Don't worry."

The next morning dawned sunny and calm. The storm had spent itself. It was hard to imagine the fury that had been visited on the Orkneys—or the persistent questions it would leave. The "mystery" of Lord Kitchener's death (or indeed the improbable rumor that he had actually struggled ashore) would be raked over for years.

International agents and would-be agents would vie with each other for the honor of having sunk the *Hampshire*. One of the more imaginative was Fritz Duquesne, who referred to himself as "Master Spy." He convinced at least one writer that he was aboard the *Hampshire*, masquerading as the Russian officer Count Zakrevsky.

At sea, he claimed, he had opened a porthole in his private cabin and flung a magnesium torch into the lashing seas. This, his fanciful tale continued, attracted a waiting U-boat which promptly torpedoed the cruiser. Duquesne further claimed that he had struggled ashore as the mysterious "thirteenth survivor." For that matter, others were also to claim that distinction: a man called Green, who said he was a servant of one of the officers; another person with the appropriate name Gulliver; a mechanic who labeled himself "The Big Artificer," and doubled as a spy for Colonel Walther Nicolai's *Nachrichten Abteilung*, or intelligence department.

Ernst Carl, a German who performed some espionage work in England, later wrote his memoirs. In them he wove the impassioned fabric of an amour with "Ethel," whom he described as a Sinn Feiner, fighting for Irish independence. One thing led to another. Although Carl cared not a whit about Ireland, he was in favor of anyone who was battling England. With the help of other Sinn Feiners at Kirkwall, Carl asserted, he had smuggled two time bombs aboard the *Hampshire*, hidden in blankets.

A man who obviously enjoyed his work—and his autobiography—as a conoisseur would savor fine wine, Ernst Carl further elaborated that, in the spring of 1916, he had even met Lord Kitchener. He had called on the war minister in his London apartment, the agent claimed, disguised as a French antique dealer.

Such accounts rolled on and on, like desultory flashes of lightning on a summer horizon. Scotland Yard and the Admiralty joined in pronouncing all the stories "entirely imaginary."

Kitchener's death was directly related to four tragic coincidences: his own towering impatience, Jellicoe's poor judgment, carelessness in minesweeping, and absurd good luck on the part of the mine-sowing U-boats.

As a final "amen" to the futility and blind waste of it all, Russia was beyond saving. Neither Kitchener, nor Great Britain with all her resources, could have bolstered the sagging imperial armies. The Bolsheviks, already emboldened to desperate acts, would sign a separate peace, at Brest Litovsk, the following year.

(7)

*Spurlos Versenkt!**

⊕ As October came to the western shores of the Atlantic, so did the World Series. In crisp weather, the opener game was played at Braves Field, Boston, October 7, 1916, before a customarily hysterical throng. The home team, the Red Sox, skinned through to a 6 to 5 victory over the Brooklyn Dodgers.

In the autumn sunshine, the war seemed far away. Even more unreal was the political campaign and the forthcoming election by which the nation must choose between President Wilson, "the man who kept us out of war," and Supreme Court Justice Charles Evans Hughes, Republican former governor of New York, who was in many ways unproven, Olympian and inscrutable.

And yet, on that very Saturday afternoon, even as the shouts of the fans echoed over the Boston stadium, a breath of Europe's struggle was felt in nearby Newport, Rhode Island. Shortly after noon, the diminutive overage United States Navy submarine *D-2*, on patrol between Brenton Reef and Block Island at the approaches to the fleet anchorage at Narragansett Bay—America's own Scapa Flow—observed a conning tower break the surface. The stranger kept coming up, until the American sailors were soon staring at the largest craft of its kind they had ever seen. It was more than 200 feet long, and it mounted two deck guns of medium caliber.

Hans Rose, a tall, dapper, younger model of Admiral Scheer, had brought the giant *U-53* across the Atlantic from Wilhelmshaven in seventeen days. The fourth ranking U-boat

*"Sunk without trace."

Wanamaker's and World Series—headliners of October, 1916. The War
seemed far away.

The Chicago Daily Tribune.

THE WORLD'S GREATEST NEWSPAPER

FINAL EDITION

VOLUME LXXV.—NO. 164. C.　　MONDAY, JULY 10, 1916.—TWENTY PAGES.　　＊ ＊ PRICE ONE CENT.

GERMAN U-BOAT IN U. S.

FRENCH ARMY AT THE GATES OF PERONNE

Capture of Biaches Gives Chance to Attack Rail Center.

BRITISH PRESS ON.

Mother Killed by "Joy" Auto; Two Boys Dead

Careening Car Smashes Into Family on Motor Jaunt.

DAY'S TOLL HEAVY

LARGEST TYPE OF GERMAN SUBMARINE

According to Advices from Berlin the Supersubmarine That Reached Hampton Roads Yesterday is Built Along the Lines of the Vessel, the Conning Tower and Bridge of Which is Pictured Here. These Vessels Have a Sailing Radius of 3,000 Miles, Being Submarine in Daytime and Torpedo Boats at Night.

CRAFT DEFIES WAR PERIL OF SEAS IN 16-DAY TRIP

Brings Cargo and Envoy of Kaiser Said to Carry Letter to Wilson.

CAPTAIN TELLS STORY.

WASHINGTON VIEW OF DEUTSCHLAND TRIP

Jake Lights Up as Loop Meteor; Then Grows Dim

ATTEMPTS TO ASSASSINATE PRESIDENT OF ARGENTINE

Trip of Submarine Stirs Problems at Washington

THE WEATHER.

MONDAY, JULY 10, 1916.

Chicago Tribune

The arrival of the *Deutschland,* the first submarine to cross the Atlantic, created a stir in Baltimore in June, 1916. Built as a submarine merchantman, she unloaded 750 tons of chemicals and dyestuffs.

172

ace, Rose, who was thirty-five, had already been awarded the Iron Cross for sinking more than thirty Allied and neutral ships.

From his conning tower, Rose asked in good English if he had permission to enter "any" east coast port. Lieutenant George C. Fuller, commanding the *D-2*, replied, "Negative!" The recent Naval Academy graduate was a man of few words. But he appreciated protocol; he had an obligation to furnish the visitor an escort.

"Follow me!" he instructed. The little craft then led the husky visitor past Fort Adams into Newport harbor, threading through the gathering swarm of sailboats and steam yachts, whose occupants had never seen one of the much-publicized U-boats at first hand.

Alongside the cruiser *Birmingham*, the *U-53* dropped anchor and its captain went ashore, heavy with medals and even side arms, to make two courtesy calls: upon Rear Admiral Austin M. Knight, commandant of the Second Naval District, and Rear Admiral Albert Gleaves, who headed the Destroyer Force of the Atlantic Fleet.

The German officer was not prepared for so elderly a commandant as Admiral Knight, who was possibly the oldest officer on active duty. The white-moustached veteran of over forty years of naval service had led the Cuban north coast blockading fleet during the Spanish-American War. He was even better known as author of the fledgling naval officer's bible, *Modern Seamanship*. Gleaves, fifty-nine, but four years Knight's junior, was more robust in appearance, with fierce eyes, a martinet's disposition, and a moustache that made Hans Rose feel *gemeinsam*, among friends. While commanding the torpedo boat *Cushing*, Gleaves had had the curious distinction of being moored alongside the battleship *Maine* when she blew up in Havana harbor.

The patrician Knight surprised his caller by his primary concern as to the whereabouts of the cargo-carrying submarine *Bremen*. The first of this giant type, the *Deutschland*, had recently sailed from Baltimore after unloading 750 tons of chemicals and dyestuffs.

When Rose replied that he did not know (and, indeed, could not, since presumably the *Bremen* had been lost in the minefields off the Orkneys), the admiral asked if he needed fuel, provisions, or possibly water. The German replied "No!" to each offer.

"Medical attention?"

Again Rose shook his head, with an indifferent brush at his narrow swatch of moustache. "We require nothing."

"You don't need repairs?" Knight, unfamiliar with underwater vessels as well as with the efficient new Diesel engines, could not understand how anything which floated could have been *seventeen days at sea* and need nothing—not even mechanical parts. However, he ventured one last thought.

"Surely there must be something, some service, some courtesy . . . ?" Knight was of the old navy, where customs, traditions, and manners were everything. He would no doubt, in time of war, have given over his own cabin to a captured enemy of similar rank. Suddenly, his eyes brightened and he asked, "Yes, perhaps you wish to be interned?"

Admiral Gleaves, appalled at a suggestion which must have sounded preposterous to a submarine ace, turned his head and glowered. Rose simply reached into his jacket and handed Admiral Knight a letter.

"This," he said, "is for Ambassador von Bernstorff in Washington." He did not hint as to the contents and the recipient did not inquire.

In exchange, Admiral Knight presented Captain Rose with a bundle of Boston, Providence, and New York newspapers, and furnished a yeoman to carry them. Expansively, the German officer invited the Americans "and their ladies" to board his *U-53*.

There was a scurrying in Newport homes during the next hour as the wives of senior naval officers prepared to visit the underseas craft. Once aboard, they found an immaculate, efficient fighting ship, painted and polished until it shone inside and out. She was a proud and formidable sight. While the women sipped Rhine wine, their husbands stared at such *pièces de résistance* as the six large, glistening torpedoes beside their tubes, the Diesel engines, and tier upon tier of storage batteries —guaranteeing possibly three days' submergence.

Well within the twenty-four-hour international limit for a

man-of-war's stay in a neutral port, the *U-53*, flags still flying, took her leave of Newport before 6:00 P.M. Escorting ships watched her past Brenton Reef, until, slowly, majestically, she commenced to submerge, down, down . . . like a vanishing Excalibur . . . until there was only the sheen of bubbles in the muted evening light where her wake had been.

In Washington, the British ambassador, Sir Cecil Spring-Rice, rushed to the State Department. The *Deutschland*'s leisurely stay had aroused the Englishman enough. Now he came with new protests for Secretary of State Lansing. But attention, especially along the eastern part of the nation, had already returned to the World Series.

The activities of the merchant submarine *Deutschland* (below), which landed in Baltimore harbor in June, were purely business. But Captain Hans Rose mixed business with pleasure when he brought his *U-53* to Newport four months later: he invited the ladies of the town to tour his ship. On board they found a polished, efficient interior—and of course, Rhine wine.

Conning tower of an unidentified German submarine. From a tower such as this, gentleman pirate Hans Rose pronounced doom to Allied merchant vessels. "I am sorry, but we must sink you," he would inform his victims in fluent English. Then he would wait for the merchant crew to abandon ship, fire his torpedoes, and, if time permitted, tow the enemy crew to safety.

Saturday night passed. The ocean off the New England coast lay calm, the moon was bright, as unusually heavy week-end sailings filled the sea-lanes with Europe-bound traffic. At 6:30 A.M. in daylight, the 4,400-ton British freighter *Strathdene,* down to her Plimsoll mark with war goods for France, took her final bearing on Nantucket Shoals lightship, forty miles southeast of Nantucket Island. After that there would be nothing but the miles and miles of the Atlantic Ocean until Captain George Wilson picked up the channel buoys leading into Bordeaux.

But before the *Strathdene* had steamed a mile farther, a monstrous submarine, with "U-53" in glistening white characters on its bulbous conning tower, surfaced a few hundred yards to starboard. A shell went crackling across the freighter's bow.

This meant but one thing to Captain Wilson: "Stop!" He did not even wait for a boarding party, as he rang the order to abandon. As the last boats were pulling away, the submarine commenced shelling the *Strathdene* at the waterline. Laden as she was, she was an easy target.

The crew rowed toward the bright red lightship, whose shocked wireless operator was even now flashing word of this wholly unexpected attack—right in America's front yard!

Next, the steamer *Kansan*, inbound for Boston, was halted. This time, Rose sent an officer on board. When he found the American-flag vessel was carrying a cargo of soda, he let her proceed. However, the British steamer *Stephano*, New York to Newfoundland with eighty-five passengers and 3,500 tons of cargo, had the misfortune next to navigate past the Nantucket lightship.

Gallantly, Captain Rose towed the *Stephano*'s lifeboats, bearing passengers and crew, to the lightship before sinking the vessel. Hurriedly, he let go the lines as the *West Point*, another freighter flying the Union Jack, wallowed into view.

Distress messages had brought the vanguard of the Newport destroyers, the *Fanning*, to the scene. Half-manned, the 750-ton destroyer, one of the first to be converted to oil, and equipped with a gyrocompass, had slipped her mooring and raced through the flat, early morning seas under forced draft. Others of the squadron were not far behind.

"It was an unbelievable sight," recalled Lieutenant (jg) George Fort, chief engineer of the *Fanning*. "The *U-53* alternately sinking ships, then towing some of the lifeboats to the lightship, all of us standing by, helpless, like spectators at a dog fight. They were international waters.

"Rose opened sea valves and placed scuttling charges—to do the job as cheaply as possible. However, one of the vessels refused to sink. He flashed to one of our destroyers: 'Get out of my way, I'm going to torpedo the ship!'

"Imagine!"

By late afternoon, fifteen American destroyers were patiently standing by this scene of legal mayhem. And two more ships had been added to Rose's list of victims, the Dutch freighter *Bloomersdijk*, and the Norwegian tanker *Christian Knudsen*. From the latter, the *U-53* obtained a quantity of fuel before casually sinking her.

The 216 survivors of the five sunken ships—all who had been aboard—were removed by the destroyers from the little lightship *Nantucket*, which was almost swamped by their weight. Among their number was a large family from Newfoundland. Rose dipped his colors, as a gesture of continuing *sangfroid*, then hauled all flags in and slowly submerged.

Soon, in the gloom of approaching evening, there was nothing but debris in the wake of the *U-53*—and the stark proof of the capabilities of the modern submarine. The *U-53* had dramatically answered the question which had, in the first place, inspired her long voyage: could a U-boat complete a war mission of nearly 8,000 miles without being compelled to refuel? This was the reason for sending Rose to Newport, certainly not the delivery of a letter to von Bernstorff.

Admiral Gleaves's destroyers headed for port, with their unaccustomed passenger lists.

As Rose knifed homeward, to take on more torpedoes and receive the plaudits of his emperor, America reacted with shock. How *could* Germany have dared bring the war within earshot of her coasts? And the ease with which the effrontery had been accomplished!

Jolted especially, one writer noted, were the "contentment-at-any-price people."

Humanity was being sorely tested by many assaults this summer of 1916. The crack of a firing squad in Bruges, Belgium, for example, reverberated across the North Sea to England. It sent the simmering fires of "Atrocity!" once again flaming.

Captain Charles Algernon Fryatt, middle-aged master of the British merchant vessel *Brussels*, accused of having previously attempted to ram the *U-33*, was executed in July as a *franc-tireur*, a civilian allegedly attacking the military. He thereby followed in death many of the citizens of such cities as Louvain, which had been burned because its inhabitants sniped at the invading armies.

That Fryatt—a gentle, popular man in his home village near Harwich—was the father of seven children, ranging upward from infants, made the deed seem even more shocking and

Count Nikolaus zu Dohna-Schlodien addresses the crew from the deck of his ship, the German raider Moewe.

Admiral Scheer praises Captain Karl Nerger on the deck of the Wolf. Nerger's marathon cruise—64,000 miles without touching port—had made naval history.

With pipe, sou-wester, and forged papers, Count Felix von Luckner eluded blockade by posing as a Norwegian fisherman.

more personal to Englishmen. Coming after the shooting of Edith Cavell, also in Belgium, the "murder," as it was referred to in London's newspapers, brought the same cry for blood as the *Baralong* shootings had in Germany. Public demonstrations in Trafalgar Square and elsewhere throughout the British Isles called for "the hanging of the kaiser and von Tirpitz!"

The Allies already held thousands of prisoners of war, taken on the western front. Why not pick a dozen or even one hundred by lot—and shoot them in reprisal? Germany was quick to reply that she harbored just as many British and French prisoners, and she would line them against walls in the ratio of two for each executed German.

Sober minds prevailed and a blood bath was averted. And no more merchant captains were condemned by military courts.

Germany's aggressiveness on the sea-lanes, however, was far from pacified. Unchastened, as Jellicoe seemed to think, Admiral Scheer exhorted the shipyards of Wilhelmshaven and Kiel to exertion at the highest pitch. He chafed and fumed through each moment which saw his High Seas Fleet languishing in port, waiting for repairs to be completed and for new ships such as the massive *Bayern*, to join him.

"Our efforts," he wrote, "were centered on putting to sea again as soon as possible for a fresh advance." By August, in little more than two months after the great battle at Jutland, the High Seas Fleet *was* ready. On August 18, Scheer led it out of Wilhelmshaven, intending, as previously, to raid the east coast of England. It was augmented by two new battleships in addition to the mighty *Bayern:* the *Grosser Kurfürst* and the *Markgraf*. Swarms of zeppelins droned overhead and U-boats scurried ahead and on the flanks of the cruisers and destroyers.

Admiral Jellicoe hastened out of a sick bed to order the Grand Fleet from harbor once more. The next day, August 19, two light cruisers, the *Nottingham* and the *Falmouth*, were torpedoed and sunk by U-boats. The German battleship *Westfalen*, hit by two torpedoes from an English submarine, was able to make port.

Scheer, realizing that the Grand Fleet was massing in strength and apparently satisfied with his two kills, swung homeward when only sixty miles east of Hull. To some it might have seemed unbelievable, but, nonetheless, the commanding British admiral had allowed his adversary to slip out of his closing grasp. Overly deliberate action and continuing poor communications had enabled Scheer to be off the Frisians, steaming toward the Jade Channel, when his British opponent realized, again, that he was far too late.

In a few weeks, the reluctant admiral of the Grand Fleet was "kicked upstairs" as first sea lord. There, in the curious reasoning of Empire, it was assumed that he could do less harm. The aggressive Beatty was given command of the fleet, as Britons, professional and nonprofessional, were already lining up in pro- or anti-Jellicoe camps.

All signs pointed to a continued acceleration of U-boat warfare, which had already accounted for 1,000 merchantmen. Germany started 1917 with a fleet of 111 submarines, 46 of which were constantly at sea. In a few weeks she maintained 75 on the hunt. Their crews were increasingly proficient, their aim deadly. Individual scores were multiplying astronomically. One craft, the *U-39* under Captain Walther Forstmann, sank more than fifty steamers in the Mediterranean in a period of three weeks.

By late January, Germany's submarines were destroying ships at a rate equivalent to more than 500,000 tons a month. It did not require a mathematician to reach the appalling conclusion that, unchecked, this would mean 6,000,000 tons a year! The cargoes lost were worth billions, and the carnage was far beyond the replacement capacity of British and French shipyards.

Added to the rapidly crumbling Russian resistance, the unprecedented success at sea finally emboldened the German Great General Staff to conclude that "the ruthless employment of an increased number of U-boats" would ensure "a speedy victory which will compel our principal enemy, England, to turn to thoughts of peace in a few months." *Schrecklichkeit*, or "terror," was wooed as an ultimate weapon of victory—demonstrated or attempted already in the subjugation of Belgium and in the executions of civilians such as Edith Cavell.

Scheer and others in the navy had assured Chancellor von Bethmann-Hollweg, a reasonable man who earnestly sought a negotiated peace, that in unrestricted submarine warfare lay Germany's only hope.

On January 31, von Bernstorff delivered to Secretary Lansing the terse announcement that, effective the next day, "all sea traffic will be stopped with every available weapon and without further notice." Promising to use her underseas fleet "to the full," Germany would allow only one United States passenger vessel a week to England. It must follow a prescribed course to Falmouth, arrive at that port on a Sunday and depart on Wednesday. It must bear, in addition to the United States flag, striped markings suggestive of a barber pole.

That did it. On Saturday, February 3, President Wilson faced a joint session of Congress and declared:

"I think you will agree with me that this government has no alternative consistent with the dignity and honor of the United States. . . . I have therefore directed the Secretary of State to announce to His Excellency the German Ambassador that all diplomatic relations between the United States and the German Empire are severed and to hand to His Excellency his passports."

Von Bernstorff confessed he was "sorry," as he started to pack. In Berlin the United States ambassador, James W. Gerard, received back his own passport.

This was not war—but it was very close to it.

That same Saturday afternoon, even as the President spoke, the 3,000-ton American freighter *Housatonic*, bound from Newport News for England with wheat, was halted by two warning shots over her bows as she approached the Scilly Islands. Her master, a tall, slender New Yorker, Thomas A. Ensor, was not entirely surprised at this misfortune since he was crossing "torpedo alley."

In minutes, a large submarine surfaced several hundred yards to starboard and sent out a searching boat with a junior officer, who boarded the freighter. He looked over the manifest, shook his head dourly, then asked Captain Ensor to return with him.

Resting his arms casually on the glistening rails of the conning tower was a dapper officer of about Ensor's height, but wearing a small moustache. He saluted smartly as his American guest climbed aboard. Masked by a bored expression, he studied the *Housatonic*'s cargo papers, then declared in good English:

"I am sorry. It is necessary that we sink you." There was the trace of a wry grin as the German added, "Keep smiling!"

Shocked at his foe's command of American slang, Ensor was rowed back to his doomed command. However, the crew of thirty-seven was afforded ample time to pack belongings and abandon, before the U-boat commenced shelling the *Housatonic*. The steamer, a twenty-six-year-old former Hamburg-American freighter, resisted her execution. Finally, a torpedo was sent as a *coup de grace*.

Ensor's surprise was then compounded. The submarine, still surfaced, loped over to the two filled lifeboats, trailing a familiar cloud of bluish Diesel exhaust.

"Here!" called the same suave officer. "I will tow you!"

He drove ahead, tossing a stern line to the Americans. For two hours, into the late afternoon, the U-boat hauled the survivors. They were nearing Penzance, on the southwest tip of England, when Ensor spotted a plume of smoke he assumed to be from a patrol boat. He watched it for several minutes, while it held the same distance and bearing. Obviously the stranger had not noticed the lifeboats, nor the submarine.

"Hey!" Ensor shouted through a megaphone to the conning tower. "Do *you* see him?"

"That fellow is asleep," came back the same fluent English, with but a trace of German accent. "But I will wake him up for you!" With that, the sailors scurried around the forward deck gun and lobbed a shell toward the horizon.

The shot did "wake him up." Now the smoke began to approach.

"Please," called the U-boat officer, "let loose the cable!" Seamen on the stern of the underwater craft hauled in the rope.

"Auf Wiedersehen!" rang across the ground swells. With mingled wonder and gratitude, Tom Ensor watched the gray waters rise over the conning tower, bubbling and frothing about the big white letters, "U-53," until there was nothing more to be seen of her.

Within the *U-53*, Captain Hans Rose, the "pirate" who couldn't bear the thought of hurting anyone, added a new incident to the voluminous notes chronicling his war experiences. Ensor had made "an excellent impression" upon Rose, as had Rose's recent hosts at Newport, though he marveled how so many Americans could be "entirely clean-shaven."

Kapitänleutnant Rose harbored postwar autobiographical plans. He had also confided, to a very few intimates, mainly Frau Rose, that he was glad to have potential character witnesses from enemy ranks, "just in case." Deutschland might not prevail *"über Alles"*; and Rose was sagacious enough to concede the possibility.

Before dusk, the trawler *Salvatore*, which had been mistaken for a patrol, was on the lifeboats. Happy and as healthy as when they abandoned their freighter, Ensor and his thirty-seven crewmen hurried up the little vessel's rope ladders and onto her slippery decks, which were redolent with herring, bloaters, and other edible denizens of the English Channel.

Scarcely a week later, the schooner *Lyman M. Law*, out of Bangor, was torpedoed in the Mediterranean. Her crew made shore safely. Then, on Sunday evening, February 25, the Cunarder *Laconia* was pounding toward Liverpool in a blinding snowstorm. The 18,000-ton liner, the largest on the transatlantic service since the loss of the *Lusitania*, carried a crew of 216 and 73 passengers. Among the latter was a well-known correspondent, Floyd Gibbons, on his way to report the Great War for the *Chicago Tribune*. His account of that night's drama was among his finest:

"The first class passengers were gathering in the lounge with the exception of the bridge fiends in the smoke-room.

" 'Poor Butterfly' was dying wearily on the talking machine and several couples were dancing.

"About the tables in the smoke-room the conversation was limited to the announcement of bids and orders to the stewards. Before the fireplace was a little gathering which had been dubbed as the Hyde Park corner—an allusion I don't quite fully understand. This group had about exhausted available discussion when I projected a new bone of contention.

" 'What do you say are our chances of being torpedoed?' I asked.

" 'Well,' drawled the deliberative Mr. Henry Cheatham, a London solicitor, 'I should say four thousand to one.'

"Lucien J. Jerome, of the British diplomatic service, returning with an Ecuadorian valet from South America, interjected: 'Considering the zone and the class of this ship, I should put it down at two hundred and fifty to one that we don't meet a sub.'

"At this moment the ship gave a sudden lurch sideways and forward. There was a muffled noise like the slamming of some large door at a good distance away. The slightness of the shock and the meekness of the report compared with my imagination were disappointing. Every man in the room was on his feet in an instant.

" 'We're hit!' shouted Mr. Cheatham.

"I looked at my watch. It was 10:30 P.M.

"Then came the five blasts on the whistle. We rushed down the corridor leading from the smoke-room at the stern to the lounge, which was amidships. We were running, but there was no panic. The occupants of the lounge were just leaving by the forward doors as we entered.

"We reached the promenade deck. I rushed into my state-room, B19, grabbed my overcoat and the water bottle and special life-preserver with which *The Tribune* had equipped me before sailing. Then I made my way to the upper deck on that same dark landing.

"I saw the chief steward opening an electric switch box in the wall and turning on the switch. Instantly the boat decks were illuminated. That illumination saved lives.

"The torpedo had hit us well astern on the starboard side and had missed the engines and the dynamos. I had not noticed the deck lights before. Throughout the voyage our decks remained dark at night and all cabin portholes were clamped down and all windows covered with opaque paint.

"The illumination of the upper deck on which I stood made the darkness of the water sixty feet below appear all the blacker when I peered over the edge at my station, boat No. 10.

"Already the boat was loading up and men were busy with the ropes. I started to help near a davit that seemed to be giving trouble, but was stoutly ordered to get out of the way and get into the boat.

"We were on the port side, practically opposite the engine well. Up and down the deck passengers and crew were donning life-belts, throwing on overcoats and taking positions in the boats. Steam began to hiss somewhere from the giant gray funnels that towered above. Suddenly there was a roaring swish as a rocket soared upward from the captain's bridge, leaving a comet's tail of fire. I watched it as it described a graceful arc in the black void overhead, and then, with an audible pop, it burst in a flare of brilliant white light.

" 'Lower away!' Someone gave the order and we started down with a jerk towards the seemingly hungry rising and falling swells. . . .

"The list of the ship's side became greater, but, instead of our boat sliding down it like a toboggan, the taffrail caught and was held. As the lowering continued, the other side dropped down and we found ourselves clinging on at a new angle and looking straight down on the water.

"Many feet and hands pushed the boat from the side of the ship and we sagged down again, this time smacking squarely on the pillowy top of a rising swell. It felt more solid than midair, at least. But we were far from being off. The pulleys twice stuck in their fastenings, bow and stern, and the one ax passed forward and back, and with it my flashlight, as the entangling ropes that held us to the sinking *Laconia* were cut away. . . .

"As we pulled away from the side of the ship, its banking and receding terrace of lights stretched upward. The ship was slowly turning over. We were opposite that part occupied by the engine rooms. There was a tangle of oars, spars, and rigging on the seat and considerable confusion before four of the big sweeps could be manned on either side of the boat. . . .

"We rested our oars, with all eyes turned on the still lighted *Laconia*. The torpedo had struck at 10:30 P.M. According to our ship's time, it was thirty minutes after that hour that another dull thud, which was accompanied by a noticeable drop in the hulk, told its story of the second torpedo that the submarine had dispatched through the engine room and the boat's vitals from a distance of 200 yards.

"We watched silently during the next minute, as the tiers of lights dimmed slowly from white to yellow, then to red, and nothing was left but the murking mourning of the night, which hung over all like a pall.

"A mean, cheese-colored crescent of a moon revealed one horn above a rag bundle of clouds low in the distance. A rim of blackness settled around our little world, relieved only by general leering stars in the zenith, and where the *Laconia* lights had shone there remained only the dim outline of a blacker hulk standing out above the water like a jagged headland, silhouetted against the overcast sky.

"The ship sank rapidly at the stern until at last its nose stood straight in the air. Then it slid silently down and out of sight like a piece of disappearing scenery in a panorama spectacle."

Among those to perish was Mrs. Mary E. Hoy, of Chicago, and her daughter, Elizabeth. They froze to death in a lifeboat in waters close to those in which the *Lusitania* made her final plunge. Mrs. Hoy's son, Austin Y. Hoy, an American businessman in London, cabled President Wilson:

My beloved mother and sister . . . have been foully murdered on the high seas. . . . I call upon my government to preserve its citizens' self-respect and save others of my countrymen from such deep grief as I now feel. I am of military age, able to fight. If my country can use me against these brutal assassins, I am at its call. If it stultifies my manhood and my nation's by remaining passive under outrage, I shall seek a man's chance under another flag.

The United States was rolling up her sleeves. Even before word of the *Laconia*'s sinking, much less Austin Hoy's impassioned cable, reached Washington, Wilson was signing into law an "armed neutrality" measure. Its first results would be the mounting of guns on merchant ships.

The German reaction was not slow. Any merchant master, threatened the *Neueste Nachrichten*, of Munich, firing on a submarine, would meet the same fate as Captain Fryatt. Undaunted, the United States Navy proceeded to arm the first vessels, including the liners *St. Paul, St. Louis, Mongolia*, and the freighter *Aztec*.

War fever, inflamed by the recent torpedoings, was sweeping America. "Preparedness parades," with torches and brassy, martial music, beat through the nation's streets into the night. "Germany is already waging war against us!" thundered old Colonel Henry Watterson, Confederate veteran and editor of the Louisville *Courier-Journal*. Billy Sunday, the evangelist, added his voice to those of many conservative preachers to demand immediate intervention. St. Luke's Episcopal Church, in Manhattan, for example, prepared a special "military service," as the choir marched pugnaciously in behind a huge American flag.

Preachers almost everywhere extolled the virtues of a "holy

crusade" until Woodrow Wilson commented in disbelief to a friend, "Our ministers are going crazy!"

The martial cry from the pulpits was stridently seconded by former-President Theodore Roosevelt, who had already organized a special businessman's training camp. "It has been a war of murder upon *us!*" he shouted before successive stomping audiences.

And to ensure hysteria at a febrile peak, the recurrent horror of international saboteurs and cloak-and-dagger men was accentuated. A *New York World* headline, for example, screamed: "Spies Are Everywhere."

The Germans did nothing to dissipate this notion, as they commenced to sabotage the machinery on their vessels trussed fast in America's ports; the giant *Vaterland* in Hoboken, New Jersey, the *Kronprinz Wilhelm* and *Prinz Eitel Friedrich* at Philadelphia (moved from Norfolk), and the *Kronprinzessin Cecilie* in Boston. Too late, federal agents seized the ships and hustled their crews off to internment.

The U. S. Navy was thereby confronted with an interesting challenge: it must find engineers who not only understood German but the complexities of foreign marine engines. These difficult barriers must be surmounted before the liners could ever put to sea again. That America would soon need them there seemed scant doubt.

During this time, Germany sent three more raiders to sea, the armed merchantmen *Moewe* and *Wolf*, both of about 5,000 tons, and the *Seeadler*, a small motor patrol ship of the regular naval forces. The latter was under command of an adventurous young lieutenant, Count Felix von Luckner, who was forced to carry his case to the kaiser when more senior officers disputed his right to captain a ship.

The first to experience success was the *Moewe* ("Gull"), under Count Nikolaus Paul Richard zu Dohna-Schlodien. She had slipped through the blockade previously, in 1915, to sink fifteen Allied and neutral ships. Now, just to be sure their enemies would be caught napping, German counterintelligence launched the preposterous rumor that the daring count, chafing under inactivity, had volunteered for duty on the western front and been killed. No Dohna-Schlodien, a name obviously respected by merchant masters, no *Moewe*—this was the propagandists' simple theory and apparently it was sound.

On her second cruise, the *Moewe* shelled, torpedoed, or scuttled six vessels in a wide zone extending from Nova Scotia south to Trindade. At that island, bitter with memories of the lost *Cap Trafalgar*, the captain took on coal from a captured collier. Dohna-Schlodien felt certain he would be watched only by "sea-eagles, man-of-war birds and boobies."

He wasn't quite correct. He soon learned that three armed merchantmen and two cruisers, the *Glasgow* and *Amethyst*, were closing in after chasing him all over the South Atlantic. He hurried from his anchorage. He was almost too late. The auxiliary *Edinburgh Castle*, which the *Cap Trafalgar* had attempted to impersonate by removing a funnel, actually sighted *Moewe*. But the German was too fast.

Count zu Dohna-Schlodien was soon streaking into the watery anonymity of mid-ocean, for Lisbon—and Wilhelmshaven.

Anti-submarine tactics were largely defensive. Here a British ship is camouflaged to avoid detection by German U-boat.

Count von Luckner, with a small, relatively slow raider, never captured many ships. His greatest fame arose from his flamboyant gallantry to survivors that he captured. With forged papers indicating that he was a Norwegian fisherman, he eluded the blockade to steam into the South Atlantic. There he operated in the vicinity of the equator, off St. Paul's Rocks.

He couldn't seem to do enough for his "guests." He had his musicians play "Tipperary," and "There's a Long, Long Trail" after meals—almost any selection which could bring tears of nostalgia to their eyes. From his own diminutive greenhouse, he presented flowers to two women who were taken off sunken ships.

There was never a prisoners' area. All were permitted the run of the *Seeadler*. Finally, he put them on board the French bark *Cambronne*, sawed off her top-gallant masts and bowsprit to slow her down, and bid her bon voyage to Rio de Janeiro.

The converted merchantman *Wolf*, under Captain Karl Nerger, had dispatched only three vessels in the Indian Ocean by the end of February. Nerger, however, would blaze a kind of "war pirate's history" by sinking 150,000 tons of shipping and cruising 64,000 miles without ever touching port. He came home safely just before the armistice. His practice of taking entire crews and passenger groups aboard almost led, at one time, to the lynching of his comrade, von Luckner. The latter, by that time a prisoner of war in New Zealand, had been accused of the destruction of the steamer *Wairuna* and all its passengers, when they were actually aboard the *Wolf*.

British hospital ships now joined the list of victims at sea, four of them in close succession: the *Donegal*, *Lanfranc*, *Asturias*, and *Gloucester Castle*, with a total loss of nearly a hundred sick and wounded. Berlin claimed the ships were really transports.

The clamor for reprisals again resounded in London, as well as Paris. As a sop to public demand, British and French planes droned off from fields in eastern France and bombed the largely open border city of Freiburg, Germany. The raid, while it didn't prove much except that the warring nations truly hated one another, was probably the first in history where large numbers of aircraft attacked an undefended city primarily for terror effect.

March arrived on an even stormier note of international tensions. A coded cable from Arthur Zimmerman, the German foreign minister, to his legation in Mexico was intercepted. While maintaining that it was his country's desire to keep America neutral, his inflammatory dispatch said:

If this attempt is not successful, we propose an alliance on the following basis with Mexico: that we shall make war together and together make peace. We shall give general financial support, and it is understood that Mexico is to reconquer the lost territory in New Mexico, Texas and Arizona. . . .

This bungling sample of German "diplomacy" and intrigue obliterated for all time Wilson's continuing efforts to mediate between the warring nations. From now on, if he was to mirror his people's desires, he had to talk at the very least of "armed neutrality."

The choruses of "Down with the kaiser!" and the almost hysterical clamor from prominent figures (led by Teddy Roosevelt) to declare war momentarily were blotted out by the shocking news on March 15 that Czar Nicholas had abdicated. Grand Duke Michael, his younger brother, was named regent. Michael tried desperately to carve a provisional government out of the remains of the old, but street riots in Petrograd, assassinations and wanton shooting, mutiny in the Imperial Navy and mass desertions and murders in the army, nullified his efforts. The old Imperial regime was dying.

Again, with blatant disregard of the consequences, Germany drew the attention of the United States back to its own concerns. In a devastating two-day onslaught, commencing on Thursday, March 15, U-boats sank four more American flag vessels—successively, like tumbled tenpins. First to go was the American Star liner *Algonquin*, en route to London with food. Next was the *City Of Memphis*, in ballast, beating westward off Cardiff. The crews of both ships reached land.

Then, the *Vigilancia*, bound for Le Havre, was torpedoed without warning off the Scilly Isles in much the same position as the ill-fated *Algonquin*. One of the lifeboats was adrift for two days, nearly 145 miles from land, before help arrived. Fifteen of her crew drowned or died from exposure in the cold spring winds.

Her hard-bitten captain, Frank A. Middleton, stormed ashore, swearing revenge. He said he would like to "line up at least fifteen Germans in New York, push them into the Hudson, then let boys throw stones at them as they drowned!"

His desire was scarcely humane, but it expressed the sentiments of most of his countrymen. When they learned next of the loss of the tanker *Illinois* in the same waters, they could boisterously second Mayor James M. Curley of Boston, who told a rally, "We love liberty more than peace!"

Before the week was out, on March 21, in the "safe zone" bordering the Dutch coast, another tanker, the *Healdton*, steaming from Philadelphia for Rotterdam, was suddenly struck. In the wintry, choppy waters of the North Sea, near the spot where the hundreds from the *Aboukir*, *Cressy*, and *Hogue* had perished, twenty-one more American citizens gave up their lives.

Wilson, as Winston Churchill reasoned, "step by step," had now been "brought to bay" by the unbelievable stupidity of the kaiser's warlords. In quick succession he had been handed four more "overt acts." He had little choice as to the next fateful step since it was far too late to consider reversing his nation's policy of "freedom of the seas." Since he could not call American merchant shipping home, he began the first draft of a declaration-of-war message.

And even as the keys of his Underwood typewriter clacked onward in a kind of threnody to violated righteousness, the torpedoes smashed home again.

The slow, quarter-of-a-century-old freighter, *Aztec*, one of the first to be armed, was wallowing toward Le Havre with a heavy cargo of food. She was seventeen miles west of the island of Ushant, struggling through heavy rain squalls and tossing seas, and Captain Walter O'Brien was mentally congratulating himself for his success in bringing the 3,700-tonner across the submarine-infested Atlantic. He strained to pick up the light of this small island, off the coast of Brest. It was a weird night, with a moon intermittently brightening through black skies and scud, driven by westerly gales.

Suddenly there was "a brilliant flash forward," a shudder, a thunderclap. The overladen vessel commenced to list rapidly. There was no use manning the guns. It was difficult enough to lower boats in these seas and in the night's all-consuming darkness.

Before a French patrol boat arrived, twenty-seven of the *Aztec*'s crew—more than half of her complement—and one navy gunner had perished. It was Palm Sunday, April 1.

The next evening, Monday, in another blustery storm, President Wilson was driven to the United States Capitol. Glistening white in the rain, the imposing seat of government was illuminated by electric lights for the first time. It was ringed by cavalry troops, sabers drawn, as the chief executive tipped his hat amid "deafening cheers" from the waiting multitudes. He hurried inside where a joint session of House and Senate listened in almost oppressive silence. For several minutes Wilson addressed the lawmakers, who were sitting forward in their chairs to catch the President's least intonations. Then, raising his familiar, distinct, professorial voice, he declared: "We shall not choose the path of submission!"

The legislators and those in the galleries could no longer contain their emotions. They were on their feet in a single motion, clapping, cheering, even stomping. Chief Justice White, a Confederate veteran with the face of a patriarch, wept without control as he applauded.

"The recent course of the Imperial Government," Wilson adjusted his pince-nez glasses and continued when the din subsided, ". . . nothing less than war against the Government of the people of the United States . . . we have no quarrel with the German people. . . . We are now about to accept gage of battle with this natural foe of liberty. . . . The world must be made safe for democracy!"

By 2:45 A.M., on Good Friday, April 6, climaxing a week's debate, both Senate and House had voted.

THE SEA CALLS YOU

The United States needed recruits to man its rapidly expanding navy. At the height of construction, 100 ships were launched in a single day.

America—at last—was in the Great War.

Germany reacted with aggrieved astonishment. She never, asserted von Bethmann-Hollweg, "had the slightest intention of attacking the United States of America . . . never desired war against the United States."

Winston Churchill, addressing the House of Commons as one of its members, praised this "God-granted aid to struggling Christendom." Privately, however, he mused as to "exactly why the United States entered the war on April 6, 1917, and why they did not enter at any earlier moment?"

But the "why" had become academic. More important was the *fait accompli*. And now, a nation which had been goading

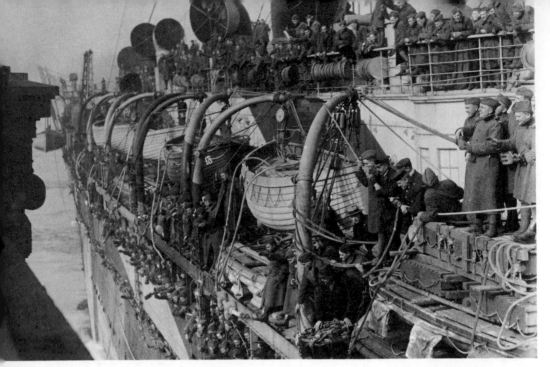

Yanks arriving in Liverpool on the *Mauretania*, sister of the *Lusitania*. Their preparedness surprised the war-weary British.

from the sidelines found herself in the thick of the very brawl she had been abetting. Actually, she was ill-prepared to fight anybody. There was much lost time to be reclaimed, if indeed it were possible to reclaim it.

"A million men to France!" became the rallying cry for an American Expeditionary Force, to be led by General John J. Pershing, a hard-bitten, square-jawed campaigner of Cuba, the Philippines, and the Villa chase in Mexico. The task facing the navy was even more dramatic. A poor third in the international "blue book" of fighting fleets, it counted only seventy capital ships, and most of these were obsolete. Germany's High Seas Fleet was still about four times as large, and more powerful in proportion.

Ready for service were 361 U. S. Navy vessels of all types, but many of these were antiquated torpedo boats (turn-of-the-century vintage) and converted yachts. However, Congress had already authorized the construction of 157 new men-of-war, including ten battleships of the largest type and six huge battle cruisers. The 32,000-ton *Mississippi, New Mexico, Tennessee* and *Idaho* were on the ways or being readied for commissioning. Two others of the same relative size, the *Pennsylvania* and her sister *Arizona*, were undergoing overhaul, while almost all the older ships were being converted from coal to oil as fast as the already overtaxed shipyards could handle them.

The strength, 4,500 officers and 68,000 enlisted men, would have to soar to 15,000 and 254,000, respectively, almost overnight.

This was the challenge at home. In London, Rear Admiral William H. Sims, tall, outspoken personal emissary of Secretary of the Navy Josephus Daniels, was learning the worst from the first sea lord, Admiral Jellicoe. Sims, as a matter of fact, had been en route to England when the United States declared war.

"It is impossible for us to go on with the war if losses like this continue," Jellicoe informed Sims. Indeed, the sinkings would peak this very April at nearly 900,000 tons.

"Is there no solution to this problem?" asked Sims.

"Absolutely none that we can see now," answered Jellicoe. He had seemingly developed an incurable inferiority complex from his inability to bag the High Seas Fleet.

Later, Ambassador Walter Hines Page added flatly, "What we are facing is the defeat of Britain."

Sims, however (as strong an Anglophile as the tough Chief of Naval Operations William S. Benson was an Anglophobe*) did not see why America's new ally should be defeated. And there *was* a solution—*convoy*. After that, if necessary, he would close off the entire North Sea with a mine barrage!

First, however, the Allies needed more patrols in the Atlantic. Little more than a week after the declaration of war, the Navy Department ordered a destroyer division, comprised of six

---

*Benson had barked his final instructions, late in March, to the departing Sims: "Don't let the British pull the wool over your eyes. It is none of our business pulling their chestnuts out of the fire. We would as soon fight the British as the Germans!"

ships, to prepare for overseas duty. They would be led—provocatively—by a handsome, dark-haired German-born officer. Commander Joseph Knefler Taussig had graduated from the Naval Academy in 1899 after distinguishing himself as an athlete and cadet officer. His prowess on the gridiron had earned him the nickname "Pig."

The Secret and Confidential orders which, in effect, cleared the navy's decks for opening action in this war, read:

TO: Commander, Eighth Division, Destroyer Force, Atlantic Fleet, USS *Wadsworth*, flagship.

SUBJECT: Protection of commerce near the coasts of Great Britain and Ireland.

1. The British Admiralty have requested the cooperation of a division of American destroyers in the protection of commerce near the coasts of Great Britain and France.

2. Your mission is to assist naval operations of Entente Powers in every way possible.

3. Proceed to Queenstown, Ireland. Report to senior British naval officer present, and thereafter cooperate fully with the British Navy. Should it be decided that your force act in cooperation with French naval forces, your mission and method of cooperation under French Admiralty authority remain unchanged.

Route to Queenstown: Boston to latitude 50 N, Long. 20 W, to arrive at daybreak, then to latitude 50 N, Long. 12 W, thence to Queenstown.

When within radio communication of the British naval forces off Ireland, call GCK and inform the Vice Admiral at Queenstown in British general code of your position, course, and speed. You will be met outside of Queenstown.

4. Base facilities will be provided by the British Admiralty.

5. Communicate your orders and operations to Rear Admiral Sims at London and be guided by such instructions as he may give you. Make no report of arrival to Navy Department direct.

JOSEPHUS DANIELS

After outfitting, fueling, and provisioning in their home naval yards, the six sailed from Boston on April 24. The voyage was stormy. Hounded by a gale that roared for a full week without the slightest abatement, the crews hung on and, as one officer recalled, ate off their laps.

When the sheltering hills of Queenstown loomed ahead at last, the Americans encountered a memorable officer of the Royal Navy—tall, graying Vice Admiral Sir Lewis Bayly, commander in chief of the coasts of Ireland. Kept on beyond retirement, Bayly, a bachelor, was a disciple of hard work. He demanded results and loathed excess talk.

"Dine in undress, no speeches!" was his dictum, even for formal occasions. He lived in a modest row cottage, not far from Admiralty House, overlooking Queenstown Harbor, and maintained, as well, an operations room in the basement of his own residence. There, he worked with what was probably the smallest staff in the British Navy—three officers.

A niece, his housekeeper and confidante, had developed a simple formula for cooling down the atmosphere when her uncle's temper soared out of limits. She would tap on the door, and announce:

"Tea is served, Sir Lewis."

With no apparent desire to curry favor, Commander Taussig made a sparkling impression on the terse, austere English admiral. Coming ashore to announce the arrival of his division, the American was asked:

"When will you be ready to go to sea?"

"We are ready now, sir!" Taussig replied.

Admiral Bayly was totally unprepared for such an answer. Fueling, ammunition, food, to say nothing of the Royal Navy "gear" that had to be installed, from special depth charge equipment to signaling "trees," hoists, and codes that would be uniform with their sisters under the Union Jack—Bayly ticked off these necessities.

"I will give you four days," he asserted, fighting down an impulse to smile.

"My boys," he thought of the Americans ever afterward. It seemed a rare compliment from an officer whom most juniors feared more than hellfire. Singularly, Bayly's affection for the navy from across the Atlantic increased at the expense of his own. At one time he sent a request to the Admiralty for "fifty

British destroyers to relieve thirty-three American." The pointed barb was in respect to his long-standing displeasure with the "short-legged" character of His Majesty's destroyers. They could not stay at sea as long as their United States equivalents.

Four days after their arrival, the American destroyers *were* at sea. And their officers reciprocated Admiral Bayly's esteem.

"Things were looking black," Taussig admitted. "In the three previous weeks, the submarines had sunk 152 British merchant ships. The night before we entered the harbor a German submarine had planted twelve mines right in the channel. The day following our arrival, one of the British gunboats from our station was torpedoed and her captain and forty of her crew were lost. Patrol vessels were continually bringing in survivors from the various ships as they were sunk."

The Queenstown "area" was a vast one, comprising 25,000 square miles of wild seas—as important to the lifeline of Britain and France as they were desirable to U-boats. Until the U.S. Navy arrived, according to Admiral Sims, "Sometimes only four or five British destroyers were operating in this great stretch of waters, and I do not think the number ever exceeded fifteen."

The United States kept sending destroyers to Queenstown until, by the end of June, thirty-seven were based there. She was also dispatching her first soldiers to the Great War: the entire First Division. This vanguard of the American Expeditionary Force sailed very secretly from New York on June 14. The convoy consisted of eighteen transports, cargo ships, and a navy collier, the *Cyclops*, guarded by no less than five cruisers, thirteen destroyers, and one converted yacht.

Admiral Gleaves himself, who had been promoted to the major responsibility of commander of the Cruiser and Transport Force, took personal command of this first great convoy. Eight days out, late at night, the armored cruiser *Seattle* ducked a white streak coming at her through the flat moonlit waters. General alarm was sounded. Deck guns opened fire. Destroyers commenced to drop depth charges. Transports scattered in many directions, like chickens in a barnyard invaded by a fox.

Searchlights glared, illuminating the transports for the suspected prowler. Luckily, in spite of all the unwitting assistance tendered by his quarry, the U-boat, if one there had been, did not score. All in all, Admiral Gleaves concluded, the "hand of providence" must have led the procession, triumphant and unharmed, into St.-Nazaire on June 26.

There, a member of the United States diplomatic delegation to Paris informed him that, "unless the United States troops or ships really accomplish something shortly, the French are beaten . . . they are much discouraged and so hard up for men that a recent order requires every man under sixty to do his part one way or another."

Gleaves, appalled at the French Navy, wrote, ". . . in a rundown condition; they have only one destroyer at Dunkirk, and in a recent destroyer action these boats, built for thirty-five knots, could only make eighteen, and two of them were put out of commission during that action."

While the United States Navy was third in the international standing, it wasn't "run-down." Its potential was far from that distressing state. To its already announced expansion, 1,000 more warships would be added; in the hurry and flurry of war, naval science would leapfrog ahead. The 43,000-ton battleship would be born, as well as the assembly line for lesser craft: specifically, Henry Ford's 200-foot, eighteen-knot "tin Lizzies of the sea," the Eagle boats.

Merchant ship construction kept pace, as American industry strained to replace Britain's disastrous losses. Yards mushroomed throughout the nation. In a few, such as sprawling Hog Island in Philadelphia, production-line technique was adapted even to so massive and cumbersome a vessel as an ocean-going freighter. Workers proved that such a steamer could be built in less than two weeks. At the peak, 100 ships, in all the nation's yards, were launched in a single day. Soon, both the navy and the merchant marine of the United States would take first place among the world's fleets.

It was an odd summer, this first one of war. Like the British, in those early months of 1915, Americans could not quite bring themselves to toss the last spadefuls of earth upon the bones of yesterday. Within sound of the steam-riveter or the "All hands, hear this!" whistles from the fleet, life persisted with a maudlin, almost hysterical nostalgia for what certain sets had known as their "status quo." Along the shores of Narragansett Bay, as the gray warships nosed out into an ocean where the struggle for life was real, Newport was headlined in one newspaper as "at Height of Social Season."

Even among the millionaires, however, there were decisions to be made. For example, the high command of the Newport Country Club, after taking thought, broke with tradition. Members of the armed forces stationed in Newport even temporarily, it ruled, so long as they were commissioned officers, could take part in the annual golf tournament.

In Germany, there was considerably more worry than that over golf balls and who was to hit them. One chancellorship fell, another assumed the seals of office. Von Bethmann-Hollweg, who had failed in his attempts to keep the United States out of the war, was succeeded by a middle-of-the-roader, Dr. Georg Michaelis.

Addressing the Reichstag on July 19, the new chancellor unwittingly dramatized a *double-entendre* when he declared that U-boat warfare "has done more than we expected." It certainly had. And a young submarine officer, Karl Doenitz,* was among those who understood just *what* it had done.

"The introduction of the convoy system in 1917," he wrote, "robbed it [the submarine service] of its opportunity to become a decisive factor. The oceans at once became bare and empty . . . then suddenly up would loom a huge concourse of ships, thirty or fifty or more of them surrounded by a strong escort of warships of all types."

If the solitary U-boat possessed a commander with strong nerves, he might succeed ultimately in sinking one or two of the assemblage—at best a poor percentage.

By autumn, the United States Navy, aided by her Allies, had delivered nearly 150,000 doughboys to France, without a casualty. However, nothing in war is ever absolutely certain. On

---

*Doenitz, who had been aboard the *Breslau* in her dash through the Dardanelles at the outbreak of war, was a prisoner at the time of the armistice. A generation later he was to lead Germany's navy in a greater conflict, head a tottering Nazi government, and be condemned at Nuremburg as a war criminal.

Better known a generation later as an admiral in Hitler's navy, Karl Doenitz began his career as a young officer aboard the kaiser's *U-39*. In the introduction of the convoy system in 1917, he saw the decline of the submarine as a decisive weapon.

Photo courtesy of Admiral Doenitz

October 17, the *Antilles*, a 6,878-ton coastal steamer from the New York-New Orleans trade, was hit by a torpedo two days out of Brest. She was returning to the United States for another contingent of the A.E.F. The submarine had penetrated the convoy screen to score in a vital region of the old vessel's innards.

The *Antilles* sank in a few minutes, carrying with her seventy of her crew of 237, comprised of navy, army, and merchant marine personnel. Eleven days later, the *Finland*, a transport nearly twice the size of the *Antilles*, was torpedoed, also on the return lap of her voyage. She limped back to port, carrying nine dead.

Navy gunners, however, commenced to account for themselves in the best traditions of their scrappy service—almost from the "starting whistle." Only a few days after the declaration, the gun crew of the transport *Mongolia* opened fire on a partially surfaced submarine. While he couldn't claim a kill, Lieutenant Bruce Ware, commanding the armed guard, saw one of the shells bounce off the conning tower, knocking off a piece of metal. Then the U-boat crash-dived.

On June 12, the American tanker *Moreni* went down blazing, seventeen miles off Cape Palos, Spain. Tall, moustached Chief Bos'n's Mate Andrew Copassaki kept his small gun crew banging off round after round until the fire was literally scorching their uniforms and the water lapped over their ankles. Nearly 400 shells blasted back and forth during the two-hour battle.

After the steamer's crew had abandoned ship, without loss of life, the submarine came close to the boats. The admiring German captain declared that it was the best fight he had "ever seen any merchantman put up." He wirelessed the survivors' position, and apologized for not being able to tarry long enough to tow the crew to land.

One of the longest single naval battles took place two days after the loss of the *Antilles*, on October 19, when the 5,000-ton *J. L. Luckenbach*, bound for Le Havre, was attacked at dawn by the *U-62* off the Scilly Islands. It was a blistering cowboys-and-Indians thriller, in which a number were hurt but, remarkably, none was killed.

"SOS! *J. L. Luckenbach* being gunned by submarine!" was the first wireless plea, sent by the armed guard commander J. B. Trautner, a chief master-at-arms.

More than sixty miles distant, helping to screen an inbound convoy, the destroyer *Nicholson* answered.

"We are coming," radioed Lieutenant Frank D. Berrien, the *Nicholson*'s skipper. Frank, when he graduated from Annapolis in 1900, was tagged "devoid of fear" by his classmates. He was soon guiding his destroyer through the Atlantic at her top speed of thirty knots, as if determined to prove the faith of his fellow midshipmen.

"Our steam is cut off," flashed back the freighter's master, Arthur W. Street. "How soon can you get here?"

The Boston Daily Globe — EXTRA

VOL. XCIII—NO. 155   BOSTON, TUESDAY MORNING, JUNE 4, 1918—SIXTEEN PAGES   PRICE TWO CENTS

GERMAN U-BOATS SINK 11 VESSELS IN RAIDS OFF AMERICAN COAST

Fate of 220 Passengers and Crew of 130 From Coast Liner Carolina Unknown—Boston Owned Schooners Edward H. Cole and Jacob M. Haskell Among Victims—Steamship City of Columbus Reported Destroyed—No Loss of Life So Far as Known—Pursuing Warships Fire on Submarine—No Transports Attacked

FRENCH DRIVE GERMANS BACK TOWARD SOISSONS

Recapture Faverolles in Spite of Enemy Attacks—Teutons Push Two Miles Down Marne, But Are Held at All Other Points

CITY OF COLUMBUS, BOSTON BOUND FROM SAVANNAH, REPORTED SUNK BY SUBMARINE

Bristol Zig-Zags to Safety and Lands Survivors of Cole In New York

Sailors Tell of Being Held on Submarine as Captives— No Lifeboats Shelled

First Day of Equal Battle

Huns' Masses Recoil From Solid Line

British Reserves Enter Struggle

Berlin Confesses Losses of Week Are Severe

ASKS 50,000 IRISH RECRUITS

Lord Lieutenant Calls for 2000 More Monthly

Special Inducement Offered in Way of Land for Soldiers

BELIEVE THAT FIVE U-BOATS CAME OVER

Two Off Virginia and as Many Off Jersey

Another Further South—No Reports of Any Engagement

WARSHIPS FIRE ON SUBMARINES

Speedy Pursuit Follows Sinking of the Pratt

HELD CAPTIVES ON SUBMARINE

Americans From Sunken Vessels Detained

Turned Adrift in Boats—Survivors Landed in New York

VICTIMS OF GERMANY'S U-BOATS OFF U. S. COAST

SUNK

CAROLINA, passenger steamer, 5000 tons, New York for Porto Rico Line, carrying 220 passengers and crew of 130, signalled she was being attacked at 7 o'clock Sunday night when about 125 to 150 miles south east of Sandy Hook.

TEXEL, steamship, 3210 tons. Owned by W. Bull and Bussos at Rotterdam.

WINNECONNE, steamship, 180 tons, Norfolk for Providence. Sunk Sunday. Owned by American Transatlantic Company of New York. Requisitioned by United States Shipping Board last year.

HERBERT L. PRATT, American tanker 5372 tons, Mexico for New York, sunk Monday afternoon four miles off Cape Henlopen, Del. One man of crew of 33 lost.

JACOB M. HASKELL, 1382 net tons, Norfolk, Va., for Portland, Me, Capt William H. Davis, Sunday. Owned by Crowell & Thurlow of Boston.

EDWARD H. COLE, schooner, 1800 net tons, Norfolk to Portland, Capt H. C. Newcombe, Somerville, sunk 75 miles off Highland Light, N J, at 4 p m Sunday. Owned by Crowell & Thurlow, Boston.

HATTIE DUNN, schooner, 435 tons, New York for Charleston, S C, in ballast, Capt Charles Holbrook, Tenants Harbor, Me. Owned by Dunn, Eliot & Co, Thomaston, Me.

SAMUEL W. HATHAWAY, schooner. Owned by Crowell & Thurlow, Boston.

ISABEL B. WILEY, schooner, 614 tons. Owned in Bath, Me, and New York.

EDNA, schooner, found bottom side up several days ago and towed into Lewes, Delaware, also a victim. Crew landed in New York. City was two miles from Philadelphia to Santiago de Cuba.

HAUPPAUGE, schooner, 1000 tons.

BELIEVED SUNK

CITY OF COLUMBUS, passenger steamer, 5433 tons, Savannah, Ga, for Boston, carrying 52 passengers and crew of 68. Capt J. H. Diehl, formerly of Malden. Owned by Ocean Line.

ESCAPED

BRISTOL, coal laden steamship, Capt Frederick Hart, Boston for Norfolk. Owned by Coastwise Transportation Company of Boston. She escaped the pursuing U-boats, escaping by reaching shallow water.

WARSHIPS HUNTING HUN SEA RAIDERS

E. H. COLE'S CAPTAIN TELLS OF SINKING

Hart's Ship Unarmed

U-Boat Hunt Begins

Long List of Victims

Not all action was "over there." American papers announced the sinking of eleven boats by the Germans.

205

"Stick to it. Will be with you in three hours."

"Shell burst in engine room," the *Luckenbach* added. "Engineer crippled . . . fire in our forehold. They are now shooting at our antennae."

Ernst Hashagen, captain of the *U-62*, who had already recorded the war with a poet's eye, wrote: ". . . her captain defends her cargo with courage and tenacity. My men go most enthusiastically to work and are almost pleased at the howling and crashing of the shells falling about us. At last, a fight in daylight and fresh air! A brisk and lively fight in which one can see the enemy and set about him. She seems to have suffered in the action but is holding and reports, 'Still afloat and fighting!' "

The *Luckenbach*, afire, half-flooded, listing, kept up her stream of messages:

"How far are you away?" Then added, "Code books thrown overboard. How soon will you arrive?"

"In two hours."

"Too late. Look out for boats. They are shelling us!"

Then, Berrien blurted an order that was to join "Don't give up the ship!" "Damn the torpedoes!" and others of naval immortality: "Do not surrender!"

The reply was in key: "Never!"

Two hours and 427 rounds of ammunition later, the *Nicholson*, guns blazing, joined in the fight. The agonized suspense of the *Luckenbach* was at last ended.

Hashagen reported, "an ear-splitting crash on the foredeck." The *U-62* was hit solidly. It was time to go home; and in fact only superior seamanship brought his command to port.

The *Nicholson*'s assistant surgeon E. L. Rice found numerous wounded on board the *Luckenbach*. Miraculously, none had been killed. However, so many dressings had to be made and then changed periodically that the doctor, together with his corpsmen, stayed aboard the freighter all the way into Le Havre.

A month later, on Saturday, November 17, the *Nicholson* had cleared Daunt Rock lightship, seven miles south of Queenstown Sound's first channel buoy. She was loping through light swells off Roberts Head on the western approaches to the major anchorage as a moderate breeze teased from the southwest and a hazy sky hastened an early dusk. About 4 o'clock, she arrived ahead of an incoming convoy of sixteen ships, then started criss-crossing at a constant twenty knots, like a nervous Basset hound.

In the next twenty minutes, an unusual drama of the convoy lanes took place, sparked by the keen eyesight of Coxswain David Loomis, on lookout aboard the *Fanning*. The *Fanning* was one of the ships which had stood by a year ago off the Nantucket lightship while Hans Rose ran wild against Allied shipping. What Loomis saw was a "finger periscope," almost too small to be noticed against the dark shifting surface of the sea. But he recognized it nonetheless, and sang out, "Submarine!"

Bells jangled, flag hoists were run up, gunners dashed to their stations, depth charges tumbled from their stern racks like oversized watermelons tumbling from a truck. Lieutenant Arthur S. "Chip" Carpender, Annapolis '08, was not only one of the most handsome and military representatives of the U.S. Navy—"Beau Brummel" he was often called—but one of the "fightingest" in the John Paul Jones tradition.

He could not be sure, in the opening moments of attack, whether he had a true contact or not. However, Chip Carpender would "sink first" and, if necessary, ask questions or make explanations later.

The *Nicholson* logged: "4:15 sighted submarine trying to rise on starboard bow . . . 4:17 dropped depth charge and fired two shots from stern gun. Steering various courses at full speed. . . ."

At 4:20, the submarine, which had been damaged so that it could neither submerge nor escape on the surface, hove to. The crews of the two American warships were greeted with a thrilling, almost unprecedented, sight: a dozen or more of the enemy tumbling onto the sloshing, careening decks and shouting, just as their comrades sometimes did along the western front, when they had had enough: *"Kamerad!"*

The *Fanning* tossed a line to the crippled undersea craft, while keeping its guns trained. The *Nicholson*, now joined by other destroyers including the 1,000-ton *Jacob Jones*, one of the newest and fastest in the service, continued to sniff around for other possible U-boats.

The Germans, not unexpectedly, had scuttled their craft. It sank before the crew could be transferred, leaving the sailors struggling in the water. The Americans leapt in themselves to help them aboard.

Kapitänleutnant Gustav Amberger had surrendered his *U-58*, his three officers and thirty-five men. One, Seaman Franz Glinder, died of water inhalation and exposure minutes after being brought into the destroyer's sick bay. Carpender immediately consulted with his officer-prisoner Amberger. It was decided to bury the deceased at sea. This was done at once. When the rites were completed, within sight of Roche Point and the headlands before Queenstown, Carpender radioed: "Burial completed. Request berth."

Admiral Bayly, with his latent sense of humor, thought this was very funny and delighted in repeating the story: ". . . burial was completed, and they asked for berth—keeping the Germans from race suicide, you know, oh, I say, isn't that droll. Berth, what?"

Such slashing attacks against the U-boats, combined with

America's first victory at sea: *U-58* surrenders to the USS *Fanning*.

the convoy technique and the aggressiveness that the vigorous Americans had injected into the war, sent the merchant-sinking rate plummeting. From its April peak it was down to 288,000 tons a month by the end of November—or one third the gross amount counted in April.

However, as the British had discovered long since, victories never came cheaply. The United States Navy would also pay in blood. On October 16, off the Irish coast in broad daylight, the destroyer *Cassin* had taken a torpedo but was able to make port. The attack was attended by an example of heroism second to none. Gunner's Mate Osmond K. Ingram, of Pratt City, Alabama, seeing the torpedo porpoising toward the destroyer, raced for the stern to release the depth charges. Too late, he was blown to bits. Ingram was awarded the Medal of Honor posthumously, and a new destroyer was named in his honor.

On November 20, three days after the *U-58* had surrendered, the American destroyer *Chauncey* was cut in two by the British steamer *Rose*, during night-time convoy, 110 miles west of Gibraltar. The destroyer's thirty-six-year-old captain, Lieutenant Commander Walter Reno, and twenty of the crew lost their lives.

The same day, the 1,000-ton, 275-foot converted yacht *Alcedo*, formerly owned by the Philadelphia millionaire George W. Drexel, was torpedoed off the English coast. Twenty-one men perished with the *Alcedo*.

Among those to die on the former luxury yacht was a sixteen-year-old seaman, Edward Ray Gossett, who quit the High School of Commerce, in Astoria, New York, to enlist. His sorrowing mother, Mrs. Amy Gossett, told reporters of a dream the night before the tragedy. "I thought I was resting my head in a comfortable position upon two American flags," she said. "Suddenly a hand appeared from space and snatched one of the flags away. I awoke with a start . . . I had a feeling that something had happened to my boy."

The greatest shock came as Christmas neared, on December 6. The *Jacob Jones* was one of six destroyers returning from Brest to Queenstown after escorting a convoy through the channel. She carried a complement of 108 officers and men under the command of Lieutenant Commander David Worth Bagley. Bagley, brother-in-law of Secretary Daniels, was the brother of Lieutenant Worth Bagley, the first naval officer to lose his life in the Spanish-American war. The most handsome member of the Naval Academy's Class of 1904, Bagley was stamped by the yearbook *Lucky Bag*: "Our pride, our pet, our fair-haired baby boy."

At 4:20 P.M., in flat seas, twenty-five miles southeast of Bishop's Rock, a torpedo was sighted, 1,000 yards distant. Bagley ordered the helm hard over. Two shots were fired from number four gun, although the submarine could not be seen. The thirty-knot destroyer could not, however, evade the onrushing torpedo. It hit below the waterline, exploding a fuel tank.

The doomed *Jacob Jones* sank in eight minutes. The wireless was carried away. No distress messages could be transmitted.

Only forty-four of her relatively large crew survived. The odd part of this latest toll of the war, however, was to come. As night, black and bitter, cloaked the waters off this western tip of Great Britain, the submarine continued to loiter nearby. Its commander—Hans Rose—was transfixed by the spectacle of his latest victim.

He finally hauled two of the crew out of the water when it appeared that they would never succeed in gaining the safety of a raft or boat. (He later landed them in Helgoland for medical attention.)

Rose also observed some sobering acts of heroism, particularly on the part of the American officers. Ensign Stanley Kalk, for example, of Omaha, Nebraska, swam in the icy waters from raft to raft, both to equalize the weight and to help haul survivors up onto them. Later his shipmates paid their own laconic tribute to Kalk, who perished from exertion and exposure: "He was game to the end."

Rose could not stand idly by any longer. About two hours after the torpedoing, one of the bedraggled men he had plucked from the waters warned, "You better get out of here! We sent off a message and destroyers will probably be here shortly." Before scooting, Rose radioed to nearby Lands End on the coast of England: "Destroyer *Jacob Jones* sunk, 49:20 N, 60:18 W. Rescue survivors. UUU"

"Look After My Folks"

NAVY RELIEF SOCIETY

OFFICIAL RELIEF ORGANIZATION OF THE U.S. NAVY

CARES FOR THE NAVY'S
WIDOWS AND ORPHANS

Navy Relief poster, World War I. Even the victors paid with blood.

Explosion of German submarine, viewed from conquering ship.

Later, the German commander explained, "I sent out this radio message because I was cruising on the surface amongst survivors and in the hope it might increase the breach which, I was given to understand from the statement of one of the prisoners, existed between the British and American naval personnel."

The spectacle of the drowning foe tore at the U-boat commander's heart; he wrote, "A few yards from the *U-53* a man was struggling with death . . . he looked over towards us. He gave no cry for help, no cry of anguish, none of fear. Silent, resolute, heroic, he went down as we passed, dead for his country."

Hans Rose's remorse was magnified in this strange drama.

Two hours after his first call, he sent another message crackling through the cold darkness of the early northern evening: "Survivors on board. Three rafts still at large!"

Regretting that he had no more room for the other crewmen, Rose continued in his notes: "We had to deal with honorable enemies, men who had unselfishly risked their lives without hope of reward in the service of their fatherland."

Finally, however, he realized that lingering twenty-five miles off the English coast for nearly four hours was an act of madness. Reluctantly, he ordered *U-53* into the anonymity of deep water —and cut for Wilhelmshaven.

"I went away," he penned in the intimacy of his diary, "with a heavy heart."

Rescue ships, responding to the German captain's appeal, arrived before midnight to pick up most of the survivors. Bagley, however, and five half-frozen companions rowed until they reached land—nearly twenty-four hours after the torpedoing.

And so, in the stark revelation of this struggle at sea, at least one of the warriors had paused—and understood that it was not in his soul to "sink without trace."

(8)

"...no more baffling mystery..."

⊕ Seemingly, *spurlos versenkt* figured in the disappearance of the collier *Cyclops*, the greatest loss the United States Navy experienced in the war.

There had been other sinkings earlier in 1918. In February, the newly launched, 14,400-ton *Tuscania* was torpedoed off the rocky north coast of Scotland, the first major disaster sustained by the A.E.F. Almost all the 116 doughboys who perished were members of the 20th Engineers Regiment, fresh from training on the bare American University campus in Washington.

The telegraphs tapped out the messages: "The Secretary of War [or Navy] regrets to inform you. . . ." The cold official requiem was intoned for a mounting number of Americans, young men who came from Eddyville, Nebraska, and Lehighton, Pennsylvania; Edgemoor, South Carolina, and Hatfield, Arkansas; Connersville, Indiana, and Ashland, Oklahoma; Fountain City, Tennessee, and Maquoketa, Iowa . . . from whistle stops, towns, and cities of the United States. These were the navy heroes, the nation's newest war dead whose names would appear, one by one, on memorials hitherto reserved for and sacred to '98, the War for the Union, and the Revolution.

Once more, mothers and fathers said extraordinary things.

"We had only one boy to give to our country and he was only a little past eighteen years of age," wrote Mr. and Mrs. Burt L. Hedglin, of Eddyville, Nebraska. "He went with his own free will and accord, and with our blessing. I regret that I have only the one boy to give. . . . It was God's will that he should be sacrificed on the altar of his country, and we will accept His will in the matter.

"I know that the boy did what he could."*

On an April evening, the war came home as well to Chambersburg, Pennsylvania. Spring had just come to the Pennsylvania valley town, which had been burned during the Civil War, and the scent of blossoms was in the air. Mrs. Guy P. Asper, whose husband was one of the community's best known doctors, remembers that knock on the door of her brick home on Queen Street which forever ended any illusion that war casualties happened only to other families.

She hurried from a small dinner party to be confronted by a familiar face from the Western Union office. She tore open the envelope handed her to read the "regrets" from the secretary of the navy. Dr. Burt J. Asper, her husband's thirty-year-old kid brother, a navy surgeon on the *Cyclops*, was missing.

In a daze, Mrs. Asper returned to the table. Then, after hesitating a moment, she whispered to Guy: "Burt's lost. . . ." She remembers how her husband pushed back his chair as though he had been expecting it.

"We must tell Lee," he said. Dr. Asper was referring to Burt's bride of a few weeks, Lee Christy, a Baltimore girl. The bride herself was living in Gettysburg, where Burt had been practicing medicine before being commissioned in the navy.

Early the next morning the Aspers took the train to Washington and hurried to the Navy Department. Their worst suspicions about this shipwreck, or whatever it was, were confirmed.

"They acted so peculiarly in Secretary Daniels' office," Mrs. Asper recalls. "There was something odd, we felt, from the start. No one wanted to talk, to answer our questions. . . ."

Indeed, there *was* something odd: a giant collier displacing more than 20,000 tons with 309 souls aboard had vanished

---

*Seaman Floyd H. Hedglin left college to enlist. He was accepted by the navy after the army rejected him because he was too short. He was one of twenty-six lost in the torpedoing of the homeward-bound transport *President Lincoln* on May 31, 1918. See also Appendix 2 for the account of one of the officers taken prisoner by the *U-90*, who subsequently escaped from a POW camp in Germany.

Heroes of the war were boys like Floyd Hedglin, eighteen, of Eddyville, Nebraska, who was killed in the torpedoing of the *President Lincoln*. His parents regretted that they had only one son to give for their country.

without trace in calm seas and in a zone which was later proven to have been clear of submarines or mines. The mystery, woven of many components, possibly began when the future master of the *Cyclops* arrived in San Francisco from Bremen, Germany, in 1878. John Frederick Georg Wichmann had persuaded his older sister, Hilga, and his brother Herman to arrange for his passage as cabin boy to the United States to escape the beatings and rages of his father.

The boy, barely sixteen, found a friend in a retired sea captain named Worley. This man became a second, but appreciative, parent, and instilled in John a great love of the sea. The pair spent long hours sailing back and forth across San Francisco Bay in the shadow of the Golden Gate, until much of the old salt's skill in sail-setting and basic ship-handling had been imparted to his willing protégé.

While the young immigrant received no formal education he somehow taught himself the English language, certainly exceeding the proficiency of Worley. While he tended to lapse into his native German in waterfront saloons, he could express himself surprisingly well in English, both written and spoken.

Troops at mess on deck of *President Lincoln*. Twenty-six never made it home.

The *President Lincoln's* crew man lifeboats as their ship goes down.

Georg Wichmann spent his late teens and early twenties on sailing ships beating to the Philippines and Australia. These were his shadowy years, attended by dark rumors and a mystery not uncommon to the brawling days along California's gold coast and the rough products of these times.

It is more certain that he operated or worked in a saloon (which he said he won in a poker game) on the corner of Clay and Polk Streets, San Francisco, in the late 80's. Then he returned to his beloved Pacific as master, successively, of the yachts *Aloha* and *Detolina*. The *Detolina* was owned by Festetics Detolna, who claimed to be an Austrian count. He was a swashbuckling soldier of fortune, sporting a bushy moustache almost as imposing as Wichmann's.

About the time he completed his naturalization in 1890, Wichmann entered the Naval Overseas Transport Service—operator of the navy's colliers, transports, and other supply ships. A far haul from the polish and gentility of the Naval Academy or even a ship of the line, this service was fashioned for Wichmann. Its vessels, reminiscent of the slavers of an all-too-recent yesterday, were manned by the riffraff of the world's waterfronts. Crewmen did not have to be American citizens (prior to the La Follette Act of 1915), or even literate beyond the manual ability to sign their names with an X.

Georg Wichmann thrived. He could prove that he was rougher and tougher than the next man should the situation demand. And it often did. If he said, "I can lick both of you!" he meant it. When he drank, he drank a lot, but could hold the fiery stuff like a bottomless tankard.

Soon, the chevrons of a warrant officer rested above the biceps of Wichmann's left arm. He was in line to command tugs and similar small work boats. As a result of rapid promotion at the time of the Spanish-American War, Georg Wichmann, the immigrant who had received no formal education, won a lieutenant's commission. He was an officer on the transport *St. Mark* which, with a certain brazenness, steamed in and out of the Spanish fleet in the Philippines until Admiral George Dewey eliminated that enemy entirely.

After the war, Wichmann commanded colliers, taking

charge successively of larger ships of this type. Colliers were dirty and often hard to handle because the coal shifted about. They attracted crews as unkempt and disorderly as the ships themselves. Few commanding officers would accept colliers, with their slovenly roistering crews.

While captain of the *Leonidas,* Georg married Selma Schold, of Bremerton, Washington. The ceremony took place in Pensacola, Florida, in February, 1906. He was to prove that he could be as devoted and sentimental a husband as he was an iron-fisted, often irascible ship-handler. He wrote love letters which were so tender that even his friends would have sworn they could not have been composed by a man who could flatten a saloon adversary with one blow, or drain a third of a bottle of whisky in a swallow.

Two years later, in San Juan, Puerto Rico, while he was commanding the *Abarenda*, his third mate, Witchardt, was murdered by the ship's carpenter, a waterfront ruffian named Dixon. While Wichmann was absolved of having any connection with the homicide, the court of inquiry expressed mild curiosity as to why the master did not pilot a better disciplined ship.

However, the naval transport service was in desperate need of masters. Georg was not only kept on, but put in line for the next major command. Now he complained that he was sick of being called Old Dutch and Dutchman. There were already anti-German rumblings in the United States as Kaiser Wilhelm II, thumbing the pages of aggressive Hohenzollern genealogy, decided to do some saber rattling of his own.

In 1909, while his ship was at Port Orchard, Washington, a suburb of Bremerton, Georg Wichmann assumed the name George Worley, in token gratitude toward the man who had launched him on his career.

The next year, fate and his own background brought George Worley and a special kind of ship together. He was chosen master of the 542-foot-long, 10,000-ton *Cyclops,* the first of three new-type colliers ordered by the navy for the overseas transport service. Her two vertical, triple-expansion steam engines could drive her at fourteen knots, fast enough to keep up with most of the wallowing fleet. Her innovations were topped by "self-trimming" holds: a system of water ballast tanks on and below decks for maintaining the ship in proper balance and equilibrium, irrespective of the sea and amount of cargo. Fourteen kingposts towering upward in pairs along the *Cyclops'* great length gave the collier the incongruous appearance of a huge sailing schooner. A generous sixty-five-foot beam was designed to lend further stability.

The *Cyclops* started her seaborne life under a dark omen, in the estimation of superstitious sea folk. Mrs. Walter H. Groves, daughter-in-law of Henry S. Groves, president of William Cramp and Sons, Philadelphia, the *Cyclops'* builder, splintered her champagne bottle into glittering fragments on the collier's broad starboard bow. The crowd cheered, but the ship would not budge.

Shipwrights, in pique and embarrassment, hurried beneath her keel, straining against the additional jacks by means of which they hoped to ease the mountainous burden off the ways. For ten long, agonized minutes the timber creaked, the men sweated—and cursed mutedly—while lovely Mrs. Groves fingered her orchid and forlornly held onto the broken neck of the champagne bottle. She seemed to be wondering if—just possibly —she had not swung it hard enough.

Then, to the consummate relief of everyone, the *Cyclops* emitted a rasping screech and slid into the muddy Delaware River like a giant sea lion. Now the rain, which had been threatening, began. The Philadelphia *Public Ledger* reported the next morning, Sunday, May 8, 1910:

MONSTER COLLIER

CYCLOPS LAUNCHED

That November, Worley guided her to sea. Like his other colliers, the *Cyclops* and her crew of semi-wild men had to be reined constantly and with unfaltering determination.

In spite of technical innovations and her vaunted ballast tanks, the *Cyclops* tended to cavort like a mustang when heavily or improperly loaded, though she could carry 10,000 tons of coal. Her roll was once clocked at forty-seven degrees.

However, the *Cyclops* proved herself from the start a valuable and efficient vessel—as long as there were sailors of strong fiber and stomach to stick with her. Samuel Dowdy, who had

Commander George Worley, his wife Selma, and daughter Virginia on deck of his ship, the *Cyclops*. A heavy drinker and tough fighter, Worley was a devoted family man.

served on her as chief engineer, wrote in the July, 1915, *American Marine Engineer* an article headed, "Splendid Record of U. S. Naval Auxiliary Ship *Cyclops*."

Lieutenant Dowdy pointed out that the big vessel could coal a squadron of dreadnoughts, plus ten torpedo destroyers for a cruise of 4,000 miles. She had already won the coaling record for the fleet: 574 tons to the battleship *Arkansas* in one hour flat, without a pause.

Worley's eccentricities, meanwhile, increased. He became a naval legend in his time. Some of his crewmen swore that their captain, in alcoholic rages, had chased them about the decks of the *Cyclops*. Lieutenant Mahlon Tisdale, an Annapolis graduate who once performed temporary duty on the collier, witnessed Worley standing, massive wrench in hand, at the entrance to an engine room hatch. Rough seas, projecting the ship into a series of snap rolls, had panicked the coal heavers who were trying to rush topside.

There were those, however, who could endorse Worley's own boast, "I treat 'em like a father!" He had been known to lend the sailors shoes, oilskins or underwear, even money when needed. For the thirsty, there was always a bottle of beer in the master's ice-chest, or even a slug of whisky.

Charles S. Ashby, Jr., of Norfolk, was one of those whom Worley treated like a son. The commander of the *Cyclops* saw something of himself in the slightly built eighteen-year-old seaman recruit who had once knocked a husky bos'n's mate onto the deck for calling him a liar! Worley not only removed the bos'n's mate but made a point of granting extra shore leaves to Ashby thereafter.

Outbursts of Worley's unique humor on several occasions brought testy dispatches from a literal-minded Navy Department. Once a petulant demand caught up with the *Cyclops* from the chief of naval operations, which began:

TO MASTER, *Cyclops*
SUBJECT: lion aboard

You are hereby ordered to remove at once . . . !

Worley, in the taverns along the Atlantic Ocean, had convinced his wide-eyed listeners that he did not "keep no goddamn pussy cat on my ship!" Instead, he had boasted, he harbored a tame lion, gift of an African chieftain.

There was about as much truth to this yarn as to a much older and more hallowed one involving Ponce de León and the fountain of youth. Not content, however, at having pulled the navy's leg about jungle animals, he let it be known that the kaiser himself had once come aboard in Kiel, inspected the collier, and left. The kaiser had, Worley said, praised the machinery as well as Commander Worley's superb management of this "smart ship."

Worley's apparent affection for his homeland did him no good after the outbreak of war in Europe. His admiration was outspoken for the German Army and Navy. He spent considerable time drinking with the officers of interned or tied-up German ships and entertained them in his new brick home in one of Norfolk's better residential districts. For Worley, his house was most conveniently located. It was within walking distance of the Norfolk and Western Railway's coal piers, where the *Cyclops* regularly filled her capacious bellies, and of the ferry across the Elizabeth River to the Portsmouth Navy Yard, the collier's berth.

Worley was especially friendly with the officers of the erstwhile raider, *Prinz Eitel Friedrich*, interned in the same naval yard. Worley, in fact, intelligence reports were to note, appeared "to act more or less as sponsor to masters of interned German ships."

A neighbor, Charles Ayledotte, once complained that George Worley had upbraided him for defending the Allied cause. And a yeoman on the *Cyclops*, Paul Roberts, was shocked at Commander Worley's "hilarious" reaction to successive German victories. It was Roberts' duty to keep the master informed of daily news dispatches.

Especially unusual was George Worley's habit of socializing and confiding in selected crewmen, while ignoring his fellow officers. An oiler, Otto Fink, who had been a German army reservist, was an especial friend of Worley's. However, their tête-à-têtes in the master's cabin were assumed to be inspired by nothing more sinister than a mutual thirst.

When America entered the war, George Worley could no longer *prosit!* with his interned friends. He went to France with the first convoy, carrying the First Division. But after returning from St.-Nazaire in late July, the *Cyclops*, peculiarly enough, made no more voyages across "the big pond."

Worley's conduct or reported conduct on his one crossing resulted in a petition to the Navy Department by certain of his crew members for an investigation. Dr. Burt Asper, the assistant surgeon, apparently spearheaded the complaints, a factor which caused the captain to protest that he was "a victim of a plot on the part of certain officers and men on board the *Cyclops*."

"... no more baffling mystery ..." • 223

Serious accusations were bounced off Worley's tough hide: he had endangered his command in the submarine zone by showing lights and also through his "continual" inebriety; he had rigged up an unorthodox light atop one mast which, some sailors speculated, could be used for signaling U-boats; he had threatened to run his ship into Rotterdam and deliver it to the Germans. . . .

And then there were those, including the ship's paymaster, Ensign Carroll G. Page, a quiet-mannered, sensitive Vermonter, who testified that he had always "gotten along well" with Worley. Ensign Page, emphasizing that the collier carried "one of the toughest crews," expressed his conviction that "a very hard-boiled captain" was needed. The paymaster for one had "a great deal of respect for Captain Worley's ability."

In his defense, Worley wrote to the Navy Department: "I do not believe that the evidence in this case is sufficient to send a stray dog to the pound, much less sufficient to request the removal of a commanding officer who has been in the Auxiliary Service for 17 years. . . ."

The inquiry found that Worley *did* drink too much, probably showed "favoritism" in granting shore liberty, but did not use insulting language or chase his crewmen at gunpoint, as charged by a few subordinates. And if, indeed, too many summary courts or punishments of confinement with bread and water appeared on the *Cyclops'* log, these entries were likely not disproportionate to those on similar vessels of the transport service, or even in the navy's ships of the line. Besides, this was war, and masters were needed to run "tough" ships.

The inquiry was at an end; the books were closed. Even so, the *Cyclops* was kept tethered within hailing distance of east coast naval bases. She coaled navy ships from Nova Scotia to the Carolinas. Her removal from the "Atlantic Train" was somewhat surprising in view of the growing "bridge to France." Ships of every size and function were needed, especially colliers.

However, the *Cyclops* was rushed north to Halifax with coal, emergency food, and medical supplies after the explosion, December 6, of the ammunition ship *Mont Blanc* in the Nova

Scotian port. The blow-up had devastated much of the city. While in Halifax, Worley fell, aggravating an old hernia to such extent that he could not walk without leaning on a cane.

When he came home to Norfolk, he told his wife and his eleven-year-old daughter, Virginia, a real "daddy's girl," that he would undergo an operation after his next voyage, followed, he hoped, by a year's leave. Worley had never been sick in his life. Even at her tender age, little Virginia thought her father was showing "real panic at the thought of having an operation."

He made tentative arrangements for leasing or selling his house and motoring back to Port Orchard for a vacation after his surgery. This in itself was surprising since Worley—who could handle one of the largest ships on the seven seas— had never learned to drive an automobile, or even a team of horses!

George Worley was singularly gloomy this Christmas season, 1917. He limped about on his cane and uttered melancholy thoughts like a man condemned.

Then, just before New Year's Day, the *Cyclops* received orders to shake off the soot of the industrial Norfolk area and put to sea. Running as a merchantman, she would deliver coal to Brazil and bring back a commercial cargo of manganese. She would be under charter to the United States and Brazil Steamship Company. The ore itself was consigned to the United States Steel Products Company, a subsidiary of the United States Steel Corporation.

The South American Shipping Company, of 78 Broad Street, New York, had arranged the transaction—at a purchase price of $15 a ton—with the navy. This importer in turn represented the E. G. Fontes Company, of Rio de Janeiro, listed as owner of the Morre de Mina Mines where the manganese originated.

A subdued, melancholy Commander Worley bade good-bye to his friends on January 7. To one of them, Samuel Harris, a jeweler, he said, "Harris, this may be the last time you will see me. I may be buried at sea."

Harris thought the remark singularly odd.

There were other circumstances. His daughter, Virginia,

was sick with the measles, for the third time. *If* he lingered at home, he could conceivably be quarantined. But he did not linger. . . .

On January 8, the *Cyclops* crunched through the surface ice of Hampton Roads, showing her forests of kingposts and her broad stern to the half-frozen buoys of Chesapeake Bay. Ahead were the gray combers of the winter Atlantic.

Across the same ocean all was quiet on the equally frigid and sometimes frozen western front. Russia was out of the war, torn internally by revolution. But the calm of early 1918 only masked the final massive drives soon to be launched: on the one side, a burgeoning victory push, on the other, the death throes of the nearly vanquished.

Just two weeks later, on January 22, the *Cyclops* swept past the ancient cannons of Fort Gamboa, then let go her long rusty anchor chains—down, down to the hard bottom of Bahia harbor. She had rounded the great bulge in Brazil's coastline, unchallenged by U-boats. Below decks, however, a menace apparently more implacable than the Germans continued to bob along in the *Cyclops'* unhappy wake—morale troubles.

"If I get back, I'll ask to get off *this* ship," Burt Asper wrote to his physician brother in Chambersburg. There were other similar laments.

William Wolf, a seaman, went ashore to write a more oblique letter. It was to his mother, Mrs. L. F. Wolf, of Chase Street, Baltimore. "Will be down here some time for guard duty. Now will be away until next year. We are going across from Brazil. Will." He dated it, "Palace Hotel, Bahia, January 23."

The *Cyclops* took on bunker coal within forty-eight hours and continued to Rio where she arrived January 28. The afternoon of the preceding day, just a few hours steaming from her destination, Lieutenant (jg) Louis J. Fingleton, twenty-five-year-old Portsmouth, New Hampshire, reservist, was on engineer watch when he heard a noise in the starboard engine. A former government tug crewman, Fingleton listened with mild interest and curiosity, but did nothing.

Within minutes, the high pressure steam cylinder, a massive juggernaut of machinery, burst into fragments. While the volume of the explosion caused the fo'c'sle watch to think the collier had been torpedoed, no one—miraculously—had been hurt in the engine room.

Upon reconstructing the accident, it appeared that one of the stud bolts had broken, causing the first rattle. This had set off a chain reaction, ruining the major portion of a piston engine. This huge machine could not be repaired until the *Cyclops* returned to Norfolk or Philadelphia. While the ship was designed to operate on one engine, her speed would be reduced and her navigability impaired.

An investigation was ordered by the commander in chief of the Pacific Fleet, Admiral William R. Caperton. In turn, Caperton instructed Captain George B. Bradshaw, the hard-bitten commander of his principal vessel and flagship, the armored cruiser *Pittsburgh*, to take charge of the inquiry. Texas-born "Black Jack" Bradshaw, Annapolis '89, was tall and moustached, an implacable disciplinarian whose volcanic temper made him the scourge of his every command. Conceivably frustrated because keel-hauling had long been outlawed as a punishment, he resorted to make-do's such as locking offenders in nonventilated, darkened storerooms.

Black Jack was in every respect the match for George Worley. And yet, when the *Cyclops'* master limped aboard, supporting himself with his cane, the *Pittsburgh's* captain looked down at him with mingled surprise and contempt.

"Is this man feeble, recuperating from a hangover, or what?" asked Bradshaw, himself a semireformed drinker. How, his own officers replied, had such a rough-appearing specimen obtained a commission even in a naval auxiliary service?

At least, Bradshaw could push along the inquiry and then speed this wretched character and his dirty ship on their way. He presented Worley with the formal orders:

Use every effort to expedite your departure. In case of any delay, inform the Commander-in-Chief immediately, and confer with the Naval Attaché, Rio.

While her cargo of coal was being unloaded and the manganese dumped aboard as successive holds were emptied, there were singular outbursts within the New York firm which had arranged the ore transaction. Franz Hohenblatt, the agent with the South American Shipping Company who had actually signed the papers selling the heavy mineral, in a drunken confidence, swore to a fellow employee, Harry Lambert: "Damn every one of them!"

Hohenblatt, a German alien who had taken out only his first citizenship papers, was referring sweepingly to others in the same export agency.

"They should be shot!" he postscripted, vehemently, in his thick English. "They are fools for fighting for this country!" Then he expressed regrets that the entry of the United States into the conflict had made it impossible for him to return and fight for his fatherland.

Lambert, a conservative, cautious individual, debated whether he should tell somebody about the odd, violent remarks. Then he decided he had better keep quiet. After all, if he possessed such a combustible temper, Hohenblatt might do something to *him*.

Meanwhile, officers of the Bureau of Construction and Repair in the Navy Department read with increasing dismay a cablegram, dated February 4, from the *Pittsburgh*'s board of investigation:

The main engines of the *Cyclops* are not in a satisfactory condition as regards lost motion in working parts, and the engine rooms are filled with noises from the main engines while underway.

While the flagship's board of investigation had not exhumed evidence of sabotage, Lieutenant Fingleton was blamed for not having stopped the starboard engine when he first heard the knock. Had he done so, there would have been merely a broken bolt to replace, instead of an entire engine.

However, the accident—if accident it had been—was history. The *Cyclops* must limp home on her one good engine. The board believed the big collier could make it back to Cramp's yard, where she had been constructed, for a new cylinder and other parts. The question of whether the slow-to-react Fingleton should face a court-martial was left to the discretion of his home base at Portsmouth, Virginia.

The office of Naval Operations replied in effect to dump the cargo aboard and hurry home, instructing the commander in chief of the Pacific Fleet:

Advise William Lowry, 36 Rou da Candalaria Rio, expected readiness *Cyclops* load manganese. When loaded inform department sailing date and expected arrival Baltimore.

Black Jack Bradshaw saw to it that Lowry was informed. Then he had to haul anchor and get the *Pittsburgh* on with her patrol. She sailed, while the *Cyclops* was still loading, for the Plate River. Actually, the Pacific Fleet, too diminutive to be a true fighting force, had been created for the primary purpose of intercepting German agents, believed to be still running between Spain and South America. Since Brazil was the only belligerent among these countries, the huge continent's many neutral ports provided "safe" bases for a broad category of agents, from wireless operators to saboteurs who would continue their already proven aptitude for placing time bombs on outgoing Allied ships.

Ensign William Granat,* of the *Pittsburgh*, had assisted in apprehending two men, labeled as German agents. One he removed from an inbound Spanish passenger steamer and took back to his cruiser where the man was questioned for several days before being sent eastward again on the same neutral vessel.

The Brazilian government had long been aware of German influence in South America. And the previous September it had been discovered that Count Karl von Luxburg, the German chargé d'affaires in Buenos Aires, had been transmitting marine intelligence in the Swedish legation's own diplomatic code via Stockholm to Berlin. Von Luxburg had suggested to his neutral host that her ships ought to be "sunk without trace." Then, said he, who would know the culprit?

Everyone assumed that a thriving sabotage ring survived von Luxburg's prompt expulsion. Public demonstrations against the aggressive German population erupted in Argentina, Uruguay, and Brazil. Now, in early 1918, it was announced that "extreme measures to stamp out Prussianism in Brazil forever"

*Now Rear Admiral Granat, U.S.N. (Ret.), of Washington, D.C.

were being adopted, including taking German businesses under government control, teaching Portuguese in German schools, and possibly even closing Rio's popular German Club where the crash of beer steins and lusty *"prosits!"* reverberated late into most nights. The German Club competed with the local, boisterous Highlife Club (pronounced "Heegie-Liffey") where sailors drank, brawled, and made arrangements with the local gulls around the clock. In fact, in Highlife's steaming vortex a sailor from the *Cyclops* had brought down a wine bottle atop the head of a shipmate, killing him—thereby adding to the investigative woes of the already dismayed and harassed Black Jack Bradshaw.

In the last days of January, Worley wrote to his in-laws in Port Orchard, revealing an obsessive preoccupation with his health:

I am in hopes to get back safe and then go to the Norfolk hospital. . . . I feel that I am sick and if I don't take it in hand now, I may be laid up for a long time. As it stands now, the doctor tells me there is nothing to worry about it, but that I ought to get away from the ship life for at least a year. Selma and I talked it over and we concluded to sell our home in Norfolk and come out your way and never to leave again . . . I'll try my damndest to keep in good spirits. I did feel so bad leaving house with Virginia in bed. . . . I get to thinking about it and then it completely upsets me for a long time. . . . Our trip down here was rather pleasant but it gets tiresome, this running without lights. . . . I don't believe that another man lives who thinks more of his family than I do. . . . I worship the ground they walk on and if anything should happen to them I would surely lose my mind. The only thing that I look forth to now is the few months leave that I expect to get after leaving the hospital to recuperate. . . . I have no news regarding the war to write, only hope that the German people will soon see their error and hang the Kaiser and his whole followers and then have peace.

To Selma and Virginia he wrote in much the same vein, adding that "our starboard engine got completely on the bum and I was compelled to make port under our port engine, but made our destination in good shape." Reaffirming "I feel very blue," he noted that he was worried not only about his impending operation but about a routine eye and ear examination by the navy. "I feel sure," he observed, "that, should I be turned down on account of my eyesight, they will find something for me to do; if not, we will not starve after all. . . ." He went on to avow to his wife, "I am still as much in love with you as the very beginning of our married life, in fact more so, if that is possible. . . ."

In a last-minute decision, a civilian passenger was packed aboard the *Cyclops*: Alfred Louis Moreau Gottschalk, forty-five-year-old United States consul general in Rio. The native-born New Yorker had been a correspondent in the Spanish-American War for the *New York Herald* and the London *Telegraph*. He had then tried sugar planting in Santo Domingo and Haiti before entering the United States foreign service in 1902.

Gottschalk had acquired the reputation of exceeding diplomatic requirements in cooperating with German firms in Brazil. It was also widely believed that he had dispatched funds through a Berlin branch bank, ostensibly to the German Red Cross.

Concerning the man himself, a naval intelligence report had observed, with doubtful charity: "He is a man of no integrity of character, a man given to misrepresentation and lying according as it suited his purpose. He is unscrupulous, and a man who used every effort to further his own interest. He spent his vacations in Berlin."

Otherwise, Gottschalk was a fine choice to represent the United States in South America's largest country. Perhaps surprisingly, the consul had informed associates in the diplomatic colony that he was going to enlist in the army as soon as he had attended to his affairs in his apartment at 178 West 81st Street, in New York City. He had not said *which* army.

It somehow did not add up—as indeed little did, where the *Cyclops* was involved.

At 9 A.M. Saturday, February 16, the collier sailed from Rio, with 10,800 tons of manganese. The ore, together with 1,000 tons added to her coal bunkers, had pushed the *Cyclops* fifteen inches over her Plimsoll or normal cargo line. This meant that the huge ship was drawing thirty-one feet, as much as a battleship—or the height of a three-story house. This below-water depth, however, would help ensure a relatively roll-free passage.

". . . no more baffling mystery . . ." • 231

Even if so large a vessel—now grossing over 20,000 tons—was sent into war-torn seas with inadequate propulsion, her cargo was well insured—for a half million dollars—thus amply protecting the investment of the United States Steel Products Company, if not necessarily the navy's investment in the collier.

On February 20, the *Cyclops* returned to Bahia, where this time she took on seventy-two service passengers from the *Raleigh*. They included navy and marine corps officers and men, mostly returning for leave, mustering out, or rotation of duty from South American waters and the Pacific Fleet. Only a very few were facing disciplinary action or bad conduct discharges. In fact, according to one of the *Raleigh*'s officers,* the homebound men were "among the finest I have ever seen in the navy—excellent sailors. They could take a ship through anything."

The *Cyclops* counted 309 persons on board, crew and passengers, including the civilian Gottschalk.

The deck watch on the *Raleigh* logged the *Cyclops* out of Bahia Harbor and past Point San Antonio at 6:25 P.M., February 21. Then the cruiser cabled Naval Operations the *Cyclops'* destination and estimated arrival: "Baltimore, Md., March 7."

Through calm seas she plowed ahead at a remarkable average of ten knots. On March 3, the *Cyclops* raised the island of Barbados, and soon was feeling her way into the cramped harbor of Bridgetown, taking fixes on Pelican Island on the port beam and the big clock tower behind Needham Point to starboard.

Worley ordered an additional 800 tons of bunker coal, (although with one engine "compounded" the *Cyclops* was consuming less than forty tons a day), plus 180 tons of provisions. The American consul at this sweltering British West Indian possession, Brockholst Livingston (a great-grandson of one of the early Supreme Court justices of the same name), thought the supplies to be excessive.

"Why don't you wait for Baltimore, or any east coast port?" Livingston suggested. "The rates are much cheaper."

Commander Worley, however, was in a strange, fevered rush. He did not even make the customary call on the British

---

*Now Captain Francis S. Gibson, U.S.N. (Ret.).

port officer, Lieutenant Harold Holdsworth, and thereby gave offense to this representative of His Majesty's Navy. And just to uphold the dignity of an old and proud service, Lieutenant Holdsworth refused, in turn, to come aboard the *Cyclops* for his own courtesies and routine offer of assistance.

The morning of Monday, March 4, Worley scribbled to Naval Operations:

Arrived Barbados, West Indies, 17303 for bunker coal. Arrive Baltimore, Md., 12013. Notify Office Director Naval Auxiliaries. Comdr. Train (Atl.) 07004

Class 3   USS *Cyclops*
DNAS
                                        1145 AM   3-4-18

The collier showed her stern to Bridgetown, heading westward in an Atlantic that was as blue and calm as the Caribbean Sea. Soon, to the watchers ashore, there was nothing left of the *Cyclops* but a smudge of coal smoke on the horizon, and the hazy memory of another of many ships which had come and then departed as secretly as possible in the wartime hurry and confusion.

March moved on. The Germans stepped up trench-raiding in the Chemin des Dames and Lorraine sectors, primarily to test the strength of the new defenders, the Yanks. The latter, bloodied in the increasingly active operations near the Aisne, returned the challenge by tearing savagely into the kaiser's positions near Lunéville on the Toul front.

Warfare against civilians was also increased this spring of 1918. Before the first week of March was out, zeppelins dumped a cargo of bombs on the English east coast, and German planes left 100 dead after a raid on Paris. British airmen zoomed angrily aloft to plaster Koblenz in one of the heaviest aerial attacks of the war.

England renewed her pleas to American industry: "Send us more ships!" However, her losses continued to drop as mines, Allied destroyers, airplanes, and blimps took mounting toll of the U-boats. Germany had lost sixty-five undersea raiders in 1917, twenty so far in 1918. Considering the time, effort, and expense required to build one of the highly complex craft, Germany could not indefinitely endure this attrition.

More and more Allied merchantmen were being armed. Whether they were or not, the convoy system was providing an ever tighter defense against torpedoing. Fast steamers, able to sprint alone, were proving almost every week their incredible nerve when attacked. Early in March, for example, navy gunners on the cargo ship *Nyansa* fought a U-boat for two and a half hours, until the raider quit the contest and limped home.

With Russia out of the war, the Allies were seeking some way of isolating her key centers from Bolshevik control. There was some agitation for Japan to occupy Vladivostok, but Wilson opposed the plan on idealistic grounds. Underscoring the end of a long imperial era, the Russian capital was moved from St. Petersburg to Moscow.

Along the east coast of the United States the weather was warm and rainy, the ocean calm. Spring storms, except off New England, were strangely absent. The days ticked on.

On March 13, the young duty officer in Naval Operations, Washington, scanning his plot board, noticed that the *Cyclops* was due in port this Wednesday. He sent a routine query sparking from the lofty wireless towers of the navy in nearby Arlington, Virginia:

OPNAV TO *Cyclops*

S.C. Cipher #1 Report probable date arrival in Baltimore, Md. 17013

No answer was received. Strangely enough, the navy did not react for five more days. On March 18, the *Pittsburgh*, still at anchor off Rio, was asked how much coal was aboard the *Cyclops* when she departed South American waters. The Pacific Fleet flagship acknowledged:

Am inquiring of USS *Raleigh* and will report as soon as possible.

"CINCPAC," the commander in chief of the Pacific Fleet, advised the Navy Department two days later:

234 • "... no more baffling mystery ..."

U. S. Navy

The disappearance of the *Cyclops,* one of the most baffling events of the war, occurred in the spring of 1918. No trace of the collier, her crew, or cargo has ever been found. With 309 men on board, the *Cyclops* was the U.S. Navy's greatest loss in the war.

My sixteen five eighteen commanding officer USS *Raleigh* reports that so far as he knew, USS *Cyclops* intended proceeding Baltimore direct 13220.

Time, unrecoverable, was slipping away these final days of March, like sand in an hour glass. On March 23, Saturday, the Sixth Naval District at Charleston, South Carolina, was asked to keep calling the *Cyclops* until she answered. On Sunday, the district replied to Naval Operations:

Have been unable to communicate with USS *Cyclops* by radio from 11 A.M. Saturday to 10 A.M. Sunday. Shall I continue attempting to converse?

The Navy Department at once replied that Charleston *should* keep trying to "converse." Belatedly, the cold fear was seizing the navy's officials that they had lost a ship—a big one, the biggest casualty yet. This same Sunday, March 24, three patrol vessels were ordered out of Guantanamo, Cuba, and all naval stations south of Norfolk, including Key West, San Juan, and St. Thomas, the Virgin Islands, were ordered:

Continue efforts to communicate with *Cyclops* . . . determine her position.

On March 28, St. Thomas admitted: "No information regarding USS *Cyclops*."

The same Thursday, the Navy Department received a message from Brockholst Livingston, American consul at Barbados:

Nothing is known here whereabouts *Cyclops* since departure March 4. Cannot account for nonarrival at destination. Have asked the colonial governor institute wireless search West Indies waters.

Naval Operations then advised the *Pittsburgh*:

USS *Cyclops* left Barbados March 4 for Baltimore. Overdue since March 13. Unable get into communication with her by radio or to obtain any information as to her whereabouts.

Slowly, the Royal Navy, preoccupied with its own war, turned fitful attention to the missing American collier. The senior officer at Kingston, Jamaica, on March 29, advised the Admiralty, London:

Governor Barbados informs me that USS *Cyclops* sailed from Barbados for Baltimore 4th March. Has not yet arrived at desination.

On March 31, Admiral Benson, the hard-boiled chief of Naval Operations, told Admiral Sims in London:

For your information USS *Cyclops* loaded with manganese out of Rio de Janeiro, Brazil, touched at and sailed from Barbados 4th March for Hampton Roads, Virginia. No. 1 engine compounded. Weather that vicinity [garbled transmission] since date of departure.

Nothing has been heard of that vessel since sailing. Searching vessels and radio unable to communicate with or locate USS *Cyclops.*

April came. The navy, assuming the *Cyclops* was probably gone, started a feverish investigation. Families of all those known to be aboard the collier were queried about recent letters they might have received, especially from South America or Barbados. What about Worley? Or German sympathizers in the crew? Could *Cyclops* have been seized after a mutiny and abducted to an enemy rendezvous? Or could the captain himself have sailed the ship to Germany, without a mutiny? No possibility was considered too preposterous to be overlooked.

Intelligence officers, routinely visiting the offices of the South American Shipping Company, in lower Manhattan, asked for Franz Hohenblatt, who had arranged for the cargo of ore. They got a jolt. He was gone.

Harry Lambert, the fellow worker who had been appalled at Hohenblatt's pro-German attitude, revealed that Hohenblatt, not yet a citizen, had told of burning 700 letters he had received from Germany. "They won't get anything on me!" he had asserted.

Now Hohenblatt had disappeared, leaving no trace—at his apartment, place of employment, anywhere. He had vanished as though he had never existed.

Then, from the American consul in Barbados, a provocative dispatch arrived at both the Navy and State Departments. Brockholst Livingston had continued his investigation. He wrote:

Master *Cyclops* stated that required 600 tons coal, having sufficient on board to reach Bermuda. Engines very poor condition. Not sufficient funds and therefore requested payment by me. I have ascertained he took here ton fresh meat, ton flour, thousand pounds vegetables, paying therefor 775 dollars. From different sources I have learned the following: he had plenty of coal, alleged inferior, took coal probably more than 1500 tons. Master alluded to by others as a damned Dutchman apparently disliked by other officers. Rumor trouble en route here, men confined, one executed, also conspiracies. Some prisoners from fleet in Brazilian waters, one with life sentence.*

*The "life sentence" may have referred to the sailor who had been involved in the Highlife homicide.

U. S. Consul General Gottschalk, passenger, 221 crew exclusive of officers and passengers. Have names of crew but not of all officers and passengers. Many German names appear. Number telegraphic or wireless messages addressed to master or in care of ship were delivered to this port. All telegrams for Barbados on file head office St. Thomas.

Admiral Benson read the dispatch, scratched his grizzled chin, then reread it. Soon, he had it tapping out to London, priority, with his own postscript to Sims:

I have to suggest scrutinizing . . . while not having definite grounds, I fear fate worse than sinking though possibly based on instinctive dislike felt towards master.

On April 20, a Naval Intelligence memorandum echoed Benson in weighing Consul Livingston's dramatic report against his "possibly . . . instinctive dislike" toward Worley. It theorized that "the most probable hypothesis of explaining the disappearance of the *Cyclops* is that she had a magazine explosion."

No serious search of the Bahamas and Caribbean area was instituted until nearly mid-April. Finally, on April 15, when the *Cyclops* had been overdue more than a month, the navy decided to let the public in on what was gravely troubling it. "No well-founded reason can be given to explain the *Cyclops'* being overdue, as no radio communication with or trace of her has been had since leaving the West Indian port," stated the announcement. After noting some details of the ship itself and her passenger list, the statement concluded, "The Navy Department feels extremely anxious for her safety."

With surprising rapidity, rumors spread through the nation's newspapers that Worley, being of German birth, had either scuttled his big command or sailed her to Germany or to some rendezvous with the Imperial Navy, now commanded by Admiral von Hipper.

This suggestion was naturally disturbing to Mrs. Worley.

"Do you think," she told reporters, "my husband would prove traitor to his wife and little daughter? My husband was an American through and through." She then added that some unidentified informant had advised her that the *Cyclops* was safe.

238 • " . . . no more baffling mystery . . ."

MEMBER OF THE ASSOCIATED PRESS

Virginian-Pilot
AND THE NORFOLK LANDMARK

VOL. LXII. NO. 15.   NORFOLK, VA., MONDAY, APRIL 15, 1918.   TEN PAGES   THREE CENTS PER COPY.

Today's Weather

ENTIRE ALLIED LINE IS HOLDING FIRM;
PERSHING'S MEN SCORE; CYCLOPS OVERDUE

SAMMIES REPULSE VIOLENT TEUTON ATTACKS ON BOTH TOUL AND ST. MIHIEL LINES

American Infantry Carry Fight To Enemy On Banks Of Meuse With Bayonets And Grenades, In Hand-To-Hand Fighting

FRENCH COMMANDER COMMENDS TROOPS FOR GREAT GALLANTRY

One Detachment, Completely Surrounded By Enemy, Fight Their Way Through And Successfully Return To Trenches

With the American Army in France, April 14.—(By The Associated Press.)—Preceded by an intense bombardment of high explosives and poison gas shellplaated troops from four German companies hurled themselves against the American positions on the right bank of the Meuse north of St. Mihiel early this morning, but were completely repulsed after terrific hand-to-hand fighting.

Sammies Carry Battle To Hun Enemies

French Commander Praises Men For Bravery

Graphic Story Of Fighting About Toul

American Naval Collier Probably Lost; Fate May Be Another Mystery Of Sea

57 PASSENGERS, 15 OFFICERS AND 221 MEN ABOARD

Due In Atlantic Port March 13, Last Reported March 4, Cyclops Missing

ENROUTE HOME WITH MANGANESE CARGO

Commander, Several Officers And Enlisted Men From Norfolk And Vicinity

BIG NAVAL COLLIER CYCLOPS, overdue at an Atlantic port since March 13, and Lieutenant Commander G. W. Worley, of Norfolk, commander of the vessel.

JUST NINETEEN PER CENT OF BIG LOAN IN SIGHT

St. Louis Leads Federal Reserve District In Proportion Of Quota Subscribed

GREATER MOMENTUM TO DRIVE NECESSARY

ANOTHER DRAFT CALL FOR 49,843

To Mobilize May 1 To 10 And Will Be Sent To 11 Forts And Barracks

VIRGINIA'S QUOTA WILL REACH 756

PARIS SHELLED DAY AND NIGHT

Long Range Gun Turned On French Capital After Dark For First Time

100 WOMEN AND 150 MEN ARRESTED

Men On Cyclops From Norfolk And Vicinity

American Officers Down Hun Planes

Brought To Earth By Well Placed Shots And Both Enemy Aviators Made Prisoners

NEW YORK AGAIN STAGES BIG RAID

All Night Restaurants And White Light District Visited By Swann's Men

SENATOR STONE DIES AT CAPITAL

Passes Into Coma On Second Cerebral Hemorrhage And Fails To Rally

FIRST ATTACK LAST WEDNESDAY

IN VAIN BOCHE RECKLESSLY HURLS MEN AGAINST BRITISH TO GAIN INCH OF GROUND

Region About Neuve Eglise Scene Of Most Obstinate Battles Throughout Saturday Night And Sunday

THOUSANDS OF GERMAN DEAD LYING BEFORE BRITISH POSITIONS

Enemy Unable To Mount Stone Wall Of Defense Or Penetrate Allied Lines, But To Reverse Are Meeting With Repulses

The entire allied line in Belgium and France is holding firm.

British Defenders Insurmountable Stone Wall

Looks Like Tide of Battle Ready to Turn

Numerous Enemy Attacks Repulsed

Virginian-Pilot

The loss of the collier *Cyclops* was not announced until April 15, more than a month after she was due to arrive in Baltimore.

Where?

Neither Mrs. Worley nor anyone else could answer that. Selma Worley could not long endure the insistent questions of reporters and investigators and the accusing looks of neighbors. On May 7 she turned the key in the lock of her Norfolk home for the last time. She started westward with Virginia, for Port Orchard and a new life.*

On June 1 the *Cyclops* was declared lost and all aboard her legally dead. The signer of the marine obituary was Franklin D. Roosevelt, acting secretary of the navy.

On December 25, 1918, Admiral Sims, still in London, cabled a final amen to any theory thàt the *Cyclops* had been lost through enemy action:

From full report of Admiral Goette to Allied Naval Armistice Commission regarding loss of USS *Cyclops*, it is definite that neither German U-boats nor German mines come into the question. The only information regarding the loss of USS *Cyclops* is that emanating from American sources which state the ship left Barbados in March, 1918, and has not been heard of since.

Neither of these requiems, however, was sufficient to staunch the rumors that flowed on and on. The collier had been torpedoed by a Brazilian destroyer. She was variously at Kiel, at Antwerp, in the Adriatic, off Colombia, in Antarctica—a vertible flying Dutchman of the World War. Bottles with messages purportedly from the sinking *Cyclops* washed ashore from Puget Sound southward, and through the Gulf up along east coast ports to Bar Harbor, Maine. When checked, the names scribbled inside did not represent anyone on board.

Planking, an imagined life preserver or two inscribed with the name *Cyclops*, even an entire barnacled wreck on an isolated Bahamian key were reported to the Navy Department. Most of these fragments—of illusion—were seriously investigated to no avail. As late as 1920, a destroyer was dispatched to Riding Rock Key, in the Bahamas, to search for what was allegedly the entire

---

*Mrs. Worley married Robert Stanton, a grocer in another Bremerton suburb, in 1921. She died in 1957, without ever learning what had happened to her first husband.

hull of the *Cyclops*. Only the familiar flotsam of the South Atlantic was found on Riding Rock's glistening white sands.

Perhaps the most elaborate theory concerned a "disappearing fortress," a kind of battleship-submarine, mounting turrets, which supposedly surfaced long enough to blow the *Cyclops* out of the water with salvos of 15-inch shells. The *American Weekly* and other publications seized on this fable and embellished it with imaginative illustrations reminiscent of a crossbreed of the *Arabian Nights* and Jules Verne.

A contributor to *The National Marine*, George Noble, delivered himself of the ultimate preposterous theory. He wrote:

"About the only possible explanation incapable of contradiction is that gargantuan squids—monster cuttlefish treated of in fiction and in fact—may have reared themselves out of the sea and, instead of winding their tentacles around the hulls and rigging and crushing the structure to matchwood before dragging it to their lair at the bottom, may have helped themselves to the ship's people as delicately and effectually as one plucks gooseberries off a bush."

Secretary Daniels personally replied, in whimsical vein, to an astrologer who had offered his services in divining the fate and location of the *Cyclops*. Poems appeared. One, of considerable length, commenced:

> Perhaps she plies through Arctic wastes,
> On some dim quest with Franklin's men*
> Or sees a new Pacific's blue,
> As those on Darien. . . .

What, indeed, had become of the *Cyclops*?

The fact that not one ship, insofar as could be established, ever sighted the *Cyclops* on the last lap of her voyage from Buenos Aires to Baltimore suggests that she may have sunk within a few hours after clearing Barbados. Rough weather apparently played no role in the disaster. The German assertion that their navy did not sink or capture her will have to be accepted as true.

*The writer, T. H. Ferril, was referring to Sir John Franklin, lost in 1848 with all members of his 150-man Arctic expedition.

The suggestions that Worley kidnapped his big collier were fantastic. Had he been able to do so, how could he have eluded American and British patrols? From his conversations before leaving Norfolk, especially with reference to his last letters, there is little doubt that George Worley was a sick man, physically in need of surgery and sorely troubled in mind. Surely, he had no business making the last voyage and should have disqualified himself when he received the fatal orders. On the other hand, there seems no logical way to link the captain's health directly with the disappearance of his ship.

One of the most popular theories was that a sudden cargo shift, for reasons not fully clarified, turned the *Cyclops* turtle. Commander Mahlon S. Tisdale, for one, who once had served briefly on the collier, wrote in the *U. S. Naval Institute Proceedings* in support of his capsizing theory. A contributing complication, he mused, might have been open manholes, causing water to flood into the holds.

While the manganese—disproportionately heavy in relation to its bulk—was stored atop wooden dunnage in the holds, it was not divided by bulkheads to keep it from tumbling about. The ore in the holds tended to form peaks.

Conceivably, although Tisdale was not aware of the factor, the one properly functioning engine may have gone awry, or the steering mechanism could have jammed. Without the starboard propeller to compensate, the *Cyclops* may have heeled suddenly, thereby causing the manganese to tumble to one side, giving the vessel a list from which she was unable to recover.

The navy's own Bureau of Construction and Repair at that time, however, tended to be of an opposite mind. It ruled that "the amplitude of roll . . . would have been comparatively small." In other words, deep-loaded as she was, with proportionately less freeboard, the *Cyclops* nonetheless should have been stable.

Whether the engine breakdown was somewhere, somehow, in the chain of circumstances leading to tragedy, whether this was a "natural" occurrence or otherwise cannot be resolved. The navy board in Rio refused to speculate on the possibilities of sabotage.

Neither Lieutenant Fingleton, though not a very alert officer, nor any other engineer officer was implicated. A few twists of a wrench by any member of the "black gang" would have started the machinery tearing itself apart. No unusual skill, training, or brains were required.

That the *Cyclops* went down with incredible speed—probably within fifteen seconds—is attested by the fact that no SOS was ever received and not even the smallest parcel of wreckage, provenly from the collier, was ever found. According to Captain Francis S. Gibson, of Annapolis, a lieutenant on the *Raleigh* when the *Cyclops* called at Bahia, the collier must have "hit something at the wrong angle." He believes she plummeted down in ten, rather than fifteen, seconds.

For a time, significance was attached to a requiem notice in the always-full obituary pages of the Rio newspapers. Listing a mass to be said for the repose of the soul of Consul Gottschalk, "lost when the *Cyclops* was sunk at sea," the otherwise routine announcement was supposedly published at least a week before there had been any official word of the collier's disappearance. However, this trail, which might logically have led to enemy agents—for who else would possess prior knowledge—went suddenly cold when dates were rechecked. Actually, the notice had been published several days *after* the navy had announced the disappearance.

Even if this had proved to be a false scent, the suspicion had in all probability blundered in the right direction. The oversight and surprising degree of ineptitude lay in not exploring this exceedingly fertile tangent.

Strangely forgotten in the continuing hypotheses concerning the *Cyclops* is the climate of espionage and sabotage in which the huge ship cleared Rio. Ignored, even in Naval Intelligence's own investigation, was the fact that the United States Pacific Fleet had been designed primarily to protect our ships and sea-lanes, as well as those of our new ally Brazil, from enemy intrigue. Overlooked too was the fact that the *Pittsburgh* alone, in that very period, had intercepted two German agents.

The Germans had already proved themselves masters of cloak-and-dagger tactics and sabotage. A major achievement was their destruction of Black Tom Pier in New York harbor in the summer of 1916, when millions of dollars' worth of ammunition, the mile-long dock structure itself, warehouses, barges, ships, and trains had been blown sky-high. Prior to that, a group of professional plotters led by the dashing Captain Franz von Papen, military attaché at the German Embassy in Washington, had manufactured at least 400 ingenious fire bombs* deep in the sanctuary of the interned *Friedrich der Grosse* at Hoboken. These had caused fires, or more extensive destruction, including total loss, on forty outbound Allied merchant ships. Von Papen's group included the notorious saboteurs, Dr. Walter Scheele, Paul Koenig, Franz von Rintelen (who, romantically, thought of himself as "the dark invader") and Wolf von Igel.

And what was the connection of the shadowy Franz Hohenblatt, of the South American Shipping Company, who had disappeared after burning his 700 letters from Germany, saying, "They won't get anything on me!" Was the role of this German, who had arranged for the cargo, a mere coincidence? Did his liaison in Rio extend beyond the firm loading the ore, the E. G. Fontes Company?

The Italian Navy had, by official finding, lost two major battleships to Austrian saboteurs—the new, 22,000-ton dreadnought, *Leonardo da Vinci*, which blew up and sank at her Taranto pier, and the 13,400-ton *Benedetto Brin*, which burned for no apparently natural reason at her own mooring.

A few days after Christmas, 1915, the 13,500-ton armored British cruiser, *Natal*, caught fire and sank at Scapa Flow with heavy loss of life including her commanding officer, Captain E. P. C. Black. While the Admiralty closed its books on the *Natal* with the oblique finding, "defective powder," the feeling persists to this day that the cruiser was sabotaged.

Shortly before the *Cyclops* disappeared, a plot to dynamite ways at Hog Island in the Delaware River, the greatest emergency shipbuilding yard in the country, was broken at apparently

---

*These were the first "cigar" or "pencil" bombs, so-called from their shape. A hollow lead cylinder was filled with picric and sulphuric acid, with a copper disc separating the two chemicals. When the acid ate through the copper, the chemicals combined, ignited, and sent a tongue of flame spurting several inches through a wax plug.

the last minute. Hundreds of rounds of explosive were confiscated, but the agents themselves escaped.

It seems singular, at the very least, that the possibility of German marine sabotage was not considered seriously in the *Cyclops* case—particularly since a United States fleet had been created and dispatched to the South American east coast to meet that very threat. A pencil bomb in conjunction with a stick of dynamite in the manganese cargo could have blown a gaping hole in the side of the heavily laden collier and sunk her in a few seconds.

Chemists list manganese as "an extreme oxidizing agent." Mixed with coal dust, of which there was an oversupply in the *Cyclops'* holds, the ore becomes flammable. However, for combustion, a spark, flame, or flash explosion is needed.

Assuming that a secret agent had turned this trick and that he survived the war, there is no reason why he should ever have boasted of his sabotage, or why his government should have admitted inspiring such an example of *spurlos versenkt*. As a matter of fact, agents on their way to overseas assignments, especially in the British Isles and the Mediterranean underbelly of Europe, frequently were lost when the submarines transporting them were depth-charged and destroyed.

What had happened to the *Cyclops?*

She was the sixteenth United States Navy vessel, and the first steam propelled one, to vanish without a clue to her fate. The seventeen-gun frigate *Saratoga*, in 1780, had been the first to disappear.

Since to this day there are no physical clues, circumstantial evidence alone remains to be weighed. Many unlikely factors can be eliminated. That the big collier broke up in a storm is manifestly absurd on two counts: there was no storm, and the *Cyclops* had proved herself rugged in eight years of bucking North Atlantic gales. That she turned turtle all of a sudden is not much more reasonable. After all, new stabilizing tanks had been engineered into her design.

"Personally," wrote Dr. H. D. Stailey,* of Santa Rosa, Cali-

*In a letter to the author. The former Lieutenant Stailey was aboard the *Raleigh* in Bahia in 1918.

fornia, "I cling to the theory of an internal explosion from a bomb as the most likely cause . . . no radio messages re trouble were received by anyone; hence her radio was either out or there was no time to use it. What then? Something sudden and drastic. Some had the idea that she may have broken up in a storm, being heavily laden. This could hardly occur without her being able to send messages re the storm, unless her radio was out. Hence, my best conjecture would be an internal explosion—a bomb or boiler—and a rapid sinking."

His view is shared by other naval officers who watched the *Cyclops* lumber into oblivion and whose specific duty was to prevent sabotage on American ships by German agents.

Secretary Daniels wrote, "There is no more baffling mystery in the annals of the Navy than the disappearance of the USS *Cyclops*." Successive navy chieftains merely altered the frustrated phraseology of Josephus Daniels' amen: "The disappearance of the *Cyclops* is as baffling a mystery today as it was in March, 1918."

Tantalizing, vexing, yes. But, in retrospect, and now that naval intelligence files have finally been opened, is it really so "baffling"? Possibly a select few (including Franz Hohenblatt), if still alive, are in a position to answer this question.

(9)

Padlocking an Ocean—
the Great Mine Barrage

⊕ How could the Allies close the North Sea?

"Dig the Germans out of their holes like rats!" Winston Churchill suggested. He mirrored his nation's frustration at the manifest inability to lock up the German ports or otherwise stifle the U-boats. For more than half of 1918, merchant shipping losses averaged monthly a costly one third of a million tons.

Peppery Admiral Sims, seconding the former first lord of the Admiralty, added, "The way to destroy a swarm of hornets ... is to annihilate them in their nests, and not to hunt and attack them, one by one, after they have escaped into the open. What the situation needed was ... a swift and terrible blow which would end the submarine menace overnight!"

But what?

While convoys were generally effective, they were inherently defensive. Their primary purpose was to keep the U-boats away, rather than to ferret them out. The American coal-burning battleship squadron which steamed into European waters in early 1918 would be of no aid in this specialized type of sea warfare. Only once in fact did its skipper, Rear Admiral Hugh Rodman*

---

*Rodman, a gruffly humorous Kentuckian who was but sixteen when he entered the Naval Academy in 1875, became legend in the wardrooms of the Royal Navy, perhaps more for his naiveté than his seamanship. Paying a courtesy call upon Grand Admiral Beatty, who with Jellicoe, Scheer and von Hipper was among the highest ranking naval officers in the world, Rodman asserted, "I don't believe much in paper work. Whenever you have anything to bring to my attention, come and see me." Beatty in silent bemusement measured this very junior admiral, the "Uncle Hugh" of Panama Canal building days, then replied, "I'll do exactly that, Admiral."

aboard the modern 27,000-ton flagship *New York*, pipe the four other battlewagons out of Scapa Flow in futile pursuit of raiding German battle cruisers.

In April, a daring raid on the important enemy submarine base at Zeebrugge was led by Admiral Roger Keyes, who had fought valiantly at Gallipoli. Royal Marines assaulted dockside defenses under murderous counterfire. A submarine, filled with high explosives, was blown up under a railroad viaduct while three block-ships were scuttled in the harbor channel near the lock gates of the Bruges Canal.

The lives sacrificed in this Victoria-Cross-type of slam-bang action were to no telling avail. The next day the U-boats were throbbing out of the canal as before, skirting the sunken vessels. The gates had not been seriously damaged.

Secretary Daniels had been prodded by the navy's Bureau of Ordnance to "stop the submarines at their source," even as Sims had counseled. Aided by such genius as that of Thomas A. Edison, the bureau had recently made giant strides in electrically detonated mines, especially those with wire antennae which could be triggered by a submarine fifty or more feet distant.

"Is it not practicable to blockade German coast efficiently and completely," Daniels cabled Sims in London, "thus making impossible the egress and ingress of submarines? The steps attempted or accomplished in this direction are to be reported at once."

Yes, it was "feasible," Sims answered, adding there was "not a London Club in which the Admiralty was not denounced for its stupidity in not adopting such a perfectly obvious plan." The Royal Navy then reaffirmed that a mine barrage across the top of the North Sea—230 miles from the Orkneys to Norway— was "quite impracticable." Spokesmen insisted that Britain had tried to mine this broad expanse of cold rough water only to be permanently discouraged by "bitter and expensive experience."

On the other hand, the British public did not share the Admiralty's despair. Newspaper and magazine artists had for so long been graphically depicting such a U-boat snare that it was assumed that the North Sea, in all or part, could readily be mined. That is, it *might* be someday, somehow, before the war ended, *if* someone managed to get around to issuing the proper order.

But no order, proper or improper, was ever given. With a magnificent patience, characteristic of their race and like no other westerners upon the face of the earth, Britons waited, and waited. The German undersea raiders meanwhile continued to slip northward around the lonely, rocky Shetlands and Faeroes, then into the Atlantic to bang away at merchantmen.

Admiral Joseph Strauss, former head of the United States Navy's Bureau of Ordnance, who had graduated from Annapolis in 1885, summed up the British objections, with understanding:*

"The proposal by the United States that we lay a mine-barrier across the North Sea was not received with enthusiasm by the British. The reason for this is complex: first, and most potent, was their reluctance to interpose anything to the northward that might hamper the movements of the British fleet, either, I presume, in chase or retreat. Although the sea area left to them would in any case be immense, so was their fleet immense in numbers of ships and sea-room required for its free operation. It has been said that Jellicoe's great caution at one phase of the Battle of Jutland was due to an edict from the authorities at London that the fleet *must* survive. In carrying out an injunction of that kind, it necessarily admits that the enemy's fleet may survive also, and that is not what fleets are built for. There was some possibility that the proposed barrage would hamper the British fleet, but the risk was remote, and without some risk little can be accomplished. Something had to be done about the submarine menace, and that, the battle fleet could not do; our proposal *did* offer a probable remedy for an appalling condition.

"Behind the reason given above, there also lay the reluctance of the British to accept a scheme which did not originate with them; this arose not only from the natural conceit of a powerful nation with a long history of successful contests at sea, but also from the question of 'face,' a quality long held dear to

*From his unpublished memoirs, made available to the author by his son, Rear Admiral Elliott Strauss, U.S.N. (Ret.).

the English nation. Face is important to any country; it sells their goods and gives them strength at international conferences."

Sims himself seemed to become momentarily infected with defeatism because he subsequently advised Secretary Daniels, "I cannot too strongly emphasize the fact that during nearly three years of active warfare this whole question had been the most serious subject to consideration by the British Admiralty."

The British Admiralty then went so far as to advise Sims that the United States Navy "can more profitably concentrate on other work."

That did it. The gauntlet was down. The Bureau of Ordnance opened its scientific throttles wide and worked around the clock. By the first of August, 1917, the wonderful Mark VI mine was ready operationally. Carrying 300 pounds of TNT, the mine was lethal at distances of nearly 100 feet. It could be moored so that it would float either just below the surface or at depths of 240 feet, while its deadly electrical antennae would ensure detonation even if the U-boat had safely steered past the mine itself.

The Royal Navy was advised. Jellicoe hesitated. Maybe . . . but he was not at all convinced. Hot-tempered Chief of Naval Operations Benson raged. This temporizing did nothing to alter his antipathy toward the English. Cabling Sims to "have a heart-to-heart talk" with the Admiralty, he concluded: "No time is to be lost!"

By mid-September, the Navy Department finally received a cautious green light from London. The British at least would not interfere with American minelaying attempts. After all, the Grand Fleet had not been seriously challenged since Jutland. It might never again have to steam forth in all its magnitude. Thus the question of dodging minefields might not arise.

The next month, Admiral Henry Mayo, commanding the Atlantic Fleet, returned from England with the final arrangements, by which the Royal Navy would assume only a minor responsibility for placing the North Sea barrage. That a super-mine, more or less, had been invented, was not enough. Contracts for their assembly-line manufacture—100,000 mines at least— had to be let; a fleet had to be created to lay them; a special depot must be built to load this awesomely destructive cargo; and overseas bases from which the minelayers would operate had to be staffed.

Actually, the United States munitions industry had been accelerating ever since 1915 when Allied orders made the business of explosives and mass death a booming concern. The Mark VI could go into production so rapidly that 10,000 or more would be ready for shipment by the first part of 1918. St. Julien's Creek, near the Portsmouth, Virginia, Navy Yard, was selected as the depot site. It was accessible by rail or sea from the mine factories. Docks were hammered into being to allow the loading of 1,000 mines a day onto a train of twenty-three cargo vessels, already being adapted to handle the heavy lethal spheres.

The most colorful aspect of the grandiose, ambitious operation, however, was the minelaying fleet: ten weary, tatterdemalion ships. The flagship was the less-than-5,000-ton "protected cruiser" *San Francisco*, launched in 1889. Her companion was the slightly larger thirty-one-year-old *Baltimore*, which had accompanied Dewey into Manila Bay. Both relics, noted Captain Reginald R. Belknap, Annapolis '91, commanding the new mining squadron, were "years older than many of their officers and crew."

Snatched from service on the "outside line" from New York to Boston were two elegant if seasoned wooden Eastern Steamship liners, the 3,800-ton *Massachusetts* and the *Bunker Hill*. As workmen, with scant sense of maritime nostalgia, began to rip out the plush sofas, chandeliers, brass cuspidors, and other especial refinements of the snug cabins, the navy, with equal absence of sentiment, changed their names, respectively, to *Shawmut* and *Aroostook*. Sin would never again be as accessible, or such a bargain on the overnight journey from Boston to New York, or vice versa.

Two less magnificent coastal steamers were at the same time requisitioned from the Old Dominion Line, serving Norfolk out of New York. These were the *Hamilton* and the *Jefferson*. Three freighters of the Southern Pacific Line, plying in Caribbean and Gulf waters, were also requisitioned.

In April, Admiral Strauss sailed to England to inspect the

two bases of the new mining squadron, one at Inverness and the other at Invergordon, on Moray Firth at the eastern extremity of the famed Caledonian Canal. This canal, a major inland waterway, connected the Atlantic with the North Sea across the roof of Scotland. Strauss recalled:*

"I called by appointment on Admiral Sir David Beatty on the *Queen Elizabeth* [at Scapa Flow] and remained with him for an hour and a half discussing the mine situation. Beatty was at that time a man of forty-seven. His rise in his profession had been phenomenal: a commander at twenty-seven, rear admiral at thirty-nine, vice admiral at forty-three and then an admiral when I met him. His advancement was due entirely to merit, and not, as I learned, to any family influence. He was a man of medium stature and gave the impression of being a little stout and was of the dark Irish type. He was wholly lacking in geniality, and that contributed a little, I suppose, to his undoubted unpopularity in the British Navy. His rapid rise in his profession may have had something to do with it, although, as I have said, it was well earned. This advancement might have been well received had Beatty been of a prominent family, but unfortunately for him, he was not. I had heard echoes enough of that fact to make me think that it had an important bearing on his lack of popularity.

"During our long interview Beatty showed his skepticism of the value of the barrage, but was willing to do everything to make it a success. He agreed with me that it was necessary to mine up to the coast of Norway, and even thought we should have a base on Norwegian territory, but said that it was impossible politically at that time. He promised a suitable convoy to our mine squadron during its operations. I asked for a sentinel patrol of our areas, say a dozen fishing vessels that could warn the fleet of attempts to sweep the field by the enemy, but he was noncommittal about that.

"He showed a minute knowledge of the whole scheme, and I left him with a high opinion of his ability and force, and the opinion that he would win if he got a chance. I was enthusiastic

*In his unpublished memoirs.

Blockading the North Sea meant long hours of inactivity, and infrequent port calls imposed a limitation on supplies. Here, crewmen on the British battleship *Royal Oak* receive rum allowance.

about the value of the barrage, but in saying goodbye, he remarked, 'I am glad to find someone who believes in this barrage.'

"This remark staggered me a little; it meant to my mind, that no British officer favored it, and that I was the only American officer that he had met who approved it, and that the disapproval must have included Sims, who was the contact officer between the United States and the Admiralty. As regards Sims, this assumption was confirmed later by Sims himself. Well, the British government had subscribed to the scheme and I went ahead with it with a whole heart.

"The magnitude of the task assigned to the Mine Force was

Padlocking an Ocean— • 253

not my greatest concern; it was outweighed by the hidden determination on the part of our British allies not to permit its accomplishment, and at least to make it abortive by withdrawing from their share of the work, which would have left a gap in the fence eastward from the Orkneys extending to a distance of over fifty miles. On May 1, I asked Clinton-Baker* how many mines had been planted in that area, and he replied, 'That had all been washed out.' I answered, that the whole scheme wasn't worth a damn unless it was understood at the outset that Area B was to be mined, and that Sims agreed with that view, and that I would recommend that it be abandoned unless the agreement was carried out. Clinton-Baker seemed to agree with me heartily. Later in the day, Captain [O. E.] Murfin, base commander, informed me that Clinton-Baker told him that their minelayers were working in Helgoland Bight while waiting to see what was to be done in Area B. It left the impression in Murfin's mind that all work in Area B had been suspended awaiting a decision whether any further work would be done in Area B or not. The situation was serious and I left the next day to lay the whole matter before Sims."

In spite of Admiral Strauss's misgivings, nonetheless, the American squadron was overseas by late spring, and at work in early June. Captain Belknap, the squadron commander, wrote:

"One may imagine with what feelings we saw our own great ships file out of Scapa Flow, form line on our quarter, and slowly disappear in the haze as they swept off to the southeastward. It will be readily understood that the way had to be made smooth for the mine planters. As long as it was so, all would go well; but a single well-placed torpedo or mine, or a few enemy shells, would certainly finish one vessel, and probably destroy all ten of them. Each mine planter carried from 21 tons to 120 tons of high explosive, a total of nearly 800 tons in the squadron, many times more than the amount that devastated Halifax. With this on board, the squadron was hardly a welcome visitor anywhere."

Before it was finished, in early autumn, the squadron would have sown more than 60,000 mines, representing approximately

*Admiral L. Clinton-Baker, who had been captain of the battleship *Hercules* during Jutland.

10,000 tons of high explosives, from the Orkneys to Norway, along a belt anywhere from fifteen to thirty-five miles wide. The British, under Clinton-Baker, placed 13,000 mines.

Enemy action was unexpectedly lacking. Only two lives were sacrificed in the whole dangerous operation. A bos'n was swept to his death when his leg became ensnarled in a paravane cable, and the commander of the sweeper *Bobolink*, Lieutenant Frank Bruce, was killed while trying to haul aboard a "defective" mine being retrieved for repair. Yet, about 3 percent of the mines could have been expected by all odds to explode prematurely.

One morning, six mines exploded under and around the sweeper *Pelican*. Its hull was ruptured and it was staggered under tons and tons of water. The sweepers' flagship, *Auk*, came alongside, threw suction hoses to the crippled craft, then started her own pumps going. A second sweeper, the *Eider*, hove to on the other beam and duplicated the procedure started by the *Auk*.

"Then a heavy head sea arose," recalled Captain R. C. Bulmer of the *Auk*, "and the pump lines were carried away. Water rose in the *Pelican*, buckling the forward bulkhead, and the vessel was liable to burst at any moment, going down in a flash. Every man on her was in danger, and it was decided to leave aboard only a few men to do necessary work. Twelve volunteers were called for. Every member of her crew stepped forward. The dozen strongest were chosen and the others, against their will, were ordered off the ship.

"Fifty miles of open sea were still to be traversed. Darkness had fallen. The crews of the *Auk* and *Eider* struggled desperately to get the lines repaired and pumps going. Men stood by with axes to cut the mooring lines, in case the *Pelican* should sink. All through the night this struggle continued, and there was a sigh of relief when day dawned with the vessel still afloat, and the ships reached the shelter of Tresness Bay."

The minelayers always worked under heavy escort by American battleships and light units of the British fleet. Submarines, appearing among the squadron on two occasions, failed to discharge torpedoes. This was fortunate during the second foray of the enemy, since two of the old American coasters had developed steering trouble in their scramble for safety, and would have been sitting ducks even for poor marksmen among U-boat commanders.

Unfortunately, the padlocking of the North Sea came too late in the war for a fair assessment of its results. "Absolute impassability never was attained or expected," in the view of Belknap. The United States Navy claimed that at least four and possibly as many as eight U-boats had either been destroyed in the minefield or damaged. The Admiralty placed the figure at a firm six and listed the lost U-boats by number. Distress messages and other intelligence sources were given as the basis of these totals.

The Germans ultimately confirmed the specific losses, but disputed the "northern barrage" as the killer. One U-boat commander, for example, declared that he could navigate the field close to the Orkneys, for he had assumed it was being laid westward from Norway. Since his hypothesis was totally wrong, the officer had merely been lucky.

"It is obvious," wrote Scheer, "on what a large scale English mine-laying was carried on, when it is considered that they set about mining the whole of the North Sea between the Shetland Islands and Norway . . . . if they had really succeeded in sowing mines sufficiently thickly in that area the Fleet would have found it an exceedingly difficult task to clear the necessary gaps there. However, the great depth of the water in this part of the North Sea made it possible for U-boats to avoid the barrier by traveling at a sufficient depth below the surface. So far as we could ascertain, we suffered no losses in U-boats from these mines."

Von Hipper disagreed with his superior, observing unequivocally that by autumn the North Sea had been closed: *geschlossen!*

At the least, there remained little doubt that the great mining effort had placed another and essential stumbling block in the path of the hitherto free-wheeling U-boats. Certainly it had helped to reduce the numbers which poured into the Atlantic each month.

The operation was carried out, moreover, in the face of apparent continuing opposition from the British. Admiral Strauss recalled:

256 • Padlocking an Ocean—

Minelaying in the North Sea was a dangerous operation. The small, antiquated mine planters carried from 21 to 120 tons of high explosives, making them especially vulnerable to enemy attack.

"On Sept. 10 I received a letter from Sims saying that friction existed between 'our people' and the British with respect to the mine-barrage. I did not reply by letter as I was compelled to go to London on other business and determined to 'have it out' there. I stated that I knew of absolutely no friction of any sort whatever between me or any of my people and the British, and could not recall a single controversial word. I asked that I be permitted to accompany Sims to the Admiralty and get the matter reduced to specific charges. We went over together to the Admiralty meeting where Admiral Sydney Fremantle took it upon himself to reply to my demand for definite complaints. He hemmed and hawed in a very embarrassed way, and finally lamely said that I did not send in reports of my operations promptly enough. I then told them in detail how and when the reports were made.

"When the returning mine-fleet was first sighted off the coast I at once sent a fast launch to intercept the ships and get from them their navigational data; this enabled me to gain something like an hour. As soon as the launch returned with the reports, my staff went to work on them without stopping for anything to reconcile the navigational data, and as soon as that was done (it sometimes took until 1 A.M.) the results were telegraphed both to the Admiralty direct and to Sims on the instant. Evidently, the Admiralty received them first, as I had had a letter from Sims complaining that the Admiralty got these reports before he did. In future, I would send the reports without the exact locations if the Admiralty wished it, and that might gain a few hours. . . .

"I read the whole matter as a scheme on the part of Beatty to discredit me. He did not like me because I had forced them to carry out the plan to which they had agreed of providing a real barrier to the exit of the submarines. Unfortunately, that did not fit in with Beatty's desire to have nothing in the way of the retreat of his fleet to the northward. It certainly could not have sprung from the aim to pursue the enemy to the northward; for to force the latter to cross what Beatty thought was a dangerous mine-field would have been highly to his advantage. Then, again, the Germans in their retreat from battle both at Dogger Bank and Jutland did not foolishly retreat to the open sea, but sought and won a refuge to the southward in their own ports where they were enabled to 'lick their wounds' in safety. My insistence on carrying out our view as to checking the depredations of the submarines was what made me an unwelcome agent of an allied government.

"General Pershing suffered under similar displeasure. 'You do as we wish and not as you wish or we will get rid of you!' is what it amounts to. Fortunately for Pershing, President Wilson and, above all, his able Secretary of War were both loyal to their subordinates and the plot to oust Pershing failed.

"I had not the slightest fear that the device of the British to get rid of me, even had it been backed by Sims, would have resulted in sending me home. I felt sure of the confidence in me of both Secretary Daniels and Admiral Benson, and I knew of their impatience with anyone who was swerved by the displeasure of the British."

This "friction" (which ultimately extended even within the mine squadron, between Strauss and Belknap) did not, fortunately, bespeak a complete lack of Anglo-American naval rapport. At one time, Admiral Bayly, going on leave from his command in Queenstown, asked Sims to take his place. The invitation was not only an expression of trust in the officer from overseas but an excellent goodwill gesture.

The Germans, too, continued to employ mines throughout the last bitter months of the war. On July 19, the armored cruiser *San Diego* smashed into a mine some ten miles southeast of Fire Island at the approaches to New York harbor.

The 13,680-ton ship assumed so steep a list on the port side that water entered the gun ports. She hung this way crazily for seven minutes, then turned turtle and sank with frightening rapidity. But only six were lost out of a complement of more than 1,100 men.

Captain H. H. Christy, the last to leave his command in the finest traditions of the sea, was highly commended for the brilliant evacuation of a ship on which it had become almost impossible to maintain footing or even balance. The *Lusitania*, with a similar list, had remained afloat for slightly more than fifteen minutes but more than half of the 1,959 persons aboard were lost. The *San Diego* was the largest American warship to be destroyed in the war.

Even in Germany's last dying gasps, as the army commenced its agonized withdrawal toward the Rhine and home, the U-boats fought like cornered panthers. On a single weekend in June two large submarines sank nine ships off the New Jersey and Delaware coasts. New York City, blacked-out, was thrown into a panic, expecting attack by sea as well as by air.

In other words, the Allies were still faced with the major challenge of not only shutting up "the hornets in their nests" but going in after the more pugnacious and recalcitrant ones. A second counterattack, after the North Sea barrage had been commenced, was made possible by special submarine-chasers ("SC" boats) and larger craft for the same general purpose, the 200-foot "Eagle Boats" built by Henry Ford. His feat marked the first application of the assembly line to marine construction, although only a dozen of the 615-ton vessels were launched in time for active service.

Virtually overnight, the emergency anti-U-boat fleet grew from nothing to squadrons totaling more than 400 boats which fanned north and south from the east coast of the United States across the Atlantic to the English Channel and into the Mediterranean. The SC's, a mere 110 feet long, were affectionately known as "Cinderellas," "mosquitoes," or "the splinter fleet," since the vessels were built of wood.

Cruising at a tedious fourteen knots, with an absolute top speed of seventeen, they thrashed and agonized their way through Atlantic gales and monstrous seas. Some barely made it across. SC 28, for example, was disabled in a storm 700 miles west of the Azores. Salvos were fired and distress signals hoisted. But rescue was nowhere in sight—not for hundreds of miles.

Since lubricating oil was exhausted, salad dressing and butter were used to coax the moving parts of the engines into action. It was of no use. The machinery was dead.

Socks and shirts were ripped up to fill the leaking seams in the crippled chaser. Finally, bedsheets, blankets, and tablecloths were spread as sails and rigged to the flag hoist and radio mast. Food and drinking water were closely rationed.

SC 28 headed east, averaging about two knots. Almost a month after the sub-chaser was disabled, Fayal, the Azores, loomed dead ahead. Her bronzed, emaciated crew was saved.

This was the only instance in the twentieth century of a warship reaching port under the sole propulsion of sail!

The feat was not the only example of unorthodox practices among the "splinters." British counterintelligence, in the early autumn of 1918, intercepted strange radio-telephone signals:

"Quack! Quack! Quack!" was the odd call.

British ships exploding German sea mines.

"Quack! Red-white-blue!" came the equally confusing reply, followed enigmatically by:

"Quack, High-low-Jack!"

Was this some Hun trick, the guttural code chatter between offshore U-boats? Queried at once, Queenstown was able, immediately, to reassure Admiralty intelligence officers that the conversation off the British Isles was from the short-range transmitters of the SC's, whose code and identification system was similar to nothing ever devised by any navy—or army—on the face of the earth. Some squadrons took their key from *Mother Goose* and *Aesop's Fables*, others from the Bible (St. James version), and a few of the still more imaginative from Edgar Allan Poe's poems and mystery stories.

However, the Cinderellas were charged with a mission which was deadly serious. They had a chance to prove this amply at the beginning of October when Captain Charles Preston ("Juggy") Nelson, Annapolis '98, was ordered to lead an expedition of twelve SC's against the Austrian naval base at Durazzo, a major U-boat lair at the entrance to the Adriatic, across from Brindisi, Italy. The "splinters" were to screen units of the British Light Cruiser Force, which would bombard the shore defenses and clear the channel of mines.

The little boats left their base on the Greek island of Corfu, less than 125 miles down the coast from Durazzo, and raced across the Straits of Otranto to pick up their big sisters of the Royal Navy. Spanning these straits, there had already been established a "mobile barrage," consisting of mines, some nets, and a continual patrol of light craft, including Italian trawlers.

"We slipped out of Brindisi at midnight (October 2)," recalled Chief Petty Officer Ray Milholland, aboard the *SC IX4*, "creeping through the mine net channel, knowing that the slightest error in blind navigation would send us roaring skyward in a fog of splinters. . . . For the rest of the night we ran at reduced speed in a general easterly direction, indicating that our objective was not very far off, and shortly after dawn headlands loomed up out of the mist. It was Durazzo."

Minutes later, the smoke from the busy port, and from the funnels of ships moored there, was seen wisping into the bright morning skies. As yet, the invaders had not been spotted.

About 8:40 A.M., the sudden surfacing of a U-boat sent depth charges tumbling from the sterns of several of the little boats and made it necessary for the attackers to reveal themselves while others proceeded to carry out their demolition of the minefields. Milholland continued:

"We went into action at once, every chaser padded in her crew's mattresses, which had been rigged around the bridge and charthouse as splinter mats. The decks had been sanded to prevent the gun crew's bare feet from slipping in their own blood later. . . .

"Not a shell was fired at us from the formidable shore batteries until we had already commenced our allotted work of countermining their extensive minefields by dumping our own depth mines over the stern.

"The first depth mine rolled off . . . then five, ten seconds went by—eternity—then, crunch! The deck plates of the engine room bounced and danced crazily as the vibrations from first the depth mine, and then the countermined Austrian mines, wrenched and tore at our thin-skinned hull. The next depth mine concussion loosened every electrical switch in the engine-room circuits.

"Instantly all three main engines died . . . we raced about madly slapping switches back into place and securing them with short pieces of tarred yarn . . . our engines roared into full throttle once more . . . but our own depth mine caught us on the outer rim of its erupting center. The fragile wooden hull writhed under us like a wounded thing, but raced on.

"Now the Austrian batteries had opened up with ranging shots, rumbling overhead like freight trains passing over a long bridge. The air vibrated and the vibration could be felt in one's stomach like the deep bass notes of a great pipe organ. A sense of the unrealness of it all settled over me. The roar of the distant guns had reached a volume that produced a weird delusion of no sound at all.

"Splash! A big shell dropped close aboard. Then another: one over, and one short; then one almost dead aboard. They had our range and speed bracketed to a hair. But we dove off at a sharp angle from the course we were on and continued dropping depth mines. . . . The savagery of the fire increased."

Then, in moments, "a slim gray enemy destroyer came streaking out of Durazzo and swung her knife-like bows straight at us, her two bow-chaser guns flashing and pitching shells around us. Our forward three-inch gun coughed back at her with a sound like the piping chirp of a young robin in all that diapason of sound."

Unexpectedly, a burst of brown smoke puffed up from the enemy's stern. She had been hit. She swerved, although her gunners continued pumping shells at the SC. Suddenly, *scafas*, little Italian torpedo boats, roared in for the kill, letting go 18-inch torpedoes at the wounded destroyer:

". . . there was a terrific explosion, boilers flew skyward, spinning like pinwheels, with jets of steam still spurting from them. Then the smother of water and flying debris settled back on the water. The destroyer had vanished."

The battle was now fully joined. Milholland found it "appalling to watch the defenses and works of Durazzo crumbling under the continual pounding of the Allied shells. And, added

In addition to planting mines, the Allies attempted to get rid of those laid by the Germans. Here, a German mine explodes astern of the U.S. minesweeper *Patapsco*.

to this destruction, came flight after flight of Italian, French, and British bombing planes—seventy-four of them!"

A gaping torpedo hole in her side, the British cruiser *Weymouth* limped off. Another U-boat was depth charged before the invaders withdrew. The assault on Durazzo was now history —this blazing prophecy of sea-air warfare to come.

On land as well, events were moving swiftly this fateful October. General Ludendorff advised a special war council that an immediate armistice was necessary. Marshal Hindenburg, the gruff stubborn mastiff, thought he could hold his sagging, punctured lines—somewhere, somehow. Statesmen of Germany, however, urged Kaiser Wilhelm to proclaim a constitutional government and discuss with President Wilson his fourteen points.

Prince Max of Baden, a liberal, became chancellor with what amounted to a "stop-the-war" mandate. On October 4, German and Austrian requests for an armistice were formally transmitted through neutral Switzerland.

Even so, it seemed almost too late. General Pershing's A.E.F. was smashing closer to the Rhine River in the Meuse-Argonne campaign, possibly the most massive and best organized and coordinated single operation of the war. Ludendorff, all too aware that his army's back was to the wall, now reasoned that Germany could gamble better peace terms by fighting bitterly to the end. He ordered counterattacks with all the strength left in his weary, depleted forces, then was himself dismissed for his impetuosity.

It was no use. Already a million and a half sick and disheartened soldiers were straggling away from their units between France and their homes. These weren't exactly desertions, but AWOL's in such mass as to be virtually uncontrollable.

On October 21, all U-boats were recalled from their war on commerce "in order to avoid anything that might make the attainment of peace more difficult. . . ."

Yet, on the same date, unbelievably enough, Scheer issued other orders:

The High Seas Fleet Is to Be Made Ready for Attack and Battle with the English Fleet.

The plan was to hit merchant shipping off the Netherlands

and Belgian coasts and then, if not challenged, sweep toward the Thames estuary and the English Channel where surely the Grand Fleet *would* be encountered.

"If the fleet suffered losses," reasoned Scheer, "it was to be assumed that the enemy's injuries would be in proportion. . . ."

It was a negative plan at best, unworthy of the careful German naval strategy of past months and years. The crews of the High Seas Fleet acquired the notion that the emperor had ordered this last-ditch sortie simply to lose his battle squadrons and thus avoid their surrender.

October 29 arrived. Minutes after midnight, the many sounds attendant to squadrons putting out swept through the High Seas Fleet and echoed off the adjacent docks and shores: the rattle of hoists, the shrill of many bos'ns' whistles, bells below decks which announced a variety of nautical punctuations, from eating to merely deck sweeping.

This was *the* day, *der Tag*. But singular discord soon erased the familiar, expectant noises, replacing them with harsher, more ominous sounds. Something was happening, something the High Command had utterly failed to anticipate.

The admirals had not considered one possibility: that there might be no fight left in their crews.

In Schillig Roads, Wilhelmshaven, young Lieutenant Friedrich Ruge, aboard the torpedo boat *B-110*, of the Second Flotilla, was standing the first watch. It was not yet 1 A.M., when he heard "lots of noise" on ships nearby . . . especially on the battleships *Thüringen* and *Ostfriesland*. He reported to his captain who ordered him to "up anchor" and see what it was all about.

In Kiel, Lieutenant Ernst Tittmann aboard the *König*, moored to the Kaiser Wharf, was awakened by something more catastrophic than mere noise. Dock workers had swarmed onto the battleship and had tried to tear down the naval ensign. In defending their ship, Tittmann recalled,* "the first officer, Lieutenant Commander Bruno Heinemann and the watch officer, Lieutenant Wolfgang Zenker, were killed while the commanding officer, Captain Karl Weniger, was seriously wounded."

---

*The accounts of Tittmann and Ruge made to the author.

Comparable violence was erupting nearby on the battleship *Markgraf*. Sounds of shouting and the sporadic crack-crack of rifle shots echoed from the Königs Weg and other thoroughfares of the old seaport, suddenly shattered by civil strife.

Fires which had not already been extinguished by the mutineers were banked on the battleships and cruisers. Anchor chains were made fast. Lights winked nervously from ship to ship: *"Wiederrufen!"* ("Orders cancelled!")

The High Seas Fleet would not sail against England this night, or ever again.

This was no spur-of-the-moment act of defiance. Fanned by Bolsheviks and extreme Socialists, the mutiny had been smouldering for several weeks, ever since a Sailors Union had established its "fleet central" on the *Friedrich der Grosse* under the nose of Admiral von Hipper and most of the High Command. Aided by the Independent Social Democratic Party, the seamen had scoffed at the first principle of military discipline by establishing a command within a command.

A minority of their own people were accomplishing against Germany what the joined might of the Royal Navy had failed to do at Jutland.

(10)

Verdict: Suicide

⊕ Lieutenant Ruge, cruising Schillig Roads on the torpedo boat, *B-110*, found to his dismay and near-disbelief that open mutiny had paralyzed at least three of the mightiest fleet vessels, the battleships *Helgoland* and *Thüringen* plus the light cruiser *Regensburg*. The *Derfflinger* and *Von der Tann* had almost slipped hawser from the authority of their officers.

On the *Thüringen* fires had been banked and electrical systems sabotaged. On this ship, along with the *Helgoland*, rebellious crewmen, armed with guns, rifles, and wrenches—even meat cleavers—sallied out to mount sporadic attacks on officers and noncoms, then barricaded themselves in their fo'c'sles to regroup for the next foray.

It was an incredible spectacle, especially to the old-line naval officers from Kiel and the Academy at Flensburg, whose very gospel had been discipline. Young Lieutenant Johannes Spiess, commanding the *U-135*, was to record one of the strangest experiences of a wholly strange night and following day. He boarded the hulk of the *Kaiser Wilhelm II* to obtain orders from Admiral Adolf von Trotha, High Seas Fleet chief of staff, to help subdue the mutiny. Blinking sleepily in his cabin aboard this office-ship, von Trotha said, in effect, "Go ahead," but refused to put it in writing.

After all, who might be in control of Germany tomorrow?

Despairingly, Spiess, who had been with Otto Weddigen at the torpedoing of the three old cruisers in 1914, moved on to the flagship of Admiral von Hipper, the *Friedrich der Grosse*. Spiess found von Hipper vague but sympathetic. In fact, the chief of the High Seas Fleet was even now preparing an appeal to the mutineers, which commenced, "We all want peace . . . we want no useless sacrifice before peace comes, but we want to stand united and with sharp weapons before the gates of our country."

It didn't sound like the old aggressive von Hipper of Jutland.

Dawn was breaking when the *U-135* and the *B-110* escorted two steamers loaded with armed soldiers, sailors, and marines to the *Thüringen* and also the *Ostfriesland*. At 500 yards, unexpectedly, the entire battery of the latter battleship was suddenly trained on the diminutive U-boat. Spiess, on the submarine's conning tower, waited to be blown into the next world . . . half a minute, a minute, two minutes. . . . The agony of this mortal suspense continued for another full minute, until finally the great cannons were depressed, and their turrets swung inexplicably back to normal positions fore and aft.

The *Thüringen*, approached by the submarine and Ruge's torpedo boat, surrendered without even token defiance. A cry rang from her decks across the roadstead:

"Don't shoot, brother!"

Both warships were boarded and their mutinous crews removed. However, one little U-boat aided by one torpedo boat, or indeed all of these craft in the navy, could not control the welling mutiny. The number of discontented men rampaging to the "cause" was too great. Ships such as the *Köln*, *Königsberg*, and *Seydlitz*, whose crews had remained loyal, presented their own special problems. "Kaiser's Blacklegs!" these patriotic sailors were called by the revolutionists; they dared not go ashore, where jeering dock workers were waiting for them with paving stones, broken bottles, ugly clubs, and lengths of lead pipe.

Mutiny spread, unchecked, through Germany's mastiffs of the sea, to the *Kaiser*, the *Markgraf*, the *Schleswig*. Battling reddened the decks of the *Markgraf* when fellow mutineers attempted to release others from the brig.

By November 4, every battleship was flying the Red flag. The capital warships had been fertile breeding grounds of mutiny. The lesser ones, almost without exception, had remained fiercely loyal. Kiel, drenched in its own blood, was placarded with proclamations from the Workers and Soldiers Committee:

The first victory is won, the first trench is taken . . . the goal of our old leaders in the struggle, Marx and LaSalle, has come a thousand times nearer to us in these last few days than in a century of effort . . . come, men and women, all of you to an imposing mass meeting, come all, all! The people are with us. Long live liberty!

More than 20,000 soldiers and sailors milled in a shouting horde to the "imposing mass meeting." Then they surged from the port area into Kiel, past the Wilhelm Platz northward to release Third Naval Squadron prisoners from the Feldstraat jail.

Prince Henry of Prussia, the kaiser's brother, saved his own life by attaching a red flag to his limousine and driving at breakneck speed out of Kiel. He was shot at by marines and other loyal sentries who were unaware of the prince's ruse, and reached the Danish border after several more close brushes.

By nightfall, Kiel was wholly in the hands of the revolutionists. At least eight died and twenty-eight were wounded in the rioting.

To the south, artillery fire rocketed through the great seaport, Hamburg, as police and loyal troops fought to quell the man-tide of insurrection. In Bremen, the supposedly most loyal of fighting men, the kaiser's marines, proved quite the opposite; they revolted and seized an army barracks.

On Tuesday, November 5, Captain Erich Raeder, who had been on Scheer's staff at Jutland, and was now with the central bureau of the navy in Berlin, left his heavily guarded offices for Wilhelmshaven. The railway system had broken down, trains crept from one signal tower to the next, their engineers never knowing when the track would suddenly end in a bomb crater or when a jagged abyss would loom where a bridge should have been.

He saw "most distressing scenes" in the home base of the High Seas Fleet, and found the so-called council of fifty-two in control of the principal ships of the fleet. Now, any lingering doubts Raeder may have entertained were dissipated. It was all over. There was no more hope, possibly, of using the U-boats or other components of the fleet ships as a "lever in any peace negotiations."

However, hoping to salvage some units of the High Seas Fleet from the mutineers, von Hipper, acting possibly on Raeder's advice, ordered all U-boats and torpedo boats out of Kiel and Wilhelmshaven—upwards of 100 in all. They knifed northward for the sanctuary of Helgoland and westward to Borkum and the Frisian Islands.

Even at Helgoland, the revolution was burning hotly. Ruge, for example, remembers that the "great iron doors" of the submarine and torpedo boat pens were "closed down."

"We were without a refuge," he recalled, "ships without a port, The flying Dutchmen, ja?"

On November 9, the squadrons were ordered back. They must submit to the ignominy, Spiess wrote, "of capitulating to the mutineers." It was a fateful Saturday, highlighted for the German Navy by one last spiteful attack: the torpedoing by the U-50 near Gibraltar of the old 17,500-ton battleship Britannia. No lives were lost.

Streaming homeward from the shattered warrens and torn barbed wire of what had been but a slightly fluctuating western front for four long frightful years of unrelieved slaughter were nearly 1,500,000 stragglers from the once unconquerable Imperial Army. Its weary, disillusioned members were ripe for any sort of revolutionary propaganda.

"On November 9," a despairing Ludendorff wrote, "Germany, lacking any firm hand, bereft of all will, robbed of her princes, collapsed like a house of cards. All that we had lived for, all that we had bled four long years to maintain, was gone. We no longer had a native land of which we might be proud. order in state and society vanished. All authority disappeared. Chaos, Bolshevism, terror, un-German in name and nature, made their entry into the German Fatherland."

Scheer added, "The evildoers who picked out the fleet as the means by which to attain their ends committed a terrible crime against the German nation."

The "terrible crime" was repeated in a growing number of

cities: Cuxhaven, Cologne, and Stuttgart, where revolutionists sought to disarm any man they saw in uniform. Most complied, willingly enough.

Berlin, that Saturday, November 9, was paralyzed by a general strike. Machine-gun detachments guarded bridges, and the telegraph offices were occupied as a huge demonstration formed more or less spontaneously. The workers (as they called themselves), soldiers, and sailors, truculently waving the ever-present red flags, marched through the Ackerstrasse and the Brunnenstrasse toward the so-called "Cockhafer (Chickenfeed) Barracks." Flanked by armed motorcars, they were augmented at every crossing by hundreds of officers who voluntarily tore off their insignias of rank and the cockades from their caps. Iron Crosses clapped against the paving like ripe chestnuts falling in autumn.

Trainloads of sailors arrived from Kiel to tumble boisterously into the marching mob, shouting, "Long live the republic!"

At the Cockhafer Barracks, the revolutionists encountered unexpected resistance from the Guard Fusiliers. After a rattling exchange of fire, three of the loyal troops lay dead and a number of their assailants were wounded.

Late that night, the curtain rolled ponderously down on the last act of the German tragedy, one with the same portent of doom, futility, and abject hopelessness as the motif of a Wagnerian opera. Kaiser Wilhelm II took pen in hand to sign his abdication papers—"for the good of Germany." He postscripted, "We must not despair of the future." He did not elaborate on *why* those of his misled subjects who had survived his war should not "despair."

Accompanied by the crown prince and an official party of ten, the former emperor, temporarily answering to "Count Hohenzollern," entrained for Holland. Through a driving winter rain, the "special" of twelve cars wailed westward until, at dawn, it paused at revolution-rocked Cologne for coal and water.

At Aachen, the royal travelers changed to limousines, crossed into the Netherlands and continued eleven more miles

Mutinous soldiers and sailors commandeer a limousine in Berlin. Germany was sick of war and had neither the will nor the means to continue the struggle.

to Maastricht, where the kaiser arrived at 10:46 A.M. There, Dutch railway coaches waited on a siding several hundred yards from the station.

Wilhelm II, in uniform but hatless, paced the rain-soaked gravel and cinder path beside the cars, smoking cigarette after cigarette as excited telegrams tapped between Maastricht and The Hague. *Should* Kaiser Wilhelm be granted the asylum he requested?

Church bells tolled in the little border village. Beyond the hedgerows, the families of Maastricht stolidly made their way to church. Conceivably, they did not even know the identity of the man who was impatiently marking time in their railway yards.

Finally, about 1:30 P.M., the red and white striped gate in front of the locomotive was slowly cranked upward, a signal that the Germans had been granted clearance. With a couple of

General Erich von Ludendorff deplored the "chaos, Bolshevism, terror" of the German revolution. Chief of staff under von Hindenburg, he had brought his armies to victory in Russia and close to victory in France.

whistles, the train started for Arnhem, seventy-five miles to the north. There, an expatriate German, Count Goddard Bentinck, who favored the Allied cause and whose relatives had fought in the British armies, awaited the abdicated kaiser in his château. The rule of the moustached, imperious Hohenzollerns on this wet November Sunday had become history.

In Berlin, rioting continued undiminished. The Imperial Bank was fired upon. It was all but impregnable, with windows shuttered and barred. Those employees who had not fled to the relative security of their homes were out marching. The emperor's royal stables were put to the torch as demonstrators danced about the several-stories-high pyre, shouting and chanting like savages at a ceremonial orgy. Fortunately, the horses were gone.

Those which hadn't become a part of the Imperial bill of fare due to the critical food shortage had preceded the kaiser to Holland. In fact, if the Socialists or Bolsheviks had any sort of intelligence network they would have ascertained easily enough that crate after crate of Wilhelm's belongings had been moving

Von Hindenburg (left) thought the war could be won on land, von Tirpitz (right), at sea. Neither was entirely right—or entirely wrong.

across the Dutch border since mid-October. Abdication, apparently, was no spur-of-the-moment decision.

However, the kaiser's departure was not greeted with unrelieved gladness or hysteria, or even considered by all Germans as necessarily an act of cowardice or desertion, as it was in the Allied capitals. Some newspapers, for example, speculated whether the switch in government was merely a "changing of autocrats." Much of the German press played the story as a quasi-royal obituary, labeling Wilhelm's act a "sacrifice," and penning lachrymose reflections on his "leadership" through the nation's dark days. Only the Socialist journals had the bad taste to suggest that the emperor himself might have played an initial role in the *Vaterland*'s giant goosestep on the road to Armageddon.

The postscript at the end of an Imperial dream was recorded by the Allied radio station atop the Eiffel Tower. It intercepted a message from the high-powered transmitter at Nauen, outside of Berlin, which had remained the major marine and naval link with the homeland:

"Nauen is in the hands of the delegates of the Soldiers and Workmen's Council. Send us your latest news!"

There was plenty.

Unable to continue the fight on land or at sea, the German government, now under the chancellorship of the Socialist Friedrich Ebert, an obscure tailor, accepted an armistice. Included in its sweeping terms, signed at 5:40 A.M. Monday, November 11, was the surrender of all submarines and the internment of the surface fleet.

The USS *Nevada*, riding easily at anchor in Scapa Flow, picked up the Eiffel Tower transmission at 6:45 A.M., little more than an hour after the signing of the momentous document:

TO: All ships and Stations, from Marshal Foch, Commander-in-Chief

Quote   Hostilities will cease upon the whole front from the 11th of November 11 o'clock French time period the Allied troops will not cross until a further order the line reached on that date and hour End Quote

At 11 A.M. the guns abruptly went quiet. An uncanny hush settled over all the sectors, from the Meuse-Argonne to Belgium. In those towns where churches still stood, a pealing of bells reverberated. Paris and London were swept by scenes of rejoicing—near-riots. In the British capital, the commotion continued for two full days.

However, the English reaction was not altogether without restraint even in this moment of heady resurrection, when the lights were, at long last, going on again. Admiral Strauss, his minelaying operation completed, was visiting friends near London.

"Before the armistice was announced," he wrote, "I had some intimation of its nearness, and at luncheon at Beaufort Castle thought to bring joy to my hostess and the few of her relations present by telling her the good news. My announcement was received in dead silence. Elsewhere I had noticed an apparent indifference to the great fact that the war was ended. For one thing, it meant the end of excitement; the reversion to the humdrum life of every day; the lack of importance of the individual. And again, I wonder if humanity does not really crave war at times; stupid and illogical as wars are, we have them often enough, God knows."

For the losers, there was reappraisal, a painful process which would continue undiminished for at least two decades.

"The German people," philosophized von Tirpitz, "did not understand the sea."

It was extreme over-simplification of the disaster which had befallen his nation, and not wholly correct.

"A curse lies on the navy," wrote Scheer, "because out of its ranks revolution first sprang and spread over the land . . . the conditions of life on the large ships, the close quarters in which the men lived, favored the propagation of this agitation, which was spread by any and every means. Further, the crews were most easily exposed to temptation because of their close connection with the homeland. But the most important and the decisive cause was this: the war-weariness of the whole nation, increased by hunger and all sorts of privations, had become so widespread that even the fighting forces had lost faith in a happy end to the war."

The 60,000 crewmen of the High Seas Fleet, added Tittmann of the *König*, had been idle since Jutland "while the army and U-boat sailors had continued to fight for their lives."

A young U-boat Lieutenant, Karl Doenitz, finishing up the war in a British prisoner-of-war camp, was to pin much of the tab for defeat on Germany's geographical position. He wrote:*

"The High Seas Fleet was denied its normal radius of action —to steam into the battleground of the North Atlantic, where, alone, a decision was possible. Only in the North Sea, our fleet presented no great danger to the Grand Fleet. The Royal Navy there had but to put into operation the war plans envisioned before 1914.

"The blame, thus, for the defeat lay not with the soldiers,

---

*In a letter to the author.

the sailors, and the officers of the High Seas Fleet, but in the continental-mindedness of our government, of our army leadership, and with the entire German people. This insular frame of mind had blinded us to the changing conditions, compared with earlier realities: we were since the Seven-Year War in 1800, in the War for Liberty, 1813-1815, in the war of 1864, 1866 and the Franco-Prussian War, 1870-1871 always victorious, because our opponents were countries on the continent of Europe and we had only an army to fight. Now our political and strategic position had been basically altered: for the first time, 1914 was a sea contest and the greatest sea might was on the side of our opponent, whom we could fight with hope of success only in the Atlantic. And this we did not understand."

Whatever the cause, Germany, beyond dispute, had lost the war, even though far too many of her citizens would interpret the armistice as a fortuitous breathing space in which to recoup and then to regroup for the next round.

On November 20, in the chilly northern dark of 7 A.M., the vanguard of a once formidable navy felt its way toward the peacetime fishing port of Harwich: twenty surrendered U-boats accompanied by two German destroyers. Commodore Tyrwhitt, who never had a satisfactory crack at the enemy, was waiting for the broken remnants of the undersea terrors. Squinting through the predawn murk and mist, one of the tars aboard the flagship *Curaçao* asked:

"Them's 'uns on the fo'c'sle?"

"Ay," a shipmate replied, "they're 'uns all right. Our fellows 'ave clean sweaters on." Many German seamen had replaced the eagle insignias on their caps with red badges.

Then a bugle sounded from the *Curaçao*. Royal Navy gunners trained on the submarines and their escort (which had come along only to take the crewmen home). The enemy colors were dipped in salute as Tyrwhitt signaled the U-boats and the two destroyers to follow him, even as his own squadron of destroyers flanked the surrendering craft. Three large seaplanes droned overhead.

Past the Ship Wash lightship and into the approaches to the Harwich Channel the fleet sailed. Then, one by one, the German colors were lowered, and white flags fluttered in a light breeze. As a supreme token of humiliation, each submarine was boarded by a British crew; the U-boat's own sailors were taken off on the two accompanying destroyers.

The next day, Thursday, marked a far more impressive surrender—that of the main units of the High Seas Fleet. It was "a silent Trafalgar," in the opinion of one witness, who watched the Royal Navy's former scourge as it "crept meekly into custody." The entrance of the ships into Scapa Flow was described by Francis T. Hunter, a young lieutenant aboard the *New York*, flagship of the American battle fleet:

"Small wonder that 4 A.M., November 21, 1918, found few asleep in all the fleet. *This* was the day! No secrecy; no doubt. The world knew. The King himself had come but yesterday to acclaim the triumph that must be ours today. Too vast a situation well to comprehend—the German High Seas Fleet had sailed from Kiel! And the King had come. Hundreds of strangers were aboard our ships. A flush of excitement covered every face, held back by a forbidding silence that seemed to suspend the motion of the very earth.

"From early evening, long lines of destroyers had preceded us to sea, hours and hours of them, out of the misty Firth of

Flagship of the German fleet, *Friedrich der Grosse* leads the German battleships to surrender at Rosyth, November 21, 1918. She had carried Scheer's flag in the battle of Jutland.

Boom at Scapa Flow. The surrendered German fleet begins internment under British guard.

Forth, followed by envious eyes. Every official ship that could turn a screw would follow shortly. Shortly! The hours were ages long. It was not until 2 A.M. that the greatest day of our lives began. The day of a thousand dreams. We seemed to be living within a highly inflated bubble, about to burst. The American flagship *New York* broke moor, swung slowly with the tide, felt the throbbing of her screws, fell into line to lead the Sixth Battle Squadron to sea.

"Gray ships in a gray dawn. Ships and ships and ships, as far as the eye could see, ahead or astern. Great monsters rising and falling on the incoming swells, by their very stateliness ac-

280 • Verdict: Suicide

claiming victory. At 4 A.M. our general alarm clanged harshly against the quiet dawn. . . . All hands to battle stations!

"Three decks below the water line men sit with 'phones, tubes, boards, pencils, and strange instruments, connected with the conning tower, the plotting room. The centre of control of fire. No 'Wooden Horse of Troy,' for Admiral Beatty. . . .

"At last dawn comes, blazing red. A low haze cuts the visibility to five short miles, but the rising sun reveals a new disposition of our forces. Admiral Beatty has divided his ships into two great lines—the northern and the southern. These two lines, proceeding on parallel courses, about two miles apart, will permit the German fleet to pass down their centre. A 'ships right and left about' will then bring both lines steaming in inverted order toward the Firth of Forth, the German line between. Either of our lines, without the other, could engage the surrendering German fleet successfully.

"On we steam at twelve knots to point 'X' in the North Sea. Eight bells strikes clearly. We know the great moment is not far distant now, and by the imposing spectacle are reassured. At last:

" 'Sail ho!'—from the foretop lookout. 'Where away?'—from the bridge. 'One point off the starboard bow,' in reply. 'Can you make it out?' 'Dense smoke, sir, seems to be approaching.'

"Twenty-five minutes later, off May Island, the tiny light cruiser *Cardiff*, towing a kite balloon, leads the great German battle cruiser *Seydlitz*, at the head of her column, between our lines. On they pass—*Derfflinger*, *Von der Tann*, *Hindenburg*, *Moltke*—as if in review. The low sun glances from their shabby sides. Their huge guns, motionless, are trained fore and aft. It is the sight of our dreams—a sight for kings! Those long, low, sleek-looking monsters, which we had pictured ablaze with spouting flame and fury, steaming like peaceful merchantmen on a calm sea. Then the long line of battleships, led by *Friedrich der Grosse*, flying the flag of Admiral Ludwig von Reuter, commanding the whole force [and who was head of Scouting Division IV at Jutland]. *König, Albert, Kaiser, Kronprinz Wilhelm, Kaiserin, Bayern, Markgraf, Prinz Regent Luitpold*, and *Gros-*

ser Kurfürst followed in formation—powerful to look at, dangerous in battle, pitiful in surrender. . . .

"This, then, is the end for which the Kaiser has lavished his millions on his 'incomparable' navy! A navy powerful enough to conquer all the navies of the world combined—bar the British. . . .

"Strangely enough, the German surrender lacked the thrill of victory. There was the gaping wonder of it, the inconceivable that was happening before our very eyes—the great German fleet steaming helplessly there at our side—conquered. . . . The one prevalent emotion, so far as I could ascertain, was pity. It carried even to our great commander in chief, who I believe was the least thrilled and most disappointed person present. In speaking to us after the surrender he remarked: 'It was a most disappointing day. It was a pitiful day, to see those great ships coming in like sheep being herded by dogs to their fold, without an effort on anybody's part.'

"And no one of his audience dissented. They were as helpless as sheep. About two hours' vigil satisfied our commanders that such was the case, and we secured battle stations. Later investigation showed that all our precautions were quite unnecessary. Not only had the powder and ammunition been removed from the German ships, but their range finders, gun sights, fire control, and very breech blocks as well. They were the husks of their former fighting selves in a miserable state as to equipment, upkeep, and repair. For example, in passing May Island at the entrance of the Firth of Forth, Admiral Beatty signalled one of the German squadrons to put on 17 knots and close up in formation. The reply came to him, 'We cannot do better than 12 knots. Lack lubricating oil.' What chance, then, of a modern engagement where a speed of at least 18 knots is sustained? Apparently they were no better off for food. Hardly had they anchored when the crews turned-to with hook and line to catch what they might for dinner!

"Guarded on every side, the German ships entered the firth at about three o'clock quietly to drop anchor outside the nets. We stood in past them, as they rode peacefully to the tide, and on to our berths, squadron after squadron, type after type, until their German eyes must have bulged in awe at such a vast array of power. Last of all came the *Queen Elizabeth*, flagship of the Grand Fleet, with Admiral Beatty."

The British naval chief then signaled: "The German flag is to be hauled down at 3:37 P.M. (sundown) and is not to be hoisted again without permission."

The silence ordered for the British and American sailors in the presence of the defeated enemy was not broken until the *Queen Elizabeth* passed down the columns of the Allied squadron. Each ship then echoed successively with lusty cheering for Admiral Beatty. Colors were dipped, the guards presented arms, ships' bands struck up the national airs of the United States, Britain, and France.

The eyes of the toughest sea dogs moistened and shone with tears. All present were overwhelmed by the emotion and meaning of the occasion.

Then, at 3:37, a bugle sounded. Down, down, came the black cross flags from the sterns of seventy warships.* The mournful notes faded against the rugged Scottish hills surrounding the great anchorage. A gull cried, then was still. Lights winked on in ship after ship in the mist and gloom of early evening.

It was all over.

The surrendered enemy fleet, "bound in misery and iron," as the *London Times* wrote, settled down to its long internment. The United States battleships, within the short space of ten days, were ready to up anchor for home. After an exchange of pleasantries between Beatty and Rodman, the "heavies" got under way. Lieutenant Hunter, who had described the surrender, continued his narrative:

"The decks of the Grand Fleet's ships were packed with humanity. Not alone were there the sailors of the ships' companies, but boatload after boatload of people from the shore had come aboard the ships which lined our channel to the sea. The

---

*The ships to be surrendered and "interned in a neutral port" grossed 364,751 tons and included nine battleships, five battle cruisers, seven light cruisers, and fifty destroyers. However, one destroyer struck a mine and sank en route.

Sixth Battle Squadron weighed anchor, broke from its maintops long streaming 'Homeward-bound' pennants and proceeded out of harbour. Our band burst forth with 'Homeward Bound' and followed it with 'Good Bye-e-e!'

"Cheers were exchanged with every vessel as we passed between the columns, while their bands played our airs, and messages of comradeship and good luck floated in a score of different versions from as many yardarms. Nor was that the end. The *New York*, followed by the *Texas, Nevada, Arkansas, Wyoming* and *Florida* in column, was escorted to May Island, twenty miles outside, by the ships of the Fifth Battle Squadron, our sister division, and the Eleventh Destroyer Flotilla. The *Barham*, Admiral Leveson's flagship, and the *Malaya* steamed to starboard, with the *Valiant* and *Warspite* to port. The destroyers took up a screening formation ahead and astern. There was music and cheering nearly all the way, culminating as we approached May Island. The British units turned gracefully outward, swinging through 180 degrees. There was a sustained roar of cheers as the great ships parted from us, and the signal force was put to it in the rapid exchange of felicitous messages. From the masthead of Admiral Leveson's *Barham* was displayed at the last the plain English hoist 'G-O-O-D B-Y-E-E-E.' Simultaneously a message was received by radio from the Commander-in-Chief, Grand Fleet:

" 'Your comrades in the Grand Fleet regret your departure. We trust it is only temporary and that the interchange of squadrons from the two great fleets of the Anglo-Saxon race may be repeated. We wish you good-bye, good luck, a good time; and come back soon!' "

He did not realize *how* soon they would return. Although Beatty himself would not live to witness it, the United States Navy would be fighting once more at the side of the Royal Navy in twenty-four tragically short years.

The High Seas Fleet was tucked away in the rocky prison of the Orkneys and all but forgotten. The Allies wrestled with peace terms for Germany which, peculiarly, did not consider herself defeated. The very name 'Versailles' became a symbol of halfway measures and frustration to those who fancied, in mingled despair and conceit, that they had won the war, and a harsh, despotic stigma to the losers.

In fact, as late as May, 1919, there seemed grave doubt that the Treaty of Versailles* would be ratified by any of the nations represented. As June commenced, there were speculations as to whether an absence of peace meant that the powers were retrogressing to war.

"America can go to hell!" stormed the increasingly vitriolic Ludendorff.

Aboard the seventy interned warships, morale of the "housekeeping" crews—only 1,800 Germans altogether—sank lower and lower. Forbidden ashore, they could not even keep in touch with the land world by radio. Transmitting and receiving equipment had been removed along with the breech blocks and range finders of the guns. For food and newspapers, the officers and men were dependent on the once-a-week steamer from Wilhelmshaven, although sometimes the captain of the water barge from Kirkwall tossed them copies of the English papers.

The inhabitants of the Orkneys did not tend to squander pity on the "Huns." Still living on the perimeter of the Royal Navy anchorage were too many widows, fatherless children, and mothers who had lost their sons in the great war at sea. They had not forgotten.

Other than the water tender and the weekly mail and provisions ship from Germany, the only other visitors to interrupt the sailors' abandonment were the large, gray, constantly foraging gulls of this northern clime and, once in a while, excursion boats. The tourists on these small ferries came to gawk at the unhappy sailors from across the North Sea and their increasingly shabby fleet as if they were animals in a zoo.

What rankled the Germans, in addition to their punishing isolation, was the fact that they had not been interned in a "neutral port," as specified in the original armistice proposal. As June wore on, the men were increasingly haunted by the fear that

*It was never ratified by the United States, which remained technically at war with Germany until the summer of 1921 when President Warren G. Harding signed into effect a special Congressional resolution declaring peace with Austria and Germany. The agreement omitted any reference to Versailles or that American anathema, the League of Nations.

they would be compelled to renew battle with their erstwhile foe. Their crews were too small to man vessels which probably could not even operate, aim guns which would not fire and for which there was no ammunition.

Since the sailors were kept more or less in the dark about the day-to-day developments in the treaty deliberations at Versailles, their commander, Admiral von Reuter, decided to prepare for the worst. This resolve was given the weight of an order about mid-May when an emissary from the Socialist government in Berlin, riding the mail boat, "suggested" to the admiral that it would be unthinkable if these rusting remnants of the High Seas Fleet, pitiful as they were, should be turned over to the British Navy. Possibly, one day, they would be used against the very people for whom they had fought. Even if that calamity did not occur, England might sell the old warships.

Quietly, from that day on, von Reuter made preparations to scuttle his fleet.

"It was very thorough," recalls Ruge, now the captain of the same *B-110* torpedo boat on which he had futilely tried to stem the mutiny in Schillig Roads. "We put explosive charges [smuggled on the mail boat] under the big sea-water condensers, which, when destroyed, would allow a torrent of water into the bilges. We set the sea cocks on a hair-turning and lubricated them heavily. We placed large hammers beside any valves which, when knocked off, would allow the water to rush in.

"We did our job efficiently on every ship—and very secretly!"

The tragic and entirely unnecessary denouement of this clandestine naval operation came on the bright, warm morning of June 21. Admiral Sir Sydney Fremantle,* commanding the watchdog squadron at Scapa Flow, decided to sail into the North Sea this sunny Saturday for torpedo and gunnery practice.

With the sun barely up and gulls screaming at the fantails of his immaculate, speedy squadron, Fremantle on his flagship *Revenge* put out from Scapa Flow. Naturally he did not advise

---

*Former commanding officer of the 3rd Battle Squadron at the Dardanelles, the hard-bitten Fremantle led a naval assemblage which was successor to the Grand Fleet. The latter had ceased to exist as a wartime entity.

von Reuter what he was up to. The stern, plain-spoken Fremantle never communicated with his former enemy except through the most junior of subordinates. Indeed he went out of his way to snub this officer of equal rank, stature, and dignity.

The German admiral watched the frothing wakes of the British fleet flattening through the eastern exits of the anchorage. Somehow, although he had observed the Royal Navy come and go hundreds of times during his long confinement, von Reuter decided that this time was *it*. England was in all likelihood steaming out to renew the war. In his distressed state, the news relayed by the water tender of a forty-eight-hour moratorium at Versailles only magnified von Reuter's phantasms of approaching doom.

From his "flagship," the cruiser *Emden*, successor to the raider of the same name, the admiral hoisted a signal: "Paragraph 11. Acknowledge!"

It was simply a code meaning, "Prepare to scuttle!"

The nearest ships replied, "Ready for sinking!"

The time was 11:20 A.M.

Incongruously enough, as the German sailors raced below to destroy condensers, open sea cocks, smash a succession of valves and pipes, and remove bulkhead rivets, an excursion boat, the *Flying Kestrel*, carrying 200 schoolchildren, poked in and out of the anchored High Seas Fleet. Exuding a gay mood in the beautiful weather, the youngsters waved ebulliently and threw candy wrappings toward the warships. The paper fluttered to the water like confetti.

There were few Germans above decks to wave back. But the children couldn't be expected to understand this significant absence. Indeed, the Royal Navy itself hadn't been able to anticipate trouble.

Shortly, von Reuter raised his final command:

"Condition Z—scuttle!"

"On all the torpedo boats," wrote Captain Hermann Cordes, in charge of these craft, "new battle flags and spotless squadron and commission pennants were hauled high. The VI Flotilla, however, did not receive the message immediately since it was anchored behind a projection of land which half hid it.

"Once the valves and sea cocks were wrenched open, their keys and handles were thrown overboard, as were entire intake valves of the condensers. Now they could not be closed again—ever! In moments the cold water was rushing and gurgling over all decks.

"The boats listed. Sea water now poured through open portholes.

"The fleet was in its death throes! One boat dipped up and down. A second shuddered, lay over on beam ends, then smashed against a neighbor as she sank. A third and then a fourth sank on even keel!"

Ashore it was a "staggering spectacle" as the ships, "in surprisingly short time began to settle down." One watcher saw a battleship, the *Friedrich der Grosse*, go under first, flying the national colors as well as the Red flag on the mainmast.

"By 1 P.M.," recalled a witness, "the scene beggared description. What an hour before had been a stately fleet, riding calmly at anchor, was now an array of reeling and rocking battleships whose doom was written in their movements.

"Here a destroyer would disappear amid a cloud of steam; there a battleship would take her last plunge and disappear in a tumult of spray. One would settle down by the stern, another would heel over until only her keel showed above the water."

Orkney islanders could discern German sailors taking to their boats as the entirely incongruous strains of "Deutschland über Alles" piped across the otherwise calm waters from the remnants of bands which the larger warships had carried into internment. The first English tugs to the scene were greeted with a peculiarly reminiscent "*Kamerad!*" from boats, and from swimmers who had jumped at the last minute. Several powered whaleboats were taking smaller skiffs in tow.

In white fury, Admiral Fremantle, who had received the incredible intelligence by radio just off May Island at the commencement of firing practice, was hammering back into the east channel at flank speed. To the custodian officer, it was almost as though he had lost his own fleet. The German men-of-war were *his* responsibility. Even a spontaneous mental image of the Huns swinging by the yardarm did not blot out a more terrifying one of himself standing before the glowering judges of a court-martial.

Ruge's *B-110* which had been anchored near the shore was among the first to plunge under. The commanding officer then made his way to a rocky vantage point to observe "the most impressive spectacle" he had ever witnessed. He watched two tugs struggling with the *Hindenburg*, which was reeling like some obese, staggering tippler. She righted, the tugs started to haul her shoreward when, with a new list and a long sigh of outrushing air from her vitals, she sloshed majestically below.

Cordes, the torpedo-boat commander, heard his men, some in small boats, others still abandoning, sounding three cheers for the fatherland for which they had offered this "death sacrifice." The shades of Wagner and all the Teuton gods of war who had bequeathed to the German people a legacy of doom, revenge, and hopelessness were hovering over Scapa Flow this beautiful June afternoon.

It was incongruous in the twentieth century. But there it was.

"The orders," Cordes continued, "to hoist the white flag in

Afraid they would have to resume fighting, the Germans decided to scuttle their fleet. Their unprecendented naval suicide at Scapa Flow—the sinking of seventy ships within two hours—far exceeded the destruction at Jutland.

the event of attack, direct or passive, from land or sea would be meticulously followed.

"However, we had little chance even to show our flags of surrender. In panicky haste, steam drifters, which had been at anchor beside the mother ships HMS *Sandhurst* and *Victorious*, joined by other armed fishing boats, tugs, salvage vessels and two destroyers, the *Vesper* and *Vega*—which cast off moorings in foaming fury—converged on the unarmed lifeboats, firing at us with cannon, machine guns, and even pistols.

"They scorned all international law, to say nothing of the dictates of humanity!

"The English Navy behaved as though insane. Sailors, engineers, officers, and even civilian personnel with them shrieked and bellowed in a crazy discord.

"There was no explanation for such conduct. They shot wild, boarded one boat only to turn it adrift in the next moment. Some even boarded our sinking ships to snatch our flags and trample upon them, or to gather up souvenirs in the final seconds before the craft submerged.

"Three of our lifeboats were sunk by gunfire. The shooting kept up even after the survivors had plunged into the water. A half-sunk torpedo boat next came under concentrated fire. Those remaining on board did not know whether to follow their shipmates into the numbing cold of Scapa Flow, in which already floated our dead.

"And through this mayhem, we could see the drifters blinking in Morse code to the shore, 'German ships are sinking!' Then, by megaphone there came the shouted command:

"'Attention the commander of the torpedo boats. Return to your ships immediately. Stop the scuttling, or we'll blast you all to hell!'

"Many crewmen could not return to their ships since water pressure forced them away. Others, who gained their craft found the weight of only a few men was sufficient to capsize the already waterlogged ships. The British replied to the Germans' entreaties:

"'Then you shall die on board!'"

Other representatives of the Royal Navy, nonetheless, were

more taciturn about the drama unfolding before their eyes. Admiral Strauss, still in the Orkneys to supervise the final clearing of the northern barrage, saw the ships going under as he gazed out of his office window at Kirkwall:

"Good heavens!" he exclaimed to a British officer of similar rank. "They're sinking. . . ."

The latter looked up. He studied the spectacle for a moment, then returned to his penciling, with the wistful acknowledgment:

"Aren't they, now?"

The main body of Admiral Fremantle's squadron was boiling into Hoy Sound. The destroyer *Spencer*, in the vanguard, hove to alongside the torpedo boat *S-132* which had resisted scuttling more stubbornly than the others. Lieutenant Commander Oscar Wehr was to quote Captain MacLean, flotilla leader aboard the flagship *Spencer*, as declaring that every officer who sank his own ship would be "shot on the spot!"

As many German officers as could be found were then rounded up and put under the guard of Royal Marines on the stern of the *S-132*. When young Lieutenant Lampe tried to break free and rush forward to protect his men, an English civilian—possibly attached to naval intelligence—fired his revolver. The bullet grazed Lampe's temple.

It was worse on the cutter *V 126*, under command of Lieutenant Zaeschmar. In spite of continual cries of "surrender!" (assuming such were needed to indicate the craft's helpless, unarmed plight) the small patrol vessel was riddled with shellfire from an armed drifter. Two warrant officers were killed, three others and two junior commissioned officers were seriously wounded.

Admiral Fremantle steamed through the sunken, half-sunken, still foundering and beached German Navy—seventy ships, virtually every one lost beyond reclaim, and within the space of two hours. Nothing like it had ever occurred in naval history. No Jutland ever approximated the physical carnage of this mass suicide.

The former enemy fleet had at last burst its bonds of "misery and iron."

National Archives

Rejoicing on Grand Boulevard, Paris, at news of the armistice, November 11, 1918.

The next day, while hitherto glum German citizens rejoiced over this "great triumph" Fremantle assembled the officers and petty officers from the German hulks on the *Revenge*, a warship appropriately named for this somber occasion. His anger raged unabated.

"Before I send you ashore as a prisoner of war," the British admiral addressed von Reuter directly, "I would like to express my indignation at the deed which you have perpetrated and which was that of a traitor violating the action of the arrangements entered into by the Allies. The German fleet was in a sense more interned than actually imprisoned. The vessels were resting here as a sort of goodwill from the German government until

292   •   Verdict: Suicide

Victory parade on Fifth Avenue, New York City, marks end of war.

peace had been signed. It is not the first occasion on which the Germans have violated all the decent laws and rules of the seas."

The butchery had stopped. Six Germans, by official count, had died, ten were wounded. An undisclosed number were "missing." Most of the crews would be herded to prison where they would languish for the next six months. There was no more talk of executions "on the spot." Reasoned counsel had penetrated through from London.

The rusty remnants of the High Seas Fleet would persist as lingering tragedians which somehow had ignored cues to leave the stage and die properly, as the script directed. On the other

Hint of a war to come: Almost unnoticed in the welcoming crowd, a minor political figure waits on a tug in the New York harbor to greet the returning crews. Franklin Delano Roosevelt was then assistant secretary of the navy.

hand, those not scuttled would join their sisters in the dark depths of the sea—but in a fashion which would have been most disillusioning to their designers.

The nation which had invented the aircraft carrier would initiate the challenge of plane versus capital ship. In February, 1921, off the Isle of Wight, the British sank the 28,000-ton *Baden*, commissioned in 1917, by aerial torpedoes and bombs. The target battleship which, like the *Bayern*, mounted 15-inch guns, had nonetheless been damaged by previous surface torpedoings and shellfire.

The Admiralty was extremely cautious in announcing this first example of a capital ship falling victim, David-and-Goliath-like, to the tiny, frail and otherwise vulnerable airplanes. Since their professional security and creeds had been shaken, the old admirals rejected the results. Their tired minds could not accept the implications for the future. In the army, the artillery generals reacted in harmony.

Lord Jellicoe, on an extended vacation in New Zealand, minimized the operation, reaffirming his faith in battleships. From the seething wreckage of Germany, the aged von Tirpitz admitted that the enemy's battleships had won the war and predicted they would sail on in their role of unchallenged supremacy.

But the British demonstration fired the imagination of several American officers, including Admiral Sims and Brigadier General William ("Billy") Mitchell, war hero and aggressively crusading exponent of air power. Mitchell had angered War Department brass by stumping noisily for more and more airplanes, even at the expense of artillery and ground forces.

Between the two outspoken officers, one representing the army, the other the navy, tests were finally arranged. Three rusty U-boats, plus the *Ostfriesland*, the *Frankfurt*, the *S-132* (on which Lieutenant Lampe had been shot), and the cutter *V-43* were patched up and hauled across the Atlantic to the Virginia Capes.

No one was overly surprised when, in July, 1921, the submarines were easily disposed of by aerial attack. They were small and vulnerable. Why shouldn't a few bombs destroy them? Depth charges had done so all through the war.

The *Ostfriesland* and the *Frankfurt*, targets of grouped army and navy planes, went the watery way of the U-boats. There should have been little doubt that air power had come into its own and that sea power was on the wane.

The Washington Conference for the Limitation of Armaments seconded at least the latter conclusion. The great maritime powers—Great Britain, the United States, and Japan—agreed, in that order, to maintain a 5-5-3 ratio of naval strength. The two Western nations meticulously honored their side of the bargain, scrapping many of their best and largest warships.

Japan, with humble obeisance to the "spirit" of the pact, dismantled old, noncommissioned relics, obsolete even at the time of her assault on Russia in 1904. She carried the farce to the preposterous extreme of tearing up blueprints of projected war vessels. But in the teeming Mitsubishi and Kawasaki yards in Kure, Yokohama, Kobe, and Sasebo, shipbuilders sweated under floodlights the night through, hastening the completion of nearly 200,000 tons of modern naval vessels (equal to the combined tonnage of American and British ships on the ways).

Japanese rearmament continued at an ever-accelerating, perilous pace. By the 30's, the war machines of Germany and Italy would be making their own strident harmony with Nippon's. The world again was steaming on a collision course for war. Forgotten in the mounting excitement and bombast of it all were the Coronels and the Falklands, the Jutlands, Dardanelles, and most assuredly the Scapa Flows. The lessons, it seemed, were never learned.

Appendix 1

The *Kent* and the *Glasgow* became implacable nemeses of the *Dresden*. They spent the winter without rest, devoting their full energies to her pursuit. On March 14, 1915, they located the elusive cruiser tucked away among the rocks, reefs, and hills of the Juan Fernández Islands, off the Chilean coast from Valparaíso.

While his lieutenant, Wilhelm Canaris, cleverly stalled for time under a flag of truce, Captain Luedecke opened the sea valves and placed scuttling charges in his anchored and almost helpless warship— a weary sea wolf, whose pack had been destroyed, unable even to scurry back to its lair. The *Dresden* was out of coal, out of ammunition, low too in the essentials of living: food and clothing.

Once Canaris had been persuaded to hurry back to his cruiser, conveying Captain Luce's grave doubts that the *Dresden* really had been interned by a neutral country, as the wily German lieutenant had insisted, the British officer's impatience prevailed. He opened fire.

The crew hastily abandoned the cruiser and swam or rowed ashore —for true internment. A few on board the *Glasgow* reported they had witnessed a singular sight: an enemy sinking, flying both her battle pennants and a flag of surrender. Captain Luedecke denied he had ever surrendered his command. With the scuttling charges and the enemy's fire, he didn't have to.

The British had wiped out the last remnant of von Spee's once formidable squadron. They had, however, lost a chance to seize an officer who would, in another war, become Adolf Hitler's *Abwehr* (Intelligence Bureau) chief, the notorious Admiral Canaris. All too late disenchanted with the Fuehrer, Canaris was hanged in the closing weeks of World War II for his part in anti-Nazi conspiracies.

Appendix 2

The loss of the 19,000-ton *President Lincoln,* a former German liner and one of the most efficient troop transports, should never have happened. She was returning from her fifth voyage to France, carrying 715 persons, including 30 officers and men of the Navy, some of whom were wounded, a few paralyzed, and many ill with influenza and varied maladies.

While she was in convoy with three other transports—the *Susquehanna, Rijndam,* and *Antigone*—her destroyer escort had taken off during the night to pick up the inbound prize among transports, the giant *Leviathan.* While the *President Lincoln* could steam along at more than fifteen knots, faster than any U-boat, she had to fetter herself to eleven knots, the speed of the slowest vessel in the convoy, the *Rijndam.* All the officers shared the misgivings of the transport's captain, Commander Percy W. Foote. And these trepidations were well-founded.

The *U-90* picked up the four unprotected vessels earlier in the evening, trailed them in brilliant moonlight for a few hours. It seemed too easy to be true. There must be a trick, speculated Captain J. Remy, relatively new to the submarine service. Were they all Q-boats?

However, he determined the convoy's base course, strangely steady, and started off on a long circle. By dawn, if the transports did not alter course, he would be off their bows and in firing position.

Among the *Lincoln*'s officers was a twenty-seven-year-old junior lieutenant, Victor G. Isaacs, an Iowan just three years out of Annapolis. Shortly before 9 A.M., May 31, a clear, cool morning, while the ship was six hundred miles west of Brest, Isaacs was finishing a leisurely breakfast. He had been both hungry and tired, since he had just come off watch at his station: two aft 6-inch guns. He recalls:*

"I was almost alone when I heard a dulled report and slight tremor followed by another perhaps three seconds later.

"Two bells had just struck.

*In a letter to and conversations with the author, and from his official reports and memoirs.

"I jumped up, rushed to my room, grabbed my life jacket, and ran aft to get to my station. I was on the starboard side and had just cleared the superstructure and was headed down the ladder to the main deck when the third torpedo struck on the port side sending a spray of water up in the air, boosting one of the lifeboats up off its davits and crashing it down on the deck. I no longer was in doubt—this explosion was much louder and I could see sailors running to their stations.

"At this time the alarm sounded because those on the bridge said they distinctly saw the wake of the torpedo. My own crews aft were already manning the guns and on order from the bridge voice tube I gave the command to fire at will.

"Of course the plan was to keep the sub underwater and thus permit the other three ships to get away...."

They made good their escape. Within fifteen minutes, the *Lincoln* presented the preposterous spectacle of a large ship half-sunk, half in action. Isaacs was calling through the speaking tube, asking for orders, since Commander Foote was still on the bridge:

"Water was approaching the main deck. They had already abandoned the ship up forward. Our guns were still firing. When I gave the order to abandon ship, my two crews at the guns and my repair gang up from the next deck from which they had been chased by the mounting water from within, threw overboard a dozen or so of the big balsa rafts and we all walked off the deck into the water only a couple of feet below us.

"At 9:30 we were well clear, and the old ship, turning over gently to starboard, put her nose in the air and went down."

After paddling about for several minutes on the raft, Isaacs heard an officer on the submarine shout, "Come aboard!" Then:

"We pulled alongside and as I rose to step out of the lifeboat, the men, realizing that I was about to leave them, perhaps never to return, raised their voices in protest and tried to restrain me. I turned to calm them, telling them not to worry, that it was only the fortunes of war, and stepping onto the gunwale I grasped the hands of those nearest me in a heartfelt good-bye and jumped on the deck of the submarine. As I walked along the deck, a German sailor came behind me and took my pistol. I then gave him the whole belt. Going up to the conning tower, I saluted the officer whom I took to be the captain. He addressed me in rather fair English as follows:

" 'Are you the captain of the *President Lincoln?*'

" 'No, sir!' I replied. 'I believe the captain went down with the ship, for I have not seen him since. I am the first lieutenant.'

" 'I am Captain Remy,' he said." *

Isaacs was taken below and given a glass of sherry to warm him up. The U-boat started for Germany. Off the Shetlands, the *U-90* was depth charged for nearly an hour by two American destroyers which Isaacs later learned were the *Smith* and *Warrington*. Both had arrived at the scene of the sinking just too late but had been implacably dogging the submarine's homeward journey ever since. Submerging to a depth of nearly 200 feet saved the *U-90,* and Lieutenant Isaacs, "although five bombs were very close and shook us up considerably."

By this time, Isaacs decided he had learned so much about inner workings of U-boats and their defenses against depth chargings that he should attempt to escape and present his intelligence to his navy or his Allies. He recalled:

"I racked my brains for ideas. I searched the ship for 'escape material.' I ransacked the drug locker in my efforts to find something to aid me in either capturing the submarine or taking my leave of it. On the plea of wanting to clean my pistol I got it back again . . . but I had only twenty cartridges and my captors numbered forty-seven. The odds surely seemed against me."

However, off the Danish coast, the determined young naval officer tried anyhow. Just about to leap overboard, he was seized by Remy and hustled firmly below. Isaacs was landed at Wilhelmshaven, then moved to Karlsruhe where the army took custody of him. He was immediately put with other Allied officer POWs in transit "stalags," or camps. From each one, Isaacs attempted to escape, abortively as had been his first try.

Isaacs was finally sent on his way by train to the American and Russian officers' camp at Villingen. "The train was making about forty miles an hour and we were passing through a valley which was rather thickly populated. The guns of the guards were pointed toward me and they did look ugly; but the window near our seat was open and I was sure that I could reach it at a bound, so if they fired they would be just as likely to hit one of the other passengers as me. It was warm and close in the carriage and one of the guards was dozing. I waited until the other slightly turned his head to answer a question put by one of the soldiers with whom he was talking. Then, jumping up, with my knapsack hanging from my neck, I leaped past both guards and tried to dive through the window. It was small, probably eighteen inches wide and

*British patrols sank the *U-90* in October. Captain Remy was not on board at the time.

twenty-four inches high; and as there was nothing on the outside of the car to hold to, I had to depend on my momentum and the weight of my head and shoulders to carry the rest of my body along. My head and shoulders went through nicely; and then with the shouts of the guards ringing in my ears I simply fell and all went dark.

"When I disappeared from view the guards must have pulled the bell-rope, for the train came to a stop about three hundred yards farther along. In the meantime I had landed on the track that paralleled the one on which the train was running. The bed was of crushed rock and the ties of steel. My head struck one tie and I was stunned, but rolled over and over; and the shaking up must have brought me again to my senses, for by the time the train had stopped I was struggling to my feet.

"Then I made a terrible discovery: my knees had apparently struck the tie next to the one that damaged my head, and when I tried to run I found they were so cut and bruised that I could not bend them. My feet, too, had been cut across the insteps, my body was all bruised and my hands and arms had small pieces of rock ground in; but in spite of all this no bones were broken. Had it not been for the condition of my knees I should have been able to make my escape; but by the time I was on my feet trying to shuffle away, the guards had descended from the train and were rapidly advancing toward me firing as they came.

"I tried to run, but could make very little headway, and soon I was exhausted. My breath came in gasps and I finally fell to the ground. I was dragging myself along by pulling on the grass when the last shot passed between my ear and shoulder and buried itself in the ground in front of me. The guards were then less than seventy-five yards away, and I just had time to turn over, raise myself to a half-sitting and half-lying posture and elevate my hands above my head as a sign that I surrendered, before they were on me.

"With fiendish fury the first guard, turning his gun end for end and grasping it by the muzzle, rushed on me, and dealt me a smashing blow on the head. It knocked me unconscious and I rolled down the hill. When I came to my senses I was lying in a shallow ditch at the foot of the hill and the guards were cursing and kicking me trying to make me get up.

"Many of the people from the hayfields nearby had gathered to watch the fun. Among them I noticed many women and children and a few old men. One old veteran with a pitchfork in his hands came running up and offered his services to the guards in case I should become dangerous. No one in all that crowd offered a word of sympathy or tried to remonstrate with my captors in the punishment they were administering—and these were the best people of Germany, the pious, church-going Baden peasants!

"And I must have made such a pitiable-looking spectacle! The blood was streaming down my face from the wound in my head where it had struck the railroad tie; my trousers at the knees had been ground into the flesh; and my hands were torn and bleeding. When they re-captured me they struck me on the head and body with their guns until one broke his rifle. It snapped in two at the small of the stock as he struck me with the butt on the back of the head.

"I was given two weeks solitary confinement, for this attempt to escape, but continued trying, for I was determined to get my information back to the navy. Finally, on the night of October 6, assisted by several American army officers, I was able to effect an escape by short-circuiting all lighting circuits in the prison camp and cutting through barbed-wire fences surrounding the camp.

"Sentries cried out: 'Halt! Halt!' several times in rapid succession to me and my companion, an American officer in the French army.

"When we dropped to the ground we whirled and ran away from the camp and past the guards who had approached to within a few feet of the bridge. As we did so, both guards fired and the one on my right had the end of his rifle so close to my head that the flash seemed to singe my hair. But neither of us was hit during the next few minutes. There was a regular hail of bullets sprinkling the side of the hill. But as we were mere shadows only a little blacker than the darkness and moving swiftly we soon were completely blended with the surrounding obscurity.

"I made my way for seven days and nights over mountains to the Rhine, which to the south of Baden forms the boundary between Germany and Switzerland. After a four-hour crawl on hands and knees I was able to elude the sentries along the Rhine. Plunging in, I made for the Swiss shore. After being carried several miles down the stream, being frequently submerged by the rapid current, I finally reached the opposite shore and gave myself up to the Swiss gendarmes, who turned me over to the American legation at Berne. From there I made my way to Paris and then London and finally Washington, where I arrived four weeks after my escape from Germany."

Isaacs made a fast trip to the United States on the *Olympic*. He arrived in Washington early on November 11. In fact, he was standing in a window of the State, War and Navy Building beside Assistant Navy Secretary Roosevelt when the crowds cheered Wilson, across the street at the White House. The armistice was official. The war was over.

The plucky lieutenant, who had come home the hard way, received a Congressional Medal of Honor for his bravery, if not necessarily his patience. After the war he made a successful career of politics, representing the San Diego, California, Congressional district for five terms. Under the legally altered name Izac, he now lives in retirement in Washington, D.C.

Notes and Acknowledgments

CHAPTER 1: The Battling Liners

Not since he was researching his first book, *The Last Voyage of the Lusitania,* has the author been aided so greatly and by so many survivors from a disaster or an engagement involving a single ship. He heard from or of approximately two dozen who served on the *Carmania* during her history-making fight fifty years ago.

Help in this quest was extended initially from a number of sources including the "Old Codgers" column of the *London Daily Mirror* and the letters-to-the-editor columns of other English newspapers, the Cunard Steam-Ship Co. Ltd., the British Legion, and, from the other side of the Great War, from Dr. Jurgen Rohwer, of the Bibliothek für Zeitgeschichte Weltkriegsbücherei (a library in Stuttgart for World War documentary books) and Rudolph Krohne, of the Okeanos Verlag publishers, Munich.

The author, first of all, owes a debt of gratitude to three persons with whom he has established virtually an old-friends' kind of correspondence. They are Mrs. Sylvia H. Ogley, of Garrison-on-Hudson, New York, whose husband, Victor Ogley, was a lieutenant on the *Carmania;* Harry Gordon Barr, of Racine, Wisconsin, the son of James Clayton Barr, the steamship-line captain of the liner; and Harold Kendall, of Montgomeryshire, Wales, who was an engineer officer on the ship.

Retired Admiral Otto W. Steffan, of Litzelstetten, West Germany, wireless chief on the *Cap Trafalgar,* gave generously of his time to write for this book the German side of the sea fight. In so doing, he has filled a long-standing vacuum in the naval archives both of the United States and Great Britain. Admiral Steffan is, perhaps, the only living survivor of the crew of the *Cap Trafalgar.*

A lively correspondence has grown up among the survivors of the sea battle as a result of the author's queries. As an example, Admiral Steffan wrote to Harold Kendall in an eloquent spirit of bygones:

"Now fifty years have passed since that time. We all have done our duty as seamen, but we are all asking why we must fight each other in two great wars. Perhaps our children and grandchildren will be more prudent. The fate of all Europe is now at stake and I hope that both nations will understand each other better in the future than in the past."

These *Carmania* survivors, too, rendered invaluable assistance as they searched in the treasures of their lockboxes and their memories: Guy A. Barber, of West Southwold, Sussex; A. J. Bowles, Essex; William Curtin, Liverpool; William Cowling, Port Isaac, Cornwall; A. D. Crowther, Perth, West Australia; Fred J. Harper, Southampton; John MacKenzie, Manor Park, London; F. J. May, Southampton; Richard Henry Richards, Penzance (communicating through his daughter, Mrs. B. Iris Russell); Wing Cdr. H. W. St. John, R.A.F. (Ret.), Peacehaven, Sussex (who would like to know about expatriate St. Johns in the United States besides the actress Jill St. John); Charles Smith, Wandsworth, London (through his brother-in-law, E. L. Searle); and Thomas Tabb, Port Isaac, Cornwall.

Further appreciation is expressed to C. J. Boyle, Liverpool; Frederick Cant, East Yorkshire, friend of an assistant wireless operator on the *Carmania*; Frank Cook; Mrs. Mabel Danskin, Dumfrieshire, niece of a crewman, Thomas Woodman (who named his daughter Carmania, and his son Noel Grant); Mrs. Rita Duncan, Crosby, Liverpool, whose husband, Engineer Lieutenant James Duncan and his cousin, James MacDonald, both served on the Cunarder (Lieutenant Duncan was among 2,500 to perish in the bombing of the *Lancastria* off St. Nazaire, June 17, 1940); R. J. Elsworthy, Devon; T. Johnston, Liverpool, son of a *Carmania* crewman; Cdr. P. K. Kemp, head of the Historical Section, the Admiralty, Whitehall, who also aided in the spadework for other chapters in this book; Peter J. Levins, Blackpool; John G. McCrohan, Ruislip, Middlesex, son of John McCrohan, Sr., who served aboard the *Carmania*; H. Novelli, Liverpool, whose father was a bos'n on the liner; J. H. Pierce, Holyhead, one of nine children left by Gunner First Class Richard Edward Pierce when he was killed on the *Carmania;* Leslie Reade, author and lawyer of London, who, as a boy, traveled on the *Carmania*, *Lusitania*, and other famed ships of the day, but somehow missed the *Titanic*, about which he is nonetheless an eminent authority; W. I. L. Roberts, North Wales; N. J. Turff, Cowes.

Many of these survivors or their friends or relatives loaned the author newspaper and magazine clippings pertaining to the unusual sea fight, and photographs, both official and personal. Many of them still treasure a souvenir booklet published shortly afterward by Cunard. Ships of that company, including the *Queen Elizabeth*, still display murals of the unusual engagement.

An answer to the question of why the *Kronprinz Wilhelm* did not continue to the side of her mortally wounded sister is found in a fascinating book written by one of her officers, a Polish-German, Alfred von Niezychowski (*The Cruise of "The Kronprinz Wilhelm,"* Doubleday, Doran & Co., Inc., New York, 1929). Telling of the frantic preparations to ready the ship for battle as her thirty-year-old captain, Paul Thierfelder, drove her through the South Atlantic, Niezychowski asserted that a cessation of *Cap Trafalgar*'s SOS's inspired the belief that the armed liner had gone down.

"Our own situation had now become critical," he wrote. "There were doubtless in the neighborhood into which we were speeding many Allied war vessels. All of them must have heard the calls of the *Cap Trafalgar* which, though in German code, had been supplemented by the *Carmania* in the British code. . . . if we arrived we would be too late to assist the German vessel which we already regarded as sunk, and would most probably be just in time to become engaged ourselves."

As it turned out, the nearest Royal Navy warships were several hours away and the *Kronprinz Wilhelm* missed the great opportunity of her own cruise: to sail in and polish off a reeling, furiously burning *Carmania* with a few rounds.

Possessed of an exceptionally good sense of humor, Niezychowski also devotes a number of pages to the great rat hunt aboard the *Kronprinz Wilhelm*.

Articles which were especially helpful appeared shortly after the battle in *The Graphic*, of London, the *Illustrated London News*, the *Times*, of London, the *London Daily Mail*, the *Manchester Guardian*, and the *Liverpool Post* (all of which have been consulted, as well, for most of the chapters in this book).

Special thanks also are due Miss Rose Coombs, Librarian, Imperial War Museum, London, for her help in this book. She was as unstinting of her time as she has been when the author has hauled aloft the distress signal during encounters with previous books. He is particularly grateful to her for furnishing, from the Museum files, a three-page typescript of the battle, written by Dr. Harry Clough, ship's surgeon.

Chapters in the following books deal specifically with the *Carmania* fight:

Chatterton, E. Keble. *The Sea-Raiders*, Hurst and Blackett, Ltd., London, 1931

Hurd, Archibald S. *A Merchant Fleet at War*, Cassell & Co., Ltd., London, 1920

Lockhart, J. G. *The Sea, Our Heritage*, Geoffrey Bles, Ltd., London, 1940

Parnis, A. "The Commission of the *Carmania*," an article in *The Nautical Magazine*, vol. 102, 1919

Wheeler, H. F. B. *Daring Deeds of Merchant Seamen in The Great War*, Harrap, London, 1918

Wyllie, W. L. *Sea Fights of The Great War*, Cassell & Co., Ltd., London, 1918

Zobeltitz, Fedor C. M. H. A. von. *Cap Trafalgar*, J. Engelhorns, Stuttgart, 1915

CHAPTERS 2 AND 3: Disaster on the Broad Fourteens
AND Revenge at the Falklands

These two chapters, encompassing the fall and early winter, 1914, are virtually one. While there is considerable documentation on the torpedoing of the *Aboukir*, *Cressy*, and *Hogue* in accounts published at the time, in standard histories, and in memoirs—both English and German—the author was unable to establish contact with anyone who served on any of the three luckless cruisers. Of the 800-some who survived there must be at least one crewman living today. Perhaps one or more will come forward upon the publication of this book.

The British are not proud of this tragedy in the war's opening weeks. "Exploit with No Parallel!" was a subheading with the *New York Times'* account. That it surely was. The Germans, understandably, wished to trumpet their victory to the world. This was accomplished through biographies of the daring U-boat commander, Otto Weddigen, including:

Eggstein, Rudolf. *Seeheld Otto Weddigen,* G. Schloessman, Leipzig, 1915

Otto Weddigen und Seine Waffe, Marinedank-Verlag, Berlin, 1915

Richter, Heinrich. *Otto Weddigen, ein Lebensbild*, Verlag von Velhagen & Klasing, Leipzig, 1915

Spiess, Johannes. *Sechs Jahre U-Bootfahrten*, E. Steiniger, Berlin, 1925

"Unser Seeheld Weddigen," A. Scherl, Berlin, 1915

Thanks to the generous efforts of the Marine-Offizier-Hilfe in Krefeld, West Germany, a locating agency for naval officers, the author was able to establish contact with survivors of both the Falklands and Jutland battles. One of them, retired Kapitän zur See Hans Kotthaus, presented graphic accounts of the Falklands battle from aboard the *Gneisenau*. Kotthaus, who lives in Bergisch Gladbach, remembers waiting in the icy water to be rescued, while albatrosses attacked the helpless survivors. He notes a peculiar difference of attitude toward a vanquished enemy by the *Inflexible* and by the *Invincible*. On the former, which saved Kotthaus, German officers were treated as guests and given the freedom of the battle cruiser. Survivors picked up by the *Invincible*, on the other hand, were kept more or less in solitary confinement, in improvised canvas cells, under heavy guard, and were refused permission to mingle even with one another.

A retired vice admiral, Otto Schenk, of Hamburg-Sasel, had served as signal officer on the *Dresden*. He vividly remembers Wilhelm Canaris as "an especially dear friend . . . the embodiment of intelligence, an officer and a person of the highest character." He recalls his escape from Chilean internment, after the sinking of his ship at Juan Fernández, and an adventurous safari through the pampas to Buenos Aires. He worked in that port as stevedore and restaurant waiter before sailing for home as an ordinary seaman in June, 1917, aboard a Norwegian bark. War's end found the indomitable Schenk in command of a destroyer.

Kurt Hartwig, the torpedo officer of the *Dresden*, now living in Weinheim, followed much the same course as Schenk. Although, like his shipmates, he had "felt the war was over for us," he nonetheless escaped to Valparaíso and returned home by way of Malmö, Sweden. He was serving in the Mediterranean on the *U-202* at the armistice.

The author also wishes to thank Hans Pfülf, of Munich, formerly aboard the *Gneisenau,* and Korvettenkapitän Friedrich Standke, of Hamburg, who was on the *Leipzig*.

M. D. Wetherall, of Windsor, England, was aboard the *Glasgow*, the only ship engaged to survive both the tragedy of Coronel and the battle at the Falklands, and then take part in the chase and final destruction of the *Dresden*. He recently wrote to me, "one of my wounds has opened again, so I am none too good."

For help with background material and photographs of liners in this period of the war, the author also wishes to thank Dr. Schindowski, of the home office of the Hamburg-American Line.

These books have material about the Falklands:

Bingham, Commodore Edward Barry. *Falklands, Jutland and The Bight*, John Murray, London, 1919

Chatterton, E. Keble. *Gallant Gentlemen*, Hurst & Blackett Ltd., London, 1931

Hirst, Lloyd. *Coronel and After*, Peter Davies Ltd., London, 1934

Irving, John. *Coronel and The Falklands*, A. M. Philpot, Ltd., London, 1927

Middlemas, Keith. *Command the Far Seas*, Hutchinson, London, 1961

Pitt, Barrie. *Coronel and Falkland*, Cassell & Co., Ltd., London, 1960

Pochhammer, Capt. Hans. *Before Jutland*, Jarrolds, Ltd., London, 1931

Spencer-Cooper, Cdr. H. *The Battle of the Falkland Islands*, Cassell & Co., Ltd., London, 1919

CHAPTERS 4 AND 5: On Safari for the *Königsberg* AND ". . . something wrong with our bloody ships!"

In the absence of a great quantity of published memoirs or analyses, contemporary newspaper and magazine accounts provided much of the grist for the *Königsberg* chapter. The following two books were, however, helpful:

Chatterton, E. Keble. *The Königsberg Adventure*, Hurst & Blackett, Ltd., London, 1935

King-Hall, Admiral Sir Herbert. *Naval Memoirs and Traditions*, Hutchinson & Co., London, 1925

Kapitän zur See Hans Apel, of Marburg, was personally helpful to the author from his perspective: the most unusual one of a man on a seagoing cruiser trapped in an African jungle.

The material available on Jutland is almost inexhaustible. The problem is entirely one of selection, especially in view of the flood of original material kindly provided the author. (The books will be included in the general bibliography.)

The Jutland fight was, at once, a naval tactician's dream and despair. It was replete with "if's," "lost chances" and blind, often undeserved luck. It is a wonder, considering the relatively confined battle area, that the two fleets did not annihilate each other—with but a few bloodied torpedo-destroyers left to limp home with word of the watery Armageddon.

Jutland remained an academic tour de force at least through the last war. Vice Admiral T. G. W. "Tex" Settle, U.S.N. (Ret.),* recalls the study of the great fight at the Naval War College, Newport. For days, the postgraduate students would sit around the maneuvering boards, pushing toy ships this way and that way, first reconstructing the battle, then trying to determine the outcome *if* Jellicoe had successfully kept on Scheer's stern.

Today, with even the carrier and the jet bomber already challenged by the rocket-firing atomic submarine, the lessons of Jutland are of purely historical interest to the Annapolis graduate. This interest, nonetheless, should endure in its proper place since there had never previously been anything to compare with the size and fury of this sea clash, and certainly never will be again.

Ernst Tittmann, of Cologne, who was a ranging officer on the *König*, looks back on the battle as an encounter which was never sought between two "fleets in being," sitting on opposite sides of the North Sea like chained mastiffs. Germany's navy was so dwarfed by her English cousin's that it couldn't even be spared to lend token protection to the kaiser's colonies overseas. In fact, von Spee's squadron was homeward-bound when it had the misfortune to encounter Sturdee's at the Falkland Islands.

Tittmann, who is a professional engineer, writes that he is so confused by "countless narratives" of the Skagerrak battle, as the Germans know Jutland, by German as well as English authors that he has come to the conclusion that each side "is writing of a wholly different battle."

Rear Admiral Werner Stichling (Ret.), of Freiburg, was serving on the cruiser *Frankfurt* in much the same capacity as Tittmann on the *König*. He postscripts the considerable information he furnished the author:

"According to my conviction, the decision of the British command [to break off the fight] is the result of common sense. The British fleet had a lot to lose and nothing to gain. The daytime battle had proven the superiority of the German shells vs. British armor. On the British side there were heavy losses suffered in the artillery duel, while the High Seas Fleet lost no warship solely to artillery shells [but a combination of shelling, torpedoes, and subsequent fires and explosions]. The British superior fleet could have, perhaps, the next day inflicted

---

*Admiral Settle, who helped the author with many chapters, served on destroyers at Queenstown during the war. He went on to fame as an altitude balloonist and airship commander.

heavy damage to the German fleet but not without heavy damage to herself.

"On the general standing of the war situation nothing would have changed, even in the improbable eventuality of the annihilation of the German fleet. The fleet was for all practical purposes paralyzed in its harbors and could never again mount a decisive assault. The British Admiralty had no reason to take any risks. One could even go so far as to say that a crushing defeat of the High Seas Fleet would have had a completely unanticipated effect. In this case, the total German ship-building capacity and the total personnel of the navy would have been put to work on the U-boat fleet."

Even the seemingly monolithic officers of the Royal Navy became emotional when the subject of Jutland was brought up.

After the war, Admiral Sturdee, the bulldog-faced victor over von Spee, was asked by an American naval officer during a dinner in London: "But Admiral, couldn't *something* have been done to put off the German fleet?"

In an incredible display of emotion, Sturdee brushed aside the silverware and momentarily buried his head in his arms. When he sat up again his cheeks were wet with tears. He remained silent, in testimony of the depths of his frustration.

Rear Admiral Elliott Strauss, of Washington, provides an interesting postscript to the *Baralong*. During the 30's, while a young naval attaché in London, Strauss happened to be lunching at a British officers' club. His host leaned over to whisper:

"That's Commander Godfrey Herbert. Was captain of the *Baralong*." After a pause, the Briton observed wryly, "He doesn't take his vacations in Germany, you know."

The account of the action, bloody enough, had magnified over the years as though the brutality of the Royal Marines needed embellishment. Now, it was said, the bodies of the slain U-boat crewmen had been stuffed in the Q-boat's furnaces in the hopes of eradicating evidence.

The author also wishes to thank Hans Bartels, of Bremen, who served on the *Derfflinger*, and August Prall, of Wuppertal, who was aboard the *Moltke*.

CHAPTER 6: "Make Way for Lord Kitchener!"

The loss of the *Hampshire*, carrying with her Britain's War Secretary, Lord Kitchener, has piqued the curiosity of Englishmen and others with a taste for mystery ever since that stormy night in the Orkneys, June, 1916. Unusually blunt speculations, considering it was wartime, filled the press. Newspaper and magazine articles asked "Why?" Books and chapters in books continue to ask the same question. The most recent in the latter category is Donald McCormick's *The Mystery of Lord Kitchener's Death* (Putnam's, London, 1959).

A graphic personal account is that of one of the survivors, William Charles Phillips, *The Loss of the "Hampshire"* (privately printed in London, 1917). The Admiralty itself published its own detailed report, *Loss of HMS HAMPSHIRE*, in 1926. Other works on the subject include:

Courtney, Charles. *Unlocking Adventure*, Robert Hale, London, 1951

Esher, Reginald B. B. *The Tragedy of Lord Kitchener*, John Murray, London, 1921

Wood, Clement. *The Man Who Killed Kitchener*, W. Faro, Inc., New York, 1932

CHAPTER 7: *Spurlos Versenkt!*

A number of retired American naval officers have been most helpful with reminiscences of the Great War. They include, in addition to Admiral Settle, mentioned in the notes to Chapter 5, Vice Admiral George H. Fort and Admiral John F. Shafroth, both of Washington.

The fabulous Hans Rose, who was Germany's fourth ranking U-boat ace at war's end, having accounted for 210,000 tons of shipping and war vessels, lives in retirement today in Winterberg. An even more famous German naval officer, Admiral Karl Doenitz, visits him at times to reminisce on their unique careers. The author thanks Rose for his helpful correspondence.

Rose is the author of his own memoirs, *Auftauchen!* (Essener Verlagsanstalt, Berlin, 1939).

The author wishes to thank Hugh King, vice president of the Luckenbach Steamship Co. Inc., for historical assistance, and to thank again Ed Gibbons, of Springfield, Va., brother of Floyd Gibbons, and Austin Y. Hoy, of Westport, Conn., who have also been of assistance in previous projects.

CHAPTER 8: . . . "no more baffling mystery . . ."

For years, the disappearance of the collier *Cyclops* has been a source of mingled fascination and frustration to the author. The mystery, which has persisted in a deep recess of his mind like a guilty conscience, was alluded to briefly in an earlier work, *They Sailed into Oblivion*—and surely the big naval auxiliary did just that.

Since the publication of that book, he has continued to track down leads. He read and reread the documents in the navy inquiry, recently removed from the "confidential" category. In this respect, he wishes to thank Elbert Huber, of the naval section of the National Archives, and Rear Admiral E. M. Eller, U.S.N. (Ret.), Director, Naval History. He also owes a debt of gratitude to John Leinbaugh, of the Federal Bureau of Investigation, who made available that agency's file on the *Cyclops*.

He wrote letters to the editors of newspapers in the United States, especially those on the east coast, and in Brazil, hoping to unearth a morsel of real evidence. He journeyed to out-of-the-way places to talk with those of an older generation who had lost a brother or even a son. He also endeavored to locate anyone who had ever set foot on or merely seen the collier, especially navy officers who watched her last sailings from Norfolk, Rio de Janeiro, and Bahia. He consumed much postage and effort writing to people at old addresses, especially in Rio where, the author is convinced, the secret of the disappearance lies.

Forty-six years have passed, however, since the disappearance. Many of those who may have been in a position to provide leading testimony are dust and, indeed, the very structures they once called home have been replaced by a new and unfamiliar species of architecture.

The trail—both "hard" leads and pure fancy—has led from remote islands on the fringes of the Antarctic to keys in the Caribbean. It has led to the Baltic and to Spain, as well as to our own Gulf and Pacific coasts. For years after the *Cyclops'* disappearance, the ship or her wreck was "seen" in these scattered areas of the earth. Enough planking, spars, and life rings were scraped off the world's beaches and rocky shores to build a small schooner—but none of these many and diverse mementoes could ever positively be identified as having originated from the *Cyclops*. Bottle messages, all spurious, washed ashore from Nova Scotia to New Orleans.

While she necessarily has no idea what happened to the *Cyclops*, Commander Worley's daughter, Mrs. Donald D. Stott, has been exceedingly helpful, especially in producing old photographs and letters from her father, whom she loved dearly. She shed an entirely new light on the character of Worley, whose personality emerges from the navy file as somewhat of a blend of Captain Bligh, Blackbeard, and Benedict Arnold, if such a preposterous crossbreed can be imagined. While the author tends, personally, to reserve judgment, he would like to quote from one of Virginia Stott's many letters to him:

"My father has never been forgotten. I have many reminders in my life of his loving indulgence toward my mother and me. Because he was my father I had a very unusual and delightful childhood. Now that I am older than he ever lived to become, I can understand him as a man who truly belonged on the sea. On shore he was a stranger, confused by the demands of conventional living. He never learned to drive a team or a car. . . ."

Mrs. Stott has generously supplied letters—written in exquisite hand—which prove incontrovertibly his exceedingly deep love for his wife, Selma. They also hint at a morose, brooding tendency, and an over-sentimentalism, as well as a penchant for self-recrimination.

Contrary to many suspicions at the time, however, this insight afforded by his daughter into her father's character and personality has convinced the author that George Worley's command of a ship which vanished under almost baffling circumstances was mere coincidence—that his presence, in itself, was in no way related to the event.

Far less constructive than Virginia Stott was Lloyd's of London whose R. C. E. Lander, the famous insurance company's shipping editor, comes up with the rather surprising intelligence:

"I regret that I have been unable to find any record of the loss of the USS *Cyclops* which is probably due to the fact that she was not a merchant vessel."

This, of course, is not wholly the case, since she was carrying an insured commercial cargo to a subsidiary of the U. S. Steel Corporation, which also, mysteriously enough, has no record of the transaction. The author thanks, however, Tom Geoghegan, of the U. S. Steel's Washington office.

The author wishes to thank, too, Charles S. Ashby, of Norfolk, father of Seaman Charles Ashby, lost on the *Cyclops;* Mrs. Guy Asper, of Chambersburg, Pennsylvania, and her grandson, Guy Asper III, serving in the navy aboard a ship of singularly little resemblance to the old collier, the USS *Forrestal;* H. H. Blackledge, Springfield, Missouri, sister of Charles Yancey Blackledge, of the *Cyclops* (and Mrs. Ruth L. Rasberry, town clerk of Commerce, Missouri, who located Mrs. Blackledge); A. M. Dennis, clerk of Bowman, South Carolina, who wrote concerning two others who perished on the collier, James E. Easterling and John Wesley Weathers; and Gerard Felix, of Meriden, Connecticut. The author interviewed Felix at some length. As an engineer aboard the Munson Liner *American Legion* in 1932, Felix talked to an Englishman in Rio who claimed to know "the three men who knocked off the *Cyclops*"—two Germans and one American. The trail, however, has grown quite cold.

Thanks also to Margaret Erickson, township clerk, Rockland, Michigan, for information concerning James Wall, of the *Cyclops'* crew; Mrs. Evelyn B. Findley, Montgomery, Alabama, sister of crewman Lee Otis Battle; Captain Edwin D. Gibb, of New York, and Captain Francis S. Gibson, of Annapolis, Maryland, both retired and both of whom served on the *Raleigh,* off Bahia; Rear Admiral William Granat, of Washington, who was aboard the *Pittsburgh;* Gerald Grosso, military affairs editor, the *Bremerton Sun;* Ernest Hargrave, now living in Worley's former residence in Norfolk, Dr. Floyd Hobbs, of Moscow, Idaho, who grew up at the same Norfolk address and who remembers that his father paid cash to Mrs. Worley for the house; D. A. Jerde, city auditor of Britton, South Dakota, relative of Paul Dobbs, of the *Cyclops;* Mrs. Stella Kraft, of Indianapolis, sister of Earl Grigsby; Mrs. Effie Liddicoat, of Ferndale, Michigan, sister of crewman John George Alschback; Miss Margaret McPherson, Kitsap County (Washington) auditor, who put the author in communication with Mrs. Virginia Worley Stott; James T. Minerd, director, Public Safety, Bound Brook, New Jersey, who wrote concerning one of the *Cyclops'* officers, Lieutenant Clarence R. Hodges, for whom a VFW post is named in his home town; Proctor Page, of Hyde Park, Vermont, brother of Ensign Carroll G. Page; Mrs. W. W. Reed, of Logansville, Georgia, sister of Fred L. Waddell (and Robert Brazil, city clerk, Rochelle, Georgia, who located Mrs. Reed); Lieutenant H. D. Stailey, U.S.N. (Ret.), of Santa Rosa, California, who was aboard the *Raleigh;* John Wagner, Norfolk, for whom the mystery has become a hobby; Mrs. Tom Walker, Wilbar, North Carolina, sister of crewman Isaac P. Dancy; E. L. Walter, Ravenna, Ohio, a nephew of William C. Brandt, of the *Cyclops;* Frank J. Walters, American consul at Barbados; Mrs. J. D. Williams, Dacula, Georgia, sister of crewman Shirley Stanley; Mrs. Norma Willis, town clerk of Ashland, Alabama, who furnished information on another crewman, Francis Olney Strong.

There are still others who in one way or another figured in the author's long quest for clues on the *Cyclops,* from neighbors and postal clerks to librarians and vital-statistics clerks in dozens of town halls. He extends thanks to all these people, who are far too numerous to mention in this list.

Gratitude is owed Mrs. Lowell Hulsebus, of Bakersfield, California, sister of the youthful Floyd Hedglin, one of the few to perish in the sinking of the transport *President Lincoln.* Though another war has come and gone, the sacrifice of the ship has been remembered in one of those rare instances of sentiment in government. While other plaques, pictures, paintings, and even statuary have come and gone, a simple bronze plate, depicting the *President Lincoln* going down and engraved with the names of those who died, remains at the front entrance of the Navy Department building on Constitution Avenue, in Washington, "Main Navy," as it has been known ever since 1917.

The author also wishes to thank again the former Lieutenant Isaacs, who proved to his German captors that "stone walls do not a prison make nor iron bars a cage."

CHAPTERS 9 AND 10: Padlocking an Ocean—the Great Mine Barrage
AND Verdict: Suicide

As noted, Admiral Elliott Strauss, of Washington, was most helpful in making available the unpublished memoirs of his father, Admiral "Joe" Strauss, the man who actually did the "padlocking" of the North Sea. Elliott, with his profound and encyclopedic storehouse of anecdotes is virtually a "must" for those who would chronicle naval history of this century—even though he himself was a boy during the Great War.

Thanks are also due John Lochhead, librarian of the Mariners Museum, Newport News, Virginia, and M. V. Brewington, Assistant Director, Peabody Museum, Salem, Massachusetts.

Admiral Sir Roger Keyes's daring Zeebrugge raid has been so adequately reported in recent books and magazine articles that the author decided that no useful purpose could be served in retelling the story, heroic as it was. However, he wishes to acknowledge the thoughtful letter sent him by the famous officer's son, of the same name, the second Baron Keyes. In the Second World War the aging admiral still had enough fight in him to organize the famous British Commandoes. An older son, Geoffrey, was killed in North Africa.

The author wishes again to express his appreciation to Admiral

316 • Notes and Acknowledgments

Doenitz, one of Aumühle's older citizens and most distinguished residents. His street address—Dora-Specht-Allee 1—is carefully printed on his stationery. This seems quite unnecessary since everyone in Holstein knows Doenitz. He attributes his good health in part to late winter trips to Padua for the mineral baths.

His extensive correspondence with the author has been excerpted in the text or paraphrased. His First World War career started aboard the cruiser *Breslau* when, with the *Goeben,* she eluded the British and fled through the Dardanelles. He was transferred to U-boats two years later. On October 4, 1918, commanding the *U-68,* he successfully attacked a Malta convoy, but the submarine was so badly damaged he had to scuttle it and surrender. His imprisonment was not long. His postwar career as architect of the new German undersea navy, as head of the fallen Nazi Germany for several days after Hitler's suicide, and his subsequent imprisonment for ten years is another story.

The bitterness which was manifest in his *Memoirs* (World Publishing Co., Cleveland, 1959) seems to have abated since then.

Admiral Friedrich Ruge reminisced of his experiences during the German mutiny and the Scapa Flow scuttling while on a lecture tour of the United States in the spring of 1964. A resident of Tübingen, he is blessed with a vivid memory and sense of humor and nearly flawless English—a source of embarrassment to most of his American hosts, who cannot reply in kind.

Admiral Ruge still thinks von Reuter outfoxed the British in the mass suicide of the fleet. Certainly, the ways were cleared for a new fleet.

Ernst Tittmann, mentioned before, writes of the "two causes" for the mutiny:

"The will to fight of the ships' companies was dulled because of the long idleness in harbor. Priority had been accorded the U-boat fleet, which also was manned by an elite, both in officers and crewmen. The cream of the High Seas Fleet had constantly to be skimmed off to compensate for submarine losses. As, finally, the western front itself crumpled, war weariness throughout the Homeland manifested itself in the fleet by open mutiny."

Unfortunately, the collapse of Germany's ability to wage war in 1918 was but the "amen" to a chapter, not the book.

Bibliography

(Starred titles indicate books from which excerpts have been taken, including those acknowledged elsewhere.)

Admiralty. White Paper No. 2710 (concerning the loss of HMS *Hampshire*), His Majesty's Stationery Office, London, 1926.

Admiralty. *Battle of Jutland—Official Dispatches,* His Majesty's Stationery Office, London, 1920.

Admiralty. *Narrative of the Battle of Jutland,* His Majesty's Stationery Office, London, 1924.

Alexander, A. C. B. *Jutland—A plea for a Naval General Staff,* High Rees, Ltd., London, 1923.

Alexander, Roy. *The Cruise of the Raider "Wolf,"* Yale University Press, New Haven, 1939.

Bacon, Sir Reginald. *The Jutland Scandal,* Hutchinson & Co., Ltd., London, 1925.

*Belknap, Reginald R. *The Yankee Mining Squadron,* U. S. Naval Institute, Annapolis, 1920.

Bellairs, C. *The Battle of Jutland—The Sowing and The Reaping,* Hodder & Stoughton, Ltd., London, 1920.

Brownrigg, Sir D. *Indiscretions of a Naval Censor,* Cassell & Co., Ltd., London, 1920.

Buchan, J. *The Battle of Jutland,* Thomas Nelson & Sons, London, 1916.

Busch, F. O. *Skagerrak und das Deutsche Marine—Ehrenmal,* Beenken, Berlin, 1933.

———. *Das Volksbuch vom Skagerrak—Augenzeugenberichte deutscher und englischer Mitkampfer,* Limpert, Berlin, 1938.

Bush, E. W. *Bless Our Ship,* George Allen & Unwin, Ltd., London, 1958.

Bywater, Hector C. *Their Secret Purposes,* Constable and Co., Ltd., London, 1932.

Carl, Ernst. *One Against England,* E. P. Dutton & Co., Inc., New York, 1935.

Chalmers, Rear Admiral W. S. *The Life and Letters of David Earl Beatty,* Hodder & Stoughton, Ltd., London, 1951.

Chatfield, Lord Alfred E., Admiral of the Fleet. *The Navy and Defence,* William Heinemann, Ltd., London, 1942.

Churchill, Winston. *The World Crisis, 1916-'18,* Thornton Butterworth, Ltd., London, 1927.

Corbett, Sir Julian. *History of the Great War,* 5 vols. (Continued by Henry Newbolt after Sir Julian's death.) Longmans, Green & Co., Ltd., London, 1920-1931.

Cornelissen, P. *Die Hochseeflotte Ist Ausgelaufen,* Lehmann, München, 1920.

Cornford, L. Cope. *The Merchant Seaman in War,* George H. Doran Co., New York, 1918.

Cruttwell, C. R. M. F. *A History of the Great War,* Oxford U. Press, New York, 1934.

Daniels, Josephus. *Our Navy at War,* Pictorial Bureau, Washington, D. C., 1922.

Der Drieg. *Zur See Nordsee,* Band V and other vols. (The German Official History of World War I at Sea, most of which was completed in the '20's.) Mittler, Berlin.

Divine, D. *The Story of Sea Warfare,* Hamilton, Ltd., London, 1957.

Doenitz, Karl. *Memoirs,* The World Publishing Co., Cleveland, 1959.

Dreyer, Sir F. C. *The Sea Heritage—A study of maritime warfare,* Museum Press, London, 1955.

Fawcett, H. W., and Hooper, G. W. W. *The Fighting at Jutland,* Macmillan & Co., London, 1921.

Fayle, C. Ernest. *History of the Great War,* 3 vols., John Murray, London, 1920-1924.

Frost, Holloway H. *The Battle of Jutland,* U. S. Naval Institute, Annapolis (printed in London), 1936.

Frothingham, Thomas G. *The Naval History of the World War,* 3 vols., Harvard University Press, Cambridge, 1924-1926.

Gibson, Langhorne, and Harper, J. *The Riddle of Jutland,* Cassell & Co., Ltd., London, 1934.

Gibson, R. H., and Prendergast, Maurice. *The German Submarine War,* Richard R. Smith, New York, 1931.

Gill, Charles C. *What Happened at Jutland,* George H. Doran Co., New York, 1921.

Hancock, H. E. *Wireless at Sea,* Marconi Marine, London, 1950.

Hanstein, O. V. *Die Seeschlacht am Skagerrak,* Vogel & Vogel, Leipzig, 1916.

Hase, Cdr. Georg von. *Kiel and Jutland,* Skeffington & Son, Ltd., London, 1921.

Hoehling, A. A. *Lonely Command,* Cassell & Co., Ltd., London, 1957.

Hoehling, A. A. *They Sailed into Oblivion,* Thomas Yoseloff, New York, 1959.

Hoehling, A. A. and Mary. *The Last Voyage of the Lusitania,* Henry Holt & Co., New York, 1956.

Horne, Charles F. *The Great Events of The Great War,* National Alumni, New York 1920.

*Hunter, Lt. Francis T. *Beatty, Jellicoe, Sims and Rodman,* Doubleday, Page & Co., New York, 1919.

Isaacs, Edouard Victor. *Prisoner of the "U-90,"* Houghton Mifflin, Boston, 1919.

*Jellicoe, Admiral Sir John. *The Crisis of the Naval War,* Cassell & Co., Ltd., London, 1920.

_____*The Grand Fleet,* Cassell & Co., Ltd., London, 1919.

Keyes, Sir Roger. *The Naval Memoirs of Admiral of the Fleet Sir Roger Keyes,* E. P. Dutton & Co., Inc., New York, 1935.

Kittredge, Tracy B. *Naval Lessons of The Great War,* Doubleday, Page & Co., New York, 1921.

Knight, E. F. *The Harwich Naval Forces,* Hodder & Stoughton, Ltd., New York, 1919.

Koeves, Tibor. *Satan in Top Hat,* Alliance Book Corp., New York, 1941.

Kuhlwetter, F. von. *Skagerrak,* Ullstein, Berlin, 1933.

Lloyd George, David. *The War Memoirs of David Lloyd George,* Ivor Nicholson & Watson, Ltd., London, 1933.

Lutzow, F. *Skagerrak,* Langen & Miller, München, 1936.

Macintyre, Capt. Donald. *Jutland,* W. W. Norton & Co., Inc., New York, 1958.

March, Francis A. *History of the World War,* United Publishers, Chicago, 1919.

*Milholland, Ray *The Splinter Fleet of the Otranto Barrage*, Bobbs-Merrill Co., Indianapolis, 1936.

Millis, Walter. *Road to War,* Houghton Mifflin Co., Boston, 1935.

Navy Times, Editors. *They Fought under the Sea,* Stackpole Co., Harrisburg, 1962.

Nerger, Karl. *S. M. S. Wolf,* August Scherl, Berlin, 1918.

Newbolt, Henry. *Naval Operations,* Vol. 14, Longmans Green & Co., London, 1928.

The Northern Barrage and Other Mining Activities, Navy Historical Section, Government Printing Office, Washington, D. C., 1920.

Official Dispatches. *Battle of Jutland,* His Majesty's Stationery Office, London, 1920.

Paine, Ralph D. *The Corsair in the War Zone,* Houghton Mifflin Co., Boston, 1920.

Perry, Lawrence. *Our Navy in the War,* Charles Scribner's Sons, New York, 1918.

Raeder, Erich. *My Life,* U. S. Naval Institute, Annapolis, 1960.

Reiners, Ludwig. *The Lamps Went out in Europe,* Pantheon Books, New York, 1955.

Reuter, Ludwig von. *Scapa Flow, das Grab der deutschen Flotte,* K. F. Koehler, Leipzig, 1921.

Robertson, Sir William. *From Private to Field Marshal,* Constable & Co., Ltd., London, 1921.

Rodman, Hugh. *Yarns of a Kentucky Admiral,* Bobbs-Merrill Co., Indianapolis, 1928.

Roskill, S. W. *H.M.S. Warspite,* William Collins, Sons & Co., Ltd., London, 1957.

*Scheer, Admiral Reinhard. *Germany's High Sea Fleet in the World War,* Peter Smith, New York, 1934.

*Schoultz, Commodore G. von. *With the British Battle Fleet,* Hutchinson & Co., Ltd., London, 1926.

Simonds, Frank H. "History of the World War," *The Review of Reviews,* New York, 1918-'20.

Sims, Admiral William S. *The Victory at Sea,* Doubleday, Page & Co., New York, 1920.

Spencer-Cooper, H. *The Battle of the Falkland Islands,* Cassell & Co., Ltd., London, 1919.

Sullivan, Mark. *Our Times,* vols. 5 and 6, Charles Scribner's Sons, New York, 1936.

Terry, C. S. (Editor). *The Battle of Jutland Bank 31 May-1 June 1916,* Oxford University Press, New York, 1916.

The Times History of the War, London, 1914-1919.

Tirpitz, Grand Admiral Alfred von. *My Memoirs,* Hurst & Blackett, Ltd., London, 1919.

Usborne, C. V. *Smoke on the Horizon,* Hodder & Stoughton, Ltd., London, 1933.

Waldeyer-Hartz, Hugo von. *Admiral von Hipper,* Rich & Cowan, Ltd., London, 1933.

Wood, Clement. *The Man Who Killed Kitchener,* William Faro, Inc., New York, 1932.

Yardley, Herbert O. *The American Black Chamber,* Bobbs-Merrill Co., Indianapolis, 1931.

These principal libraries and historical institutions were consulted: the Army Library, in the Pentagon; the British Museum; District of Columbia Public Library; Library of Congress including the Manuscript Division where the Albert Gleaves papers were primarily consulted; the Navy Library, and its able director, Frederick S. Meigs; the National Archives; and the Smithsonian Institution. The Imperial War Museum, London, has previously been credited.

The Victoria Cross and George Cross Associations were most helpful, as they have been in past projects, in tracking down records of heroes.

Among the many magazines consulted were: *Atlantic Monthly; Berliner Illustrirte Zeitung; The Century; Collier's; Current History; Das U-Boot* (published monthly in Berlin during the war for submarine personnel); *Harper's Magazine; History Today; Illustrated London News; Life; Literary Digest; London Graphic; Living Age; The Nineteenth Century and After; Outlook; Review of Reviews; Saturday Evening Post; Shipmate* (Jan., 1964, article by Eugene Wilson on the Grand Fleet); *World's Work.*

Principal wire services consulted were Associated Press, International News Service, Reuter's, and United Press. Principal newspapers consulted, in addition to those already noted, were *Boston Herald, Chicago Tribune, Christian Science Monitor, New York Herald, New York Times, New York Tribune, Paris Herald,* and the Washington, D. C., papers, the *Post* and the *Star.*

Index

Toul, 233
Trafalgar Square, 180
Trautner, J. B., 204
Tresness Bay, 255
Trinidad, 26
Trinidad Island, 23, 26, 27, 36, 190
Triumph, 85
Trotha, Adolph von, 268
Tsingtao, 60, 67
Turbulent, 149
Turff (N.J.), 305
Turkey, 83, 85, 98
Tuscania, 214
Tyland, 113
Tyrwhitt, Reginald, 46, 51, 56,
    133-134, 143, 278

U-9, 47-59
U-20, 86, 88, 90
U-27, 103-104
U-29, 59
U-33, 178
U-39, 182, 203
U-50, 271
U-53, 170-178, 183-184, 210-213
U-58, 208, 209
U-62, 204-206
U-68, 317
U-75, 158
U-90, 215, 298-300
U-135, 208, 269
U-boats (*see also specific areas, boats,
    engagements, sinkings*), 25, 41-59,
    84-90, 102, 110, 143, 159, 160,
    233-234, 247; called home, last
    days of war, 265; end of war,
    surrender, 278ff.; mutiny,
    revolution, 268ff.
Union Castle Line, 24, 93
United States (*see also specific cities,
    engagements, ships*), 9, 24, 59,
    86-91, 102-106, 142, 151;
    declaration of war, 193, 194-197;
    minelaying operations, 248-259;
    severs relations with Germany,
    182-193; and surrender of
    Germany, 283ff.; and U-boats
    (*see* U-boats, *specific boats*);

and Versailles, 285;
    "war fever" in, 188, 192, 193
United States units: A.E.F. (*see*
    American Expeditionary Force*);
    Atlantic Fleet, 250; Cruiser and
    Transport Force, 200; Naval
    Overseas Transport Service, 218,
    219; Pacific Fleet, 227-229, 232,
    234, 243; 1st Division (Army),
    200; 5th Battle Squadron, 284;
    6th Battle Squadron, 280, 284;
    11th Destroyer Flotilla, 284;
    20th Engineers Regiment, 214
United States and Brazil Steamship
    Co., 225
U.S. Naval Institute Proceedings, 242
United States Steel Corp., 225, 314
United States Steel Products Co., 225,
    232
Unity, 160, 168
Uruguay, 22, 229
Ushant, 193

V-43, 295
Valiant, 284
Valparaiso, 60, 66, 67, 71
Vanderbilt, Alfred Gwynne, 86
Vaterland, 9, 189
Vega, 290
Venezuela, 23, 26
Verdun, 108
Versailles, 284-285, 286, 287
Vesper, 290
Victoria, Queen, 93
Victoria Cross, 115, 120, 121
Victorious, 290
Victory, 160, 168
Vigilancia, 193
Villingen, 300
Virginia Capes, 295
Virgin Islands, 236
Vladivostok, 234
Volturno, 12
Von der Tann, 112, 116, 136; mutiny
    on, 268; surrenders, 281
Voorham, Captain, 55
Vyl lightship, 113

Wadsworth, 198

336   •   Index